BECOMING THE CFO

THE FIRST 90 DAYS AND BEYOND

(A Practical Playbook for the First 365 Days of Financial Leadership)

CA SHRIHARSH SONAR

BECOMING THE CFO

THE FIRST 90 DAYS AND BEYOND

Decoding the DNA of Financial Leadership for First-Time CFOs

CA SHRIHARSH SONAR

(Featuring the journey of Kael Cipher at G Z Corporation's NextAura Global)

This book is a work of nonfiction presented through illustrative characters and scenarios. All corporate names, dialogues, and events are used for educational purposes.

Cover and interior design by Shriharsh Sonar.

Disclaimer

This book is intended for education, professional development, and general guidance. It does not constitute financial, legal, investment, tax, medical, psychological, or other professional advice.

The information, frameworks, examples, and scenarios presented in this book are for learning purposes only. Readers should exercise their own judgement and consult qualified professionals before acting on any concept, framework, or recommendation discussed herein.

All companies, characters, names, dialogues, and situations — including Kael Cipher, Gemma Zessar, G Z Corporation, and NextAura Global — are illustrative composites created to demonstrate leadership and finance practices. Any resemblance to actual persons, organisations, or events is purely coincidental.

The author and publisher accept no responsibility for any action taken, decision made, or outcome arising from the use or interpretation of this book.

For Madhura —

whose quiet strength continues to guide every number I write and every truth I stand by.

Decoding the DNA of Financial Leadership for First-Time CFOs

Author's Note

Every CFO's first day feels the same: a heavy chair, a silent room, and an inbox full of history.

This book comes from years of observing finance leadership from close quarters — working across MNCs, Indian MNCs, director-driven organisations, and complex corporate structures involving functional and business reporting lines across India and overseas.

Over the years, I have worked and interacted with thousands of stakeholders across accounts, finance, taxation, business finance, operations, sales, plants, audits, government authorities, and leadership teams. I have worked with finance controllers, CFOs, SBU presidents, CEOs, plant heads, sales leaders, Big 4 auditors, tax officers, assessment and appeal authorities, and cross-functional teams across multiple locations.

I have also experienced the reality of working with dual reporting structures — functional bosses, business bosses, Indian leadership, and overseas leadership — where finance is expected not merely to report numbers, but to interpret them, defend them, challenge them, and convert them into business direction. Presenting to senior leadership and boards taught me that a CFO's role is not built only on accounting knowledge. It is built on judgement, timing, clarity, courage, and business understanding.

Over time, I saw one truth clearly: the modern CFO is no longer expected to remain confined to accounts, compliance, reporting, taxation, or treasury. The CFO is expected to become a business partner — someone who can guide CXO-level decisions, support CEOs, challenge assumptions, strengthen working capital, shape budgets and forecasts, review rolling sales forecasts, assess capital needs, explore developing markets, evaluate backward and forward integration, manage borrowings, handle auditors and authorities, lead teams across head office and plant locations, and help the organisation think with financial clarity.

Becoming the CFO is not a manual of formulas. It is a practical leadership playbook built from real corporate finance exposure, business finance experience, turnaround situations, multi-location coordination, audit interactions, tax matters, funding discussions, board presentations, and CXO-level expectations.

Through the journey of Kael Cipher, this book explores what every aspiring or first-time CFO must learn: how to see beyond the numbers and lead through clarity, judgement, and courage.

My hope is simple: that this book gives every finance leader the confidence to sit in the chair, breathe once, and begin.

— FCA Shriharsh Sonar

TABLE OF CONTENTS

Chapter 11 — Board & Audit Committee Engagement

Every boardroom question is an invitation to earn trust.

Insights 171–190

PART III — THE FIRST 180 DAYS: BUILDING THE MACHINE

Chapter 13 — Designing Finance Systems & Digital Workflows: ERP Discipline, Automation and MIS Cadence

From data entry to decision intelligence. Build visibility before velocity; introduce shared services, RPA, and analytics.

Insights 211–230

Chapter 14 — Partnering Beyond Numbers

Influencing operations, HR, and sales with data.

Insights 231–250

Chapter 21 — Ethics and the CFO's Red Lines

The most valuable asset on a balance sheet is still integrity. Knowing when to dissent or walk away.

Insights 356–372

Chapter 22 — From First-Time CFO to Business Leader

A true CFO builds an independent system — building succession, influence, and legacy.

Insights 373–382

PART V — THE CFO'S INVESTOR-GRADE SWOT MATRIX

Reader Benefit Summary

This book walks aspiring and first-time CFOs through the first year of financial leadership — from the interview room to the Board meeting, from cash crisis to capital strategy, and from technical confidence to enterprise leadership.

Blending Kael Cipher's journey with practical frameworks, it helps readers:

- Navigate the transition from **accountant to enterprise leader**.
- Master the **30/90/180/365-day rhythm of CFO leadership**.
- Build systems that endure, teams that think, and a legacy that lasts.

With **380+ insights, 30 SWOT levers,** and a boardroom-ready framework for governance, capital, global scale, and investor-grade thinking, this is a practical playbook for navigating complexity — and becoming the CFO.

What This Book Is — and What It Is Not

This book is not intended to replace technical manuals on forex management, taxation, transfer pricing, M&A valuation, treasury systems, accounting standards, audit documentation, ERP implementation, or regulatory compliance.

Those subjects require specialist depth, jurisdiction-specific interpretation, updated legal references, and professional advice. A CFO must consult auditors, tax advisors, legal counsel, bankers, technology experts, and domain specialists before making final decisions in those areas.

This book serves a different purpose.

It is written to help aspiring and first-time CFOs understand the operating rhythm, judgement framework, leadership posture, and practical sequence required to enter the CFO chair with clarity.

It does not attempt to teach every technical subject in exhaustive detail. Instead, it helps the reader understand what to notice, what to question, what to prioritize, what to escalate, and how to build credibility during the first year of financial leadership.

A new CFO does not fail only because of weak technical knowledge. He may fail because he speaks too early, acts without diagnosis, misses cultural signals, mishandles the Board, underestimates liquidity pressure, delays difficult conversations, or treats finance as a reporting function rather than an enterprise nerve centre.

This book is therefore a playbook of transition.

It touches multiple CFO domains — liquidity, working capital, governance, compliance, capital allocation, M&A, risk, tax, investor readiness, systems, ethics, and team leadership — not to exhaust each subject, but to show how they connect inside the mind of a modern CFO.

In simple terms, this book will not make you a tax expert, treasury dealer, valuation specialist, ERP architect, or legal advisor.

It will help you think like a CFO who knows when those experts are needed, what questions to ask them, how to interpret their inputs, and how to convert their advice into responsible enterprise decisions.

That is the real journey of becoming the CFO.

Introduction

Why the World Needs Better CFOs, Not Just Better Numbers

Every organisation has a balance sheet, but only a few have a soul.

And it is the CFO who, often quietly, helps decide whether that soul survives change, chaos, and time.

For decades, the finance function has been viewed as the guardian of numbers. In reality, it is the nervous system of decision-making — the place where facts become foresight. The CFO's role today extends far beyond reporting results; it influences how the organisation thinks, adapts, protects value, and leads.

Yet when many professionals finally reach the title of Chief Financial Officer, they realize something unsettling: no one ever truly taught them how to be one.

The degree prepared them to analyze, audit, and control.
The years in industry trained them to deliver, manage, and report.
But very little prepares them for the solitude, responsibility, and expectation that come with owning the enterprise's financial truth.

This book comes from that gap.

Becoming the CFO is not a textbook. It is a handbook for transition — from finance professional to financial leader. It helps the reader navigate the invisible terrain between the first day and the first year, guiding them through what to notice, what to question, what to fix, and what to build.

The book is structured as a year-long mentorship, told through the journey of Kael Cipher, a first-time CFO joining NextAura Global — a subsidiary of G Z Corporation, led by the visionary yet demanding Gemma Zessar.

Through Kael's journey, the reader encounters the same challenges every new CFO faces: limited time, incomplete data, competing egos, liquidity pressure, governance expectations, and the constant demand to deliver clarity in a fog of complexity.

Each phase of the book corresponds to a real leadership milestone:

• The First 30 Days: Listen before leading. Understand what you have inherited.
• The First 90 Days: Stabilise, communicate, and establish trust.
• The First 180 Days: Build systems and teams that think beyond firefighting.

• The First 365 Days: Institutionalise processes, shape strategy, and leave behind continuity.

At the end of each phasc, the reader will find practical deliverables — diagnostic grids, dashboards, strategy maps, scorecards, and leadership tools designed to build control, credibility, and confidence.

The world of finance leadership is increasingly unforgiving. By the 90th day, boards expect stability. By the 180th, systems must show improvement. By the year's end, the CFO must already be known for foresight, judgement, and trust.

This book is written for the first-time CFO stepping into the seat, the aspiring finance head preparing for enterprise-level accountability, the seasoned controller or VP-Finance moving from accuracy to influence, and the CEO or board member who wants to understand how a strong CFO thinks.

If read with curiosity and applied with discipline, this book will help the reader see finance not as a language of limitation, but as a language of leadership.

Because ultimately, Becoming the CFO is not just about numbers. It is about meaning — the meaning brought to decisions, the courage shown in silence, and the foresight left behind in every ledger, policy, system, and team shaped.

"Every CFO eventually realizes this: you don't just sign the accounts — you sign the company's future."

— FCA Shriharsh Sonar

How To Use This Book

This book is designed as both a narrative and a playbook.

Each part represents a real-time stage in a CFO's first year:

Phase	Time Frame	Focus	Tool / Output
I — Orientation	Days 0–30	Listening, observing, diagnosing	30-Day Action Grid
II — Stabilization	Days 31–90	Quick wins and credibility	90-Day Dashboard
III — Optimization	Days 91–180	Building systems and teams	180-Day Strategy Map
IV — Consolidation	Days 181–365	Institutionalizing finance and legacy	365-Day Leadership Review

Read it sequentially if you are beginning a CFO role, selectively if you wish to strengthen a specific domain, and practically by completing the grids, dashboards, and deliverables at the end of each phase.

Think of Kael Cipher's journey as a mirror of your own. Behind every conversation in this story lies a decision framework you can apply tomorrow morning.

PART I

THE FIRST 30 DAYS: SEE BEFORE YOU SPEAK

Theme: Observation | Listening | Diagnosis

The first month in the CFO chair is not about control — it's about clarity. Numbers are visible, but meaning hides in people, in silences, and in the systems that everyone swears are "working fine."

When Kael Cipher joined NextAura Global, his first instinct wasn't to act but to absorb. He spent his mornings reading reports that no one had touched for months, his afternoons in quiet one-to-one conversations with business heads, and his evenings mapping what wasn't being said. He learned that every balance sheet has two sides — the financial and the cultural. *One shows assets; the other reveals attitudes.*

In these first 30 days, ***a new CFO must resist the temptation to prove intelligence through speed.*** The real win lies in understanding the organisation's pulse before prescribing its cure. Your credibility won't come from new policies but from calm observation, precise questions, and the humility to learn the business you now protect.

Each chapter in this part closes with a **30-Day Action Grid**, guiding you through what to observe, whom to meet, what to read, and how to capture your first diagnostic view. The goal is simple: to see clearly before you speak loudly.

At the end of this phase, you should be able to produce your first internal milestone — a confidential **CFO Arrival Report** summarizing:

- Liquidity and solvency status
- Control and compliance maturity
- Cultural and leadership tone
- Immediate financial exposures

In the chapters ahead, you'll follow Kael through those exact steps — his first meeting with Gemma Zessar as CEO, his quiet audit of liquidity, his assessment of working capital discipline, and his first written reflections as CFO.

The month will teach one eternal lesson of leadership:

Before you fix anything, learn why it broke.

CHAPTER 1

The Call to Lead: From Accountant to Custodian of Enterprise Value

Stepping into the chair where numbers end and judgement begin.

The Awakening of Responsibility

Kael Cipher's first morning as CFO was not marked by applause but by silence.
The desk was immaculate, the skyline distant, and the company's heartbeat faintly audible through spreadsheets.
He knew this silence was not emptiness—it was expectation.

Every CFO, in those first few hours, confronts an unspoken truth: what the organisation truly needs from you cannot be downloaded from an ERP system. It must be discerned—between numbers, across meetings, beneath tone.

"Finance leadership begins the moment you stop explaining the past and start shaping the future." — **Ruth Porat**, CFO of Alphabet Inc.

1. Understanding the True Mandate of a CFO

A CFO's real mandate is not precision — it is perception.

It is to ensure that every financial outcome mirrors strategic intent. Profit is no longer the finish line; stewardship is.

Kael understood that while controllers preserve accuracy, CFOs preserve direction. His new responsibility was to ensure the organisation deserved the wealth it pursued — to make sure ambition never outran integrity.

Kael also understood that a CFO's signature was never a formality. *It was a declaration of belief — in the numbers, the controls, and the conscience behind them.*

CFO Practice Note:

• Do not define your role only by reporting accuracy; define it by the quality of enterprise decisions your finance function enables.

• Review whether financial outcomes are aligned with stated strategy, not merely whether they are technically correct.

• Treat every approval, sign-off, and certification as a statement of professional conviction, not administrative routine.

---

2. The Psychological Shift from Controller to Leader

The shift from controller to leader is not functional — it is psychological.

Controllers fix variances; leaders define vectors. Controllers focus on data integrity; leaders focus on organisational intent.

Kael had to trade the comfort of certainty for the courage of ambiguity. He would no longer be evaluated by how fast he closed the books, but by how effectively he opened conversations.

Leadership, he realized, was no longer about what he knew. It was about what he made possible for others to know.

Kael marked the transition in his own words: *leadership begins where control ends — when people stop waiting for instructions and start trusting direction.*

CFO Practice Note:

• Move from asking "Are the numbers correct?" to also asking "What decision should these numbers improve?"

• Build conversations with business heads before issuing conclusions; leadership influence begins before formal authority is used.

• Notice where your old controller habits may limit your new CFO responsibilities — especially in ambiguity, negotiation, and strategic judgement.

---

3. Strategic vs. Operational CFOs — Choosing Your Stance

Every enterprise defines its financial destiny through the lens of its CFO.

Some organisations demand operational mastery — tight liquidity, accurate forecasts, relentless efficiency. Others require strategic foresight — capital allocation, scenario design, risk framing.

The best CFOs stand at the intersection.

Kael resolved to become the bridge between precision and purpose, anchoring strategy in data without drowning it in detail. He built his early diary around two rhythms: operational fluency by day, strategic reflection by night.

His early principle was simple: *make the complex visible, then make the visible useful.*

CFO Practice Note:

• Identify whether the company currently needs control repair, growth guidance, capital discipline, or cultural reset.

• Split your first 90 days between operational review and strategic interpretation; do not let firefighting consume the entire role.

• Build a personal CFO stance statement: what you will protect, what you will improve, and what you will refuse to compromise.

---

4. Building Early Credibility with the CEO and Chairperson

Credibility cannot be demanded; it must be detected.

It begins not with the quarterly review but with the first conversation.

Kael prepared for his early meetings by reading the last three years of CEO letters and investor calls — not to memorise numbers, but to decode emotion: where the company sounded defensive, where it sounded proud, where it hesitated.

In his first executive dialogue, he spoke less of ratios and more of reality. He listened for pain points before proposing performance measures.

By week two, the Chairperson remarked, "You ask questions that make us think, not defend."

That is how a CFO earns entry — not as a gatekeeper, but as a trusted interpreter.

CFO Practice Note:
• Before meeting the CEO or Chairperson, study not only financials but tone: repeated phrases, avoided topics, public commitments, and strategic anxiety.
• In early meetings, ask diagnostic questions before proposing solutions; premature certainty weakens credibility.
• Build trust by showing that you understand the enterprise's pressure points, not merely its accounting position.

---

5. Governance and Stewardship Responsibilities

Governance is the invisible architecture of trust.

Stewardship is its living manifestation.

Kael viewed both as moral compasses disguised as procedures. He re-examined every policy through three questions:

Does it protect the organisation's reputation?

Does it encourage the right behaviour?

Would I sign this even if no one were watching?

True stewardship demands that a CFO never allows financial creativity to eclipse corporate conscience.

To govern is to preserve credibility — because credibility compounds faster than capital.

CFO Practice Note:
• Review key policies through behaviour, not wording: ask what each policy encourages people to do under pressure.
• Identify governance gaps where approvals exist on paper but accountability is weak in practice.
• Create a short list of non-negotiables early — reporting integrity, cash visibility, compliance discipline, and ethical escalation.

---

6. Role Comparison — CFO vs. Controller vs. VP Finance

Where the controller manages accuracy and the VP Finance manages efficiency, the CFO manages consequence.

The role evolves from ensuring things are done right to ensuring the right things are done.

Kael drafted a clear responsibility map: controllers owned compliance; finance heads owned process; the CFO owned purpose.

This clarity prevented duplication and cultivated accountability.

The distinction was not hierarchy. It was horizon.

CFO Practice Note:
• Clarify who owns reporting, compliance, treasury, FP&A, controls, tax, business partnering, and board communication.
• Avoid doing your team's work because it feels faster; unclear ownership creates dependency.
• Use the responsibility map to shift yourself from reviewer of details to owner of enterprise consequence.

---

7. Linking Finance to Enterprise Purpose and Culture

A CFO who cannot translate the balance sheet into belief will forever manage numbers, never inspire them.

Kael integrated the company's purpose into every dashboard — ESG metrics, diversity ratios, customer impact measures, and long-term capability indicators.

He believed that if culture was invisible, finance should make it measurable.

Purpose could not remain a poster in the hallway. *If purpose mattered, it had to show up in capital, incentives, reporting, and trade-offs.*

When finance becomes the mirror of purpose, employees see numbers as narratives — not as instructions.

CFO Practice Note:
• Identify which stated values can be translated into measurable business indicators.
• Check whether budgets, incentives, and capital allocation support the company's declared purpose.
• Use dashboards to make culture visible without reducing it to cosmetic metrics.

---

8. First-Day Priorities Checklist

Kael's opening checklist was less tactical than reflective:

• Listen before leading.
• Map allies and antagonists without judging either.
• Verify liquidity silently.
• Observe cultural tone before proposing change.
• Draft the first 100-hour diary to log every insight.

He understood that urgency is not speed. It is accuracy in choosing what deserves momentum.

The first day was not meant to prove his intelligence. It was meant to protect him from premature assumptions.

CFO Practice Note:

• Do not announce major changes on Day One unless there is an immediate control, cash, or compliance emergency.
• Quietly verify liquidity, reporting reliability, pending regulatory matters, and unresolved audit issues.
• Begin a confidential observation log from the first hour; early impressions often reveal patterns that later become normalized.

---

9. Board-Level Expectations and Early Optics

Boardrooms read body language before they read balance sheets.

The first presentation defines whether the CFO is viewed as defensive or dependable.

Kael rehearsed brevity: five slides, no jargon, every statement anchored to enterprise risk or resilience. He recognised that board interactions were not about detail, but about confidence transfer.

The numbers could be delegated. The conviction could not.

His rule was clear: *a CFO should never use complexity to hide uncertainty.*

CFO Practice Note:

• Prepare board communication around three questions: what changed, why it matters, and what decision is required.
• Keep early board packs concise; excessive detail can signal insecurity rather than command.
• If data is incomplete, say so clearly and explain the timeline for verification.

---

10. Leadership Presence in Crisis or Calm

CFOs are most visible when volatility is highest.

Presence is not posture — it is predictability.

Kael resolved that in every meeting, his tone would be calmer than the numbers on screen. In crisis, the CFO becomes the company's psychological currency.

If he panics, markets panic. If he steadies, confidence returns.

Kael reminded himself often: *during chaos, finance must become the metronome — steady enough for others to regain rhythm.*

CFO Practice Note:
• In volatile situations, communicate with frequency, brevity, and discipline; silence creates speculation.
• Separate confirmed facts from assumptions before presenting any crisis update.
• Maintain a visible cadence with the CEO, treasury, legal, communications, and board stakeholders until stability returns.

---

11. Crafting a 90-Day Personal Positioning Plan

Kael built his first 90-day roadmap around three verbs: Observe. Stabilise. Signal.

• Observe everything before acting.
• Stabilise the systems that signal trust.
• Signal his own intent through small, visible decisions.

The plan was less about projects and more about posture — showing the organisation that discipline had a heartbeat, not just a spreadsheet.

A CFO's first 90 days do not build legacy. They build permission.

CFO Practice Note:
• Divide the first 90 days into diagnosis, stabilization, and visible trust-building actions.
• Share the broad roadmap with the CEO, but avoid overpromising before your first diagnostic is complete.
• Choose early signals carefully: one liquidity improvement, one reporting improvement, and one relationship improvement can establish credibility faster than ten announcements.

---

12. The CFO as Conscience Keeper

The CFO is the last line between optimism and overstatement.

Kael knew that truth often arrives quietly, through anomalies others ignore.

He instituted a daily 10-minute "truth huddle" with his direct team — three questions only:

What did we learn today that others should know?

What risk emerged that no one wants to mention?

What decision needs moral clarity, not numerical proof?

Kael believed courage was not a speech. *It was a discipline repeated before pressure became public.*

CFO Practice Note:

• Create a regular forum where uncomfortable facts can surface before they become board issues.
• Encourage the team to report weak signals — unusual variances, delayed reconciliations, strained customer collections, or pressure to adjust assumptions.
• Protect people who raise early warnings; a silent finance team is a governance risk.

---

13. Building the Trust Account with Business Heads

Trust accrues through reciprocity.

Kael spent his initial weeks not issuing directives, but joining discussions — plant visits, product briefings, HR townhalls, sales reviews, and supply-chain meetings.

He shared insights in plain language: "If we reduce receivable days by three, we fund your marketing campaign without borrowing."

When finance enables, it earns permission to challenge.

The business did not need another controller. It needed a partner who could convert discipline into possibility.

CFO Practice Note:

• Meet business heads in their operating context, not only in finance review meetings.
• Translate financial discipline into business benefit — cash released, margin protected, risk reduced, capacity funded.
• Build trust before challenge; resistance falls when finance is seen as an enabler of better choices.

---

14. First 100-Hour Reflections Log

By the end of his first hundred hours, Kael documented patterns rather than events:

- Where emotion drove decisions.
- Where systems replaced sense.
- Where talent lacked empowerment.
- Where silence carried more information than slides.

His log became the raw data for leadership calibration — a mirror, not a metric.

He understood that first impressions are dangerous only when they remain untested.

CFO Practice Note:

- Record observations under themes: liquidity, people, culture, controls, reporting, governance, and decision-making rhythm.
- Revisit the log after 30 days and separate confirmed patterns from first impressions.
- Use the log to frame better questions, not to form early judgements about people.

---

15. Self-Audit of Values, Strengths and Blind Spots

Before auditing others, Kael audited himself.

He listed his biases, ego triggers, and knowledge gaps. He identified two truths: he was data-driven but sometimes impatient with dissent; decisive but occasionally dismissive of emotion.

Leadership begins with literacy of self.

He resolved to surround himself with colleagues who challenged him — not comforted him.

A CFO who cannot see his own blind spots eventually becomes one for the organisation.

CFO Practice Note:

- Write a personal leadership audit covering strengths, impatience triggers, technical gaps, relationship risks, and ethical non-negotiables.
- Identify two people who can challenge your assumptions without fear of punishment.
- Review your own behaviour after key meetings; the CFO's tone often

becomes the finance function's culture.

The 30-Day Action Grid (Integrated Narrative)

In the first thirty days, Kael's mission was silent alignment.
He met thirty leaders, spoke less than 30 percent of the time, mapped every critical cash flow and cultural flow, and produced his first confidential "CFO Arrival Report" for the CEO.
It contained three sections: Liquidity Health, Cultural Tone, and Governance Risk.

No targets. No projects. Just truth.

By Day 30, the CEO remarked, *"You've shown me the mirror without judgement — that's leadership."*

Leadership Reflection

Numbers measure progress; judgement measures leadership.
Kael Cipher entered his new role as a technician of finance and emerged as a custodian of trust.
He learned that to be a CFO is not to own the truth but to protect the space where truth can be spoken.

"In the end, the CFO is not the keeper of accounts — he is the keeper of confidence."
— Adapted from the Harvard Business Review, "Leading When It Counts."

CHAPTER 2

READING THE ORGANISATION'S INTENT: Vision, Strategy & Finance Alignment

Decoding strategy, culture, and decision-making DNA.

When Kael Cipher first entered the corner office in Mumbai, the walls spoke before the people did. Strategy decks lined the credenza. A "Vision 2030" poster glimmered beside a compliance calendar. But beneath the surface of every PowerPoint slide, he sensed a deeper truth — strategy is rarely what the company *writes*; it's what the company *tolerates.*

The first responsibility of a new CFO is not to re-engineer finance — it is to **read the organisation**. Because long before capital flows, *intent* flows. And unless a CFO learns how that intent moves through hierarchy, the numbers will always tell only half the story.

16. Assessing Corporate Vision Statements for Execution Reality

Every company has a vision statement. Only a few have a vision system.

Kael began by comparing G Z Corporation's official ambition — "to shape sustainable global impact through innovation and integrity" — against its actual portfolio allocation. The mismatch was evident.

High-cost, low-yield units still received funding, while the sustainability vertical that attracted ESG capital remained under-resourced.

Kael's first task was to quantify how much of G Z's investment truly aligned with its declared intent. The audit was not of finances alone. It was an audit of honesty. He wrote in his notes: ***a strategy becomes credible only when capital follows conviction.***

CFO Practice Note:

• Compare the company's stated vision with actual budget, capex, hiring, and management attention.
• Identify areas where capital allocation contradicts declared strategic priorities.
• Prepare a short "vision-to-capital" gap note for private discussion with the CEO before making public recommendations.

---

17. Mapping Stated vs. Lived Values

Values, Kael learned, are not what leadership repeats at offsites. They are what managers reinforce in meetings.

He began a value-mapping exercise by listening to how mid-level managers justified budgets, exceptions, promotions, delays, and risk-taking. If every conversation circled back to "growth at any cost," then integrity was only ink on paper.

He built a two-column log: **Stated Values vs. Observed Behaviours**.

The exercise revealed more about the company's soul than its balance sheet.

Finance, he reminded his deputies, does not merely count. *It reflects character in numbers.*

CFO Practice Note:

• Observe how managers make trade-offs when values conflict with targets.
• Compare stated values with incentives, approvals, escalation behaviour, and budget priorities.
• Use value mapping quietly at first; culture must be diagnosed before it is corrected.

---

18. Strategy Architecture: Core vs. Satellite Initiatives

A conglomerate's strength often becomes its fog.

Kael divided G Z's activities into two categories: **Core Engines**, the businesses driving most of EBITDA, and **Satellites**, innovation projects that consumed capital but created stories.

He applied a simple CFO lens: Does this initiative generate, protect, or dilute enterprise value?

Once clarified, he could trace which satellite projects deserved continuation and which ones survived only through political sponsorship. This exercise created strategic visibility before any cost optimisation began.

The objective was not to kill experimentation. It was to ensure that experimentation had purpose, ownership, and return discipline.

CFO Practice Note:

• Classify each major initiative as core, adjacent, experimental, or politically protected.

• Ask whether the initiative generates value, protects value, or merely absorbs attention.

• Review funding discipline for satellite projects through milestones, not enthusiasm.

---

19. Aligning Financial KPIs with Strategic Pillars

Too many organisations measure what is easy, not what is essential.

Kael reconstructed the KPI dashboard from the ground up, mapping each financial indicator to a strategic pillar.

If the strategy spoke of customer intimacy, he ensured metrics like customer lifetime value, repeat revenue, complaint cost, and retention-cost ratio entered the finance review.

If the strategy aimed at global resilience, he added currency diversification, supplier dependency, inventory flexibility, and geography-level margin sensitivity.

Finance became not a separate language, but the grammar of execution.

CFO Practice Note:

• Map each strategic pillar to two or three measurable financial or operational indicators.

• Remove vanity metrics that look impressive but do not influence decisions.

• Ensure each KPI has an owner, review frequency, threshold, and escalation trigger.

---

20. Detecting Early Warning Signs of Strategic Misalignment

Kael's early-warning radar was data-driven yet intuitive.

He scanned three areas weekly:

• Variances between forecast and cash actuals.
• Overperformance of non-core units.
• Unusual silence from high-margin divisions.

Discrepancies in tone and trajectory often revealed more than any spreadsheet. Misalignment rarely shouts. It whispers through numbers that look too convenient to question.

Kael marked one warning in his journal: *the costliest detours often begin as polite deviations.*

CFO Practice Note:
• Track where actual results repeatedly diverge from strategic assumptions.
• Investigate unusually smooth numbers, sudden overperformance, or unexplained silence from key business units.
• Convert early-warning signals into management questions before they become board-level surprises.

---

21. Understanding Business Model Economics

Every CFO must understand how value is truly created, captured, delayed, and lost.

Kael analysed the unit economics of each vertical: what inputs drove revenue, what costs throttled margins, how capital intensity differed across geographies, and where cash lagged behind reported performance.

His framework was simple: if he could not sketch the business model on one page, he did not yet own it.

By converting operating complexity into economic clarity, he made finance the translation engine of the organisation's DNA.

A CFO who understands only the accounts understands the past. *A CFO who understands the business model can influence the future.*

CFO Practice Note:

• Prepare a one-page economic map for every major business line: revenue driver, cost driver, margin lever, working-capital lever, and risk trigger.
• Identify where profit is reported before cash is realized.
• Use business model economics to guide pricing, capex, inventory, credit, and market-entry decisions.

---

22. Distinguishing Cost-Center vs. Value-Center Functions

Kael redefined the CFO lexicon inside the company.

Instead of casually labeling departments as cost centers, he reframed them as value centers — each expected to show measurable contribution to enterprise outcomes.

He introduced internal value charters: concise one-page statements linking each function's outcomes to growth, cash, risk reduction, capability, reputation, or resilience.

This reframing created accountability without humiliating support functions. HR, IT, legal, procurement, and administration could now articulate ROI beyond expense lines.

The language changed the behaviour. *When people are measured only as costs, they defend budgets. When they are measured by value, they defend outcomes.*

CFO Practice Note:

• Ask each major function to define its contribution to enterprise value, not only its annual cost.
• Convert support-function spending into outcome measures such as retention, uptime, compliance, productivity, or risk reduction.
• Avoid blunt cost-center language when the real goal is performance accountability.

---

23. Performing a Strategy-to-Cash Diagnostic

Kael initiated a 60-day strategy-to-cash diagnostic.

He traced how strategic priorities travelled through budgeting, execution, invoicing, collection, and cash conversion. Every drop in the funnel — from intent to invoice — indicated leakage of focus, discipline, ownership, or control.

The exercise exposed a critical insight: decisions made in strategic meetings rarely reached operational dashboards.

He summarised the finding for the CEO in one line: *if strategy does not reach cash, it never truly entered the business.*

CFO Practice Note:

• Trace one major strategic priority from board approval to budget, operating plan, invoice, collection, and reported cash.
• Identify where ownership weakens between strategy, execution, billing, and recovery.
• Use the diagnostic to expose leakage without blaming functions; the aim is system repair.

---

24. Interpreting Board Resolutions and Past Strategy Decks

Instead of starting fresh, Kael revisited five years of board decks, resolutions, and action trackers.

He marked every deferred project, unclosed action, repeated concern, and recommendation that had returned under a new title.

Patterns emerged. Similar ideas had been repackaged across years, while some unresolved risks had survived multiple leadership reviews.

It was organisational déjà vu.

Kael realized his first governance duty was not to create more plans. It was to close the open loops of the past. Continuity, not novelty, builds confidence with the board.

CFO Practice Note:

• Review at least three to five years of board packs, action trackers, and unresolved committee matters.
• Identify repeated themes that appear under different labels across years.
• Build a closure register for old commitments before launching new transformation agendas.

---

25. Aligning Capital Allocation with Enterprise Priorities

Kael introduced a discipline of Capital Alignment Reports.

Each quarter, finance would publish how deployed capital tracked against declared strategic priorities. The report compared board-approved ambition with actual capital movement across business lines, geographies, functions, and projects.

It was not about policing. It was about proving alignment.

The transparency elevated trust with the board, which could finally see how money mirrored strategy.

Kael's principle was clear: *capital allocation is the most honest version of strategy.*

CFO Practice Note:

• Build a quarterly capital alignment report showing where money actually moved versus where strategy said it should move.
• Separate growth, maintenance, compliance, innovation, and defensive capital.
• Flag capital drift early — especially when politically protected projects continue receiving funds without value proof.

---

26. Identifying "Sacred Cows" in Budgeting

Every company has budget lines that escape gravity.

Kael identified them using a three-step test: historic immunity, political protection, and data silence.

Once exposed, he did not cut them abruptly. He initiated value conversations: "If we were not funding this, what would we lose?"

This technique reframed cost-cutting as strategic reallocation, reducing resistance while restoring logic.

The objective was not to attack legacy spending. It was to ask whether legacy still deserved capital.

CFO Practice Note:

• Identify expenses that are never challenged, never measured, or always defended by senior influence.
• Ask what value would be lost if the spend stopped, reduced, or moved elsewhere.
• Reframe cuts as reallocation to higher-value priorities, not punishment of existing owners.

---

27. Observing Informal Communication Channels

Information does not travel only through dashboards.

It travels through lunch tables, WhatsApp groups, corridor conversations, late-night emails, and the people everyone consults before a formal meeting.

Kael quietly observed the informal networks: who influenced whom, who filtered what, who carried bad news, and how decisions really formed.

This social audit helped him map hidden decision nodes. When finance later intervened in tough calls, it did so through influence, not imposition.

He learned that formal authority shows the chart. *Informal authority shows the company.*

CFO Practice Note:

• Identify the informal influencers who shape decisions before meetings begin.
• Notice where bad news slows down, changes language, or disappears.
• Use informal network awareness ethically — to improve communication flow, not to manipulate people.

---

28. CFO's Role in Strategy Reviews

Kael institutionalised finance's presence in all strategic reviews.

But he deliberately avoided turning those meetings into financial autopsies. Strategy reviews were not meant to become post-mortems where finance arrived only to explain why targets were missed.

Instead, he reframed his role: to translate financial implications into decision velocity.

By presenting scenarios, not sermons, he built credibility as a business enabler — not the compliance police.

The CFO's role in strategy was not to slow ambition. *It was to make ambition financially executable.*

CFO Practice Note:

• Enter strategy reviews with scenarios, sensitivities, and trade-offs — not only historical variance reports.
• Ask how each strategic choice affects cash, capacity, risk, talent, compliance, and timing.
• Position finance as a decision partner by showing options, not merely objections.

---

29. Drafting Your CFO Strategy Interpretation Memo

Every new CFO should write a Strategy Interpretation Memo — a confidential document for personal alignment.

Kael's memo had three sections: what the company says it wants, what it truly rewards, and what it quietly avoids.

The memo became his moral compass, not for circulation but for clarity. It reminded him that leadership begins with internal honesty.

Such a memo protects the CFO from being seduced by slogans. It forces him to distinguish strategy from theatre.

CFO Practice Note:

• Write a private memo summarising declared strategy, actual behaviour, funding patterns, and avoided conversations.

• Revisit the memo after 30, 60, and 90 days to test whether your early reading was accurate.

• Use the memo to guide questions, not accusations; its purpose is clarity before intervention.

---

30. Integrating AI Dashboards for Real-Time Strategy Tracking

Finally, Kael introduced a dynamic AI dashboard integrating real-time performance, forecasts, and internal sentiment data.

It was not about replacing human judgement. It was about augmenting foresight.

The dashboard visualised alignment gaps between strategic goals and financial trends. It showed where KPIs moved against stated priorities, where risk indicators were rising, and where execution slowed before the month-end review revealed it.

It gave Kael what every modern CFO needs — a living map of intent.

But he remained cautious. *AI could sharpen visibility, but accountability still belonged to leadership.*

CFO Practice Note:

• Use AI dashboards to detect patterns, anomalies, and alignment gaps — not to outsource judgement.

• Ensure dashboard inputs are governed by clean master data, defined ownership, and controlled access.

• Review AI outputs with business context; a model can detect movement, but only leaders can interpret meaning.

30-90-Day Action Grid — Reading the Organisation's Intent

1. Conduct a 360° "vision-to-capital" alignment audit.
2. Create a Value Map comparing stated vs. lived behaviours.
3. Establish cross-functional sessions translating strategy to measurable KPIs.
4. Review five years of board minutes for continuity gaps.
5. Initiate quarterly Capital Alignment Reports.
6. Build an AI-driven Strategy Dashboard to visualise gaps in real time.

Leadership Reflection

"If numbers are the body of a company, intent is its soul."

For Kael Cipher, the first ninety days weren't about proving intellect — they were about proving *alignment.*
He realized that finance, when practiced with strategic empathy, becomes the organisation's conscience.
His goal was no longer to interpret the numbers for the company — it was to interpret the company through its numbers.

CHAPTER 3

THE FIRST 30 DAYS DIAGNOSTIC: People, Process, Priorities — Mapping Your Battlefield

Your first-month immersion plan.

When Kael Cipher officially took charge, the first thirty days weren't about issuing commands — they were about *listening to the noise beneath the numbers.*
He knew every new CFO inherits not just balance sheets, but *belief systems.*

In the first month, perception forms faster than reality. That's why his diagnostic wasn't financial — it was anthropological. He had to map how people thought, how processes actually worked, and what priorities truly drove decisions.

---

31. Conducting Stakeholder Interviews and Listening Audits

Kael began with one operating principle: empathy precedes efficiency.

He scheduled twenty-five one-to-one conversations across levels — from regional controllers to plant supervisors. Each meeting started with the same three questions:

1. What works well here?
2. What slows us down?
3. If you were CFO, what would you fix first?

The answers formed his listening ledger.

By week three, he saw patterns the numbers alone would have hidden — bottlenecks disguised as traditions, risks rationalised as culture, and frustrations that had become too familiar to be escalated.

Kael reminded himself often: *leadership is not speaking first; it is being disciplined enough to conclude last.*

CFO Practice Note:
• Conduct listening interviews across hierarchy, geography, and function — not only with direct reports.
• Ask the same core questions repeatedly so patterns become visible across conversations.
• Separate complaints from signals; repeated friction often points to a broken process, not a difficult person.

---

32. Creating the Organisation's Financial Anatomy Chart

Kael sketched what he called the financial anatomy of G Z Corporation APAC.

It showed every nerve that carried financial information: subsidiaries, reporting hubs, shared-service centers, ERP interfaces, treasury links, audit touchpoints, and consolidation routes.

This visual map replaced hundreds of slides with a single truth — where financial data began, where it changed hands, and where it broke.

It was a revelation.

Some regional entities still reported through legacy systems, making the closing process both slow and fragile. The chart became his diagnostic X-ray.

A CFO cannot repair what he cannot see.

CFO Practice Note:
• Map every entity, system, reporting route, approval point, and consolidation layer in one visual chart.
• Mark where manual intervention, legacy systems, duplicate uploads, or spreadsheet dependency enters the flow.
• Use the anatomy chart to decide which process failures are isolated issues and which are structural weaknesses.

33. Reviewing Existing Finance Process Maps

Kael next pulled out the process maps of Accounts Payable, Receivable, Payroll, Treasury, and Closing.

Most were immaculate on paper — untouched since an ISO audit years earlier.

His test was simple: "Show me how this process survives on the worst day of the month."

That question exposed cracks. Reconciliations depended on individuals, not controls. Timelines hinged on goodwill, not governance. Exceptions had become habits, and habits had begun calling themselves process.

Kael flagged each dependency in red — not to shame, but to prioritise.

The CFO's job, he reminded his team, is not to admire complexity. *It is to make simplicity scalable.*

CFO Practice Note:

• Compare documented process maps with actual execution during peak-pressure periods.

• Identify where the process depends on personal memory, informal approval, manual correction, or late intervention.

• Update maps only after observing the real process; otherwise documentation becomes theatre.

---

34. Analysing Prior Audit Reports for Recurring Gaps

Kael studied five years of internal and external audit reports, not merely for findings but for patterns.

Any issue that reappeared twice was no longer just a control failure. It was a cultural one.

Repeated non-compliance told him where attention had become routine and ownership had vanished. He created a repetition matrix, mapping which divisions had recurring remarks, which owners had delayed closure, and which root causes remained unsolved.

It became the first dashboard he presented to the Audit Committee: evidence that some risks were not operational accidents, but institutionalised behaviour.

CFO Practice Note:

• Review at least three to five years of audit findings to identify repeat issues, delayed closures, and weak owners.

• Classify recurring gaps by root cause: process weakness, system limitation,

skill gap, accountability failure, or cultural tolerance.
• Present repeat findings as governance signals, not isolated compliance defects.

35. Reading Management Letters from Statutory Auditors

Before meeting the auditors, Kael read every management letter they had issued to the previous CFO.

He highlighted comments written in cautious language — "may consider enhancing," "requires monitoring," "needs further review," "could be strengthened."

Such phrases, he knew, often masked chronic discomfort auditors hesitate to escalate bluntly.

By converting these subtleties into action items, Kael turned courtesy into control.

He wrote in the margin: *auditors often write in pencil; CFOs must learn to read in ink.*

CFO Practice Note:
• Read management letters for tone, not only technical findings; cautious language may hide serious concern.
• Convert every auditor observation into an owner, due date, root-cause note, and closure evidence.
• Meet auditors early to understand which issues worry them most but may not appear forcefully in formal language.

36. Studying Previous Three-Year Financial Trends

Numbers, like people, have habits.

Kael compared the last three years of consolidated financials: revenue growth, margin drift, working-capital turns, debt cost, accrual movement, and operating cash conversion.

He was not looking for ratios alone. He was looking for rhythm.

A sudden shift in expense patterns or accrual logic often hinted at changes in leadership behaviour. Margin stability without cash strength worried him more than a visible dip in profit.

The goal was to see whether performance had improved through capability — or merely through accounting.

CFO Practice Note:
• Compare three-year trends across revenue, margin, cash flow, working capital, debt cost, and exceptional items.
• Investigate changes in accruals, provisions, capitalization, or cut-off patterns that may explain performance movement.
• Ask whether improvement came from stronger operations, better pricing, accounting treatment, or delayed recognition of stress.

---

37. Variance Analysis Between Budget, Forecast and Actuals

Kael instituted an early variance-mapping exercise — not to assign blame, but to reveal bias.

If sales kept overshooting targets while cash lagged, he knew optimism was institutional. If expenses stayed within budget only through delayed recognition, discipline was cosmetic. If forecasts changed every month without explanation, planning had become negotiation.

He built variance narratives, asking business heads to explain assumptions, not just numbers.

Soon, variance analysis turned from arithmetic to anthropology — showing where leadership psychology inflated projections, underplayed risks, or rewarded convenient certainty.

CFO Practice Note:
• Review recurring variances between budget, forecast, actuals, and cash realization — not just P&L performance.
• Ask owners to explain the assumption behind the variance, not merely the mathematical movement.
• Track whether variance patterns reveal optimism bias, delayed escalation, weak forecasting, or incentive distortion.

---

38. Identifying the Top 10 Cash-Impact Processes

Kael narrowed focus to the ten processes that truly moved the company's liquidity needle — from order booking to customer collection, from procurement commitment to vendor payment.

He applied a risk-to-cash lens: which activities, if delayed or disrupted, could cost the company a week's liquidity?

Those ten processes became his Cash Impact Commandments.

He assigned owners, metrics, escalation triggers, and review frequency for each — converting invisible friction into visible accountability.

Cash discipline, he knew, begins where process ownership becomes measurable.

CFO Practice Note:

• Identify the ten processes that most directly affect cash inflow, cash outflow, debt usage, or liquidity visibility.
• Assign each process a named owner, metric, threshold, and escalation trigger.
• Review cash-impact processes weekly during the first 90 days; liquidity pressure usually begins as process delay.

---

39. Mapping Dependencies on Key Individuals

Legacy organisations often depend on a few "indispensables."

Kael quietly noted where processes paused when a single individual was absent.

He found one controller whose Excel macro essentially ran the monthly close. Another executive alone knew the vendor-discount algorithm. A regional finance manager carried tax payment logic in a personal notebook no one else had seen.

He introduced knowledge-redundancy mapping, ensuring no critical process rested on one person's memory, laptop, or private method.

He told his deputies: *dependence is not loyalty; it is latent risk.*

CFO Practice Note:

• Identify all processes dependent on one person, one spreadsheet, one password, one macro, or one undocumented routine.
• Create backup ownership and written SOPs for every critical finance activity.
• Test redundancy during normal operations; backup plans fail when they are first used during crisis.

---

40. Risk of Single-Point Failures within Finance

Building on that insight, Kael ordered a single-point-of-failure audit.

Each finance manager had to identify at least two backups for their top three recurring tasks. He coupled this with access-control verification to prevent fraud under cover of urgency.

This simple audit pre-empted several future crises and later became a governance model adopted by other functions.

A process is not controlled merely because it works. It is controlled when it can work without the hero who usually saves it.

CFO Practice Note:

• Run a single-point-of-failure audit across closing, treasury, tax, payroll, statutory filings, reporting, and payments.
• Assign primary owner, backup owner, and emergency reviewer for each critical recurring task.
• Link SPOF review with access-control checks so continuity does not create fraud opportunity.

---

41. Cultural Tone of Finance Team — Defensive or Proactive?

Kael's informal check was disarmingly human.

During team reviews, did people talk about what went wrong — or what could go right?

The language of finance revealed its mindset. Defensive cultures protect explanations. Proactive cultures protect improvement.

He began rewarding curiosity, not perfection. Small errors surfaced earlier because people no longer feared being punished for honesty.

That shift mattered. A finance team that hides small discomforts eventually creates large exposures.

CFO Practice Note:

• Listen to the team's language: are they explaining delays, identifying causes, or proposing improvements?
• Reward early risk reporting and root-cause thinking more visibly than perfect-looking dashboards.
• Create psychological safety for small errors; concealed minor issues often become material failures.

---

42. Designing Your First 30-Day Dashboard

By Day 25, Kael compiled a concise dashboard — a single slide summarising liquidity, open risks, control gaps, compliance exposure, cultural observations, and top ten quick wins.

No clutter. No jargon.

He colour-coded the chart using the three-signal test:

• Green = operationally sound.
• Amber = attention required.
• Red = potential exposure.

This became his talking document with the CEO — an instrument of shared vigilance rather than fear.

The dashboard did not claim mastery. It showed disciplined visibility.

CFO Practice Note:
• Keep the first dashboard limited to what the CEO must know: liquidity, risks, controls, people dependencies, and quick wins.
• Use colour coding only when the definition of each colour is clear and consistent.
• Do not use the dashboard to dramatise problems; use it to create shared prioritisation.

43. Reporting Rhythms — Daily, Weekly, Monthly

Kael synchronised reporting cadence with decision cadence.

Daily reports were reserved for liquidity. Weekly reviews covered working-capital movement, collections, payment priorities, and control exceptions. Monthly reporting focused on P&L, covenant tracking, cash conversion, and board-level variance narratives.

He discouraged presentations longer than five slides — one for numbers, four for narrative.

Consistency, not sophistication, builds credibility.

Kael's rule was simple: *finance earns trust not by forecasting once, but by showing up with rhythm.*

CFO Practice Note:
• Match reporting frequency to decision urgency: daily for liquidity, weekly for working capital, monthly for performance and governance.
• Keep each report tied to action — owner, variance, trigger, decision, or escalation.
• Avoid over-reporting; too many reports can create noise while still hiding the truth.

44. Quick Wins vs. Structural Reforms

In the first thirty days, Kael prioritised momentum over magnitude.

Quick wins included automating approval hierarchies, reconciling dormant accounts, clarifying payment terms, improving collection follow-up, and closing long-pending audit actions.

Structural reforms — ERP consolidation, policy rewrite, shared-service redesign, treasury centralisation — were logged for the 90-day plan.

Early victories bought him political capital to execute deeper changes later.

He understood the sequence: first earn trust, then ask the organisation to change.

CFO Practice Note:

• Separate quick wins from structural reforms; do not confuse visible action with transformation.
• Choose quick wins that reduce risk, improve cash visibility, or repair credibility without destabilising operations.
• Build a 90-day reform backlog for larger changes that require sponsorship, budget, systems, or behavioural shift.

---

45. Writing Your Confidential "Arrival Report" for the CEO

At the end of the month, Kael submitted a private three-page note to the CEO titled **State of Finance — 30 Days In**.

It contained no adjectives, only observations.

The report summarised liquidity condition, people dependencies, control gaps, audit patterns, cultural tone, early risks, and priority actions.

It was both diagnosis and declaration — proof that he understood the terrain he had been entrusted to lead.

The CEO's response was brief: "Welcome aboard, Kael. I trust your silence will be strategic."

Kael knew the deeper meaning: his first month had not been passive. It had been disciplined listening.

CFO Practice Note:

• Keep the first arrival report factual, concise, and confidential; avoid blame, adjectives, and dramatic conclusions.
• Structure it around current state, early risks, quick wins, unresolved

questions, and next 60-day priorities.
• Use the report to align privately with the CEO before wider organisational action begins.

30-Day Action Grid — Mapping Your Battlefield

1. Complete 25+ stakeholder listening sessions; summarise patterns, not opinions.
2. Draft the organisation's financial anatomy map with system interlinks.
3. Create a "repetition matrix" from historical audit findings.
4. Launch SPOF and knowledge-redundancy checks.
5. Publish a one-slide 30-Day Dashboard for CEO visibility.
6. Submit the confidential *Arrival Report* by Day 30.

Leadership Reflection

"In the first month, every number you see is a reflection — not of performance, but of perception."

Kael learned that diagnosis is diplomacy in disguise.
The first thirty days define whether a CFO becomes a gatekeeper or a guide.
He chose the latter — listening harder, asking slower, and building trust before tightening controls.

Finance, he realized, isn't the pulse of the organisation.
It's the *stethoscope* — the instrument that tells whether the heart still beats in rhythm.

CHAPTER 4

TREASURY AND FUNDS CONTROL — The Early Audit

Quietly verify liquidity, covenants, and banking health.

Kael Cipher believed that a company's first mirror was its cash book. On Day 10, he requested all bank balances at 10 a.m. local time — across fourteen entities, five currencies, and three time zones. What returned was a spreadsheet with twelve versions, four formats, and three disclaimers.

That was the moment he knew: **the treasury wasn't just a department — it was the bloodstream of trust.**

"Liquidity is oxygen — unnoticed when abundant, fatal when absent." —
Jamie Dimon, JPMorgan Chase

His first audit would therefore not be public. It would be *quiet, forensic,* and deeply human.

46. Bank Account Rationalisation Across Entities

G Z Corporation APAC had 87 active bank accounts.

Kael asked one simple question: "How many of these still serve a purpose?"

He discovered dormant subsidiaries maintaining accounts "just in case," legacy accounts left open after projects ended, and local teams using separate banking arrangements for convenience rather than control.

He launched a rationalisation plan, consolidating accounts by currency, jurisdiction, legal entity, and banking partner. Fewer accounts meant faster reconciliation, stronger control, lower charges, cleaner audit trails, and clearer cash visibility.

The goal was not merely cost saving. It was to re-establish cash sovereignty.

CFO Practice Note:

• Prepare a complete bank-account inventory by entity, currency, purpose, signatories, balance, charges, and activity level.
• Close dormant, duplicate, or low-purpose accounts after legal, tax, and operational review.
• Create a quarterly bank-account certification process so unnecessary accounts do not quietly return.

---

47. Cash Pooling and Inter-Entity Settlement Policy

Kael reviewed whether idle cash in Singapore could legally support deficits in Indonesia.

Within two weeks, he introduced a cross-entity cash-pooling structure — a zero-balance mechanism with daily sweeps into the group hub, subject to local regulations, tax rules, transfer-pricing discipline, and board-approved limits.

The move released trapped liquidity and reduced avoidable short-term borrowing.

More importantly, it changed treasury behaviour. Cash was no longer viewed entity by entity, but as a regional resource to be governed intelligently.

Treasury, Kael reminded his team, was not an accounting office. It was a liquidity exchange.

CFO Practice Note:

• Map surplus and deficit positions across entities before negotiating fresh borrowings.
• Review legal, tax, FEMA/local exchange-control, transfer-pricing, and board-approval requirements before pooling cash.
• Establish inter-company settlement timelines so liquidity movement does not become unresolved group exposure.

---

48. Daily Liquidity Dashboard

By Day 20, Kael implemented a **Liquidity Pulse** dashboard — a 10-minute morning ritual.

It showed inflows, outflows, available cash, bank headroom, expected collections, statutory outflows, and country-level constraints.

The colour coding was deliberate: green for control, amber for volatility, red for constraint.

For the first time, the regional CEO could see the company's cash position in one page and one language. The dashboard did not solve liquidity by itself, but it removed confusion.

In treasury, visibility is the first form of control.

CFO Practice Note:

• Build a daily dashboard covering opening cash, expected inflows, committed outflows, bank lines, and liquidity headroom.

• Define colour triggers clearly; red should mean action, not decoration.

• Review the dashboard at a fixed time daily during the first 30–60 days until liquidity visibility stabilises.

---

49. Short-Term Investment of Surplus Funds

Idle cash is lazy capital.

Kael established a short-term investment policy aligned with the group's risk appetite. He split surpluses into three tiers:

• **Operational reserves under 30 days:** overnight sweeps or money-market funds.

• **Strategic buffer for 30–90 days:** term deposits or high-grade short-term instruments.

• **Long float above 90 days:** group inter-company deposits or approved instruments at arm's-length rates.

Every investment moved through dual authorisation and was benchmarked against treasury-approved reference rates.

Kael's principle was clear: return matters, but liquidity and safety come first.

CFO Practice Note:

• Segment surplus cash by expected usage period before investing it.

• Approve instruments only after checking credit rating, liquidity, counterparty exposure, maturity, and policy limits.

• Do not chase yield with operating cash; treasury earns trust by avoiding avoidable risk.

---

50. Early Warning Indicators of Stress

Kael built a **Liquidity Radar** with five stress signals:

1. Delayed vendor payments beyond agreed terms.
2. Unexpected foreign-exchange drawdowns.
3. Rising utilisation of overdraft or working-capital lines.
4. Declining collection predictability.
5. Unusual silence from controllers or business heads.

Each trigger required a one-paragraph explanation within 24 hours.

The goal was not blame. It was early oxygen.

A CFO cannot prevent every liquidity storm, but he can prevent the organisation from discovering it too late.

CFO Practice Note:
• Define five to seven liquidity stress indicators and monitor them weekly, or daily in sensitive periods.
• Require short written explanations for trigger breaches, including owner, cause, action, and expected closure date.
• Escalate patterns, not isolated noise; repeated amber signals often become red before management accepts them.

---

51. Reviewing Banking Covenants and Compliance Calendar

Kael mapped every loan covenant against reporting dates, ratio definitions, testing frequency, cure periods, and cross-default clauses.

He converted dense legal text into a visual **Covenant Calendar** shared with treasury, FP&A, legal, and controllership.

A missed ratio could cost more than penalty interest. It could damage negotiating credibility for an entire year.

He instituted a no-surprise rule with banks: if a breach became foreseeable, they would hear it from him first.

Banks forgive difficult results faster than they forgive concealed surprises.

CFO Practice Note:
• Convert every borrowing covenant into a calendar with ratio formula, due date, data owner, review owner, and escalation date.
• Run covenant forecasts at least one quarter ahead, not only at reporting deadlines.

• Inform lenders early if stress is emerging; credibility is strongest before formal breach occurs.

---

52. Understanding Weighted Average Cost of Funds

Kael computed the weighted average cost of funds by region, currency, lender, instrument, maturity, security, and covenant burden.

He benchmarked it against peer rates, market references, and internal borrowing models.

The exercise revealed pricing inconsistencies caused by fragmented negotiations and local borrowing arrangements. Some entities paid more not because they were riskier, but because the group had never negotiated as one financial voice.

Within a month, Kael initiated a central credit-line negotiation to unify pricing.

Treasury savings rarely become headline victories. But they compound quietly into enterprise value.

CFO Practice Note:

• Calculate weighted average cost of funds by instrument, entity, currency, maturity, and lender.
• Identify avoidable spread differences caused by fragmented borrowing, weak negotiation, or outdated facilities.
• Use group-level visibility to renegotiate pricing, covenants, collateral, and unused-line charges where possible.

---

53. Interest Coverage and DSCR Monitoring

To maintain bank confidence, Kael built a rolling interest-coverage and Debt-Service Coverage Ratio tracker.

It projected coverage three quarters ahead, stress-testing for rate hikes, earnings volatility, delayed collections, and currency movement.

Every board pack included a one-page summary titled **How Long Can We Breathe?**

The title was dramatic by design. It forced leadership to see debt servicing as a living capacity, not a backward-looking ratio.

A company does not lose lender confidence on the day it misses payment. It loses it when it stops seeing pressure early.

CFO Practice Note:
• Track interest coverage and DSCR on a rolling basis, with base, stress, and severe scenarios.
• Link ratio movement to EBITDA, cash conversion, debt maturities, interest-rate changes, and covenant thresholds.
• Show future coverage risk in board packs before the lender asks the question.

---

54. Cash Forecasting Models — 13-Week and Rolling

Kael adopted the 13-week rolling forecast as the foundation of liquidity planning.

It gave treasury the right balance between discipline and agility: near enough to act, long enough to prepare.

The model was updated weekly with variance alerts for collections, vendor payments, statutory dues, payroll, debt servicing, and committed capex. It trained teams to think forward instead of explaining cash after it had already moved.

Forecasting was no longer a spreadsheet exercise. It became a management habit.

CFO Practice Note:
• Build the 13-week forecast using direct cash inflows and outflows, not only accounting assumptions.
• Update the model weekly and compare every forecast against actual movement.
• Use the forecast to trigger action: collection acceleration, payment rescheduling, credit-line drawdown, or board escalation.

---

55. Measuring Cash Forecast Accuracy

Kael instituted an accuracy metric: the difference between forecast and actual cash should remain within an approved tolerance band.

Any variance beyond the threshold required a narrative explanation and corrective plan.

Predictability, he argued, was more valuable than optimism.

A finance team that cannot predict cash with reasonable accuracy cannot make reliable promises to the CEO, banks, vendors, employees, or the board.

Forecast accuracy therefore became a leadership discipline, not a treasury statistic.

CFO Practice Note:
• Define acceptable forecast-variance tolerance for weekly and monthly cash movement.
• Require variance narratives explaining whether the miss came from collection timing, payment acceleration, data error, or business assumption failure.
• Track forecast accuracy by owner; recurring variance is a process issue, not bad luck.

---

56. Building Automation via Treasury Management Systems

Manual spreadsheets had their days numbered.

Kael piloted a Treasury Management System integrated with ERP and bank APIs for real-time balances, payment workflows, exposure tracking, and audit trails.

By the second month, most disbursements were digitally tracked and dual-authorised. Cyber controls were tightened to prevent single-signatory exposure, payment manipulation, and uncontrolled master-data changes.

Automation was not introduced for elegance. It was introduced to reduce blindness.

A treasury system is valuable only if it improves visibility, control, and response time.

CFO Practice Note:
• Prioritise automation in bank-balance visibility, payment approval, exposure tracking, and cash forecasting.
• Ensure system implementation includes access controls, maker-checker logic, audit trail, and bank API security.
• Do not automate broken processes blindly; standardise the workflow before digitising it.

---

57. Relationship Banking — Etiquette, Exposure, and Trust

Kael reframed bank relations as partnerships, not procurements.

He hosted a quarterly **Bank Roundtable** with relationship managers to share regional updates, discuss market signals, review facility utilisation, and understand lender appetite.

This transparency turned treasury into a relationship asset. Banks became informal advisors during macro turbulence because they trusted the CFO's candour before stress arrived.

Relationship banking was not social courtesy. It was strategic resilience.

When liquidity tightens, the quality of past communication becomes negotiating capital.

CFO Practice Note:

• Maintain a lender relationship map covering exposure, facility type, pricing, covenant sensitivity, and relationship strength.

• Speak to banks before renewal season or crisis; trust built only during need is too late.

• Share credible business updates regularly without over-disclosing sensitive information.

---

58. Investment Criteria for Short-Term Instruments

The new policy defined five filters before any investment was approved:

1. Credit quality.
2. Maturity discipline.
3. Counterparty diversification.
4. Instrument liquidity and exit visibility.
5. Transparency on beneficial ownership and structure.

Kael made one principle non-negotiable: treasury would not trade security for marginal yield.

Short-term investments exist to protect liquidity, not to prove cleverness.

Treasury's reputation, he said, is measured less by returns earned and more by risks avoided.

CFO Practice Note:

• Approve short-term instruments through defined filters: credit rating, maturity, liquidity, counterparty concentration, and regulatory suitability.

• Set exposure limits per bank, fund, instrument, and group entity.

• Review all treasury investments for capital protection before yield comparison.

---

59. Investment Restrictions and Internal Policy Setup

To formalise discipline, Kael issued the **APAC Treasury Policy Handbook** — a concise document covering limits, approvals, permitted instruments, prohibited instruments, counterparty exposure, reporting rhythm, and exception handling.

It became the region's first codified manual ratified by both the CFO and Group Treasury.

The handbook did not exist to make treasury fearful. It existed to make decisions repeatable.

Compliance became habit, not fear.

Policy, Kael believed, should not slow good judgement. It should prevent avoidable stupidity.

CFO Practice Note:

• Document permitted instruments, prohibited exposures, approval limits, exception routes, and reporting requirements.
• Get treasury policy approved by CFO, group treasury, legal, and board committee where required.
• Review the policy annually or after any major liquidity, fraud, cyber, or market event.

---

60. Fraud Prevention and Treasury Controls

Kael ran a surprise treasury simulation: a fake payment request sent from a masked email.

Only one assistant clicked.

He used it as a teachable moment to demonstrate why dual verification, voice back-checks, payment-purpose validation, vendor-master controls, and geo-locked authentication were non-negotiable.

The point was not to embarrass the assistant. It was to show how fast fraud enters through ordinary behaviour.

He reinforced three golden rules: verify the source, confirm the purpose, and record the trail.

CFO Practice Note:

• Test payment controls through simulations, not only policy reviews.
• Require independent verification for bank-detail changes, urgent payments, and executive payment requests.

• Protect vendor master data with restricted access, change logs, maker-checker approval, and periodic review.

61. Cybersecurity and Dual Approval in Digital Treasury

Kael partnered with the CISO to conduct penetration tests on payment gateways, treasury workflows, bank portals, and TMS interfaces.

Access controls were restructured with multi-factor authentication, role-based permissions, geo-tagging, and transaction thresholds.

No material payment could proceed without two independent approvals from authorised individuals.

Security was rebranded as credibility.

In digital treasury, a weak password can become a financial statement event.

CFO Practice Note:

• Review treasury cybersecurity jointly with the CISO, not as a finance-only control.
• Apply MFA, role-based access, dual approval, payment thresholds, and periodic user-access reviews.
• Treat cyber incidents in treasury as financial risk events requiring CFO-level visibility.

62. Centralised vs. Decentralised Treasury Models

Kael evaluated operational maturity across countries before centralising too fast.

Some markets had regulatory complexity, banking customs, and customer-payment behaviours that required local execution. Others needed tighter group control because local practices had become inconsistent.

He adopted a hybrid model: central visibility with local execution authority under defined thresholds.

It preserved agility without sacrificing control.

Kael captured the balance clearly: *decentralisation without discipline becomes anarchy; centralisation without context becomes fragility.*

CFO Practice Note:

• Assess each market's regulatory, banking, tax, operational, and talent maturity before changing treasury structure.

• Centralise visibility, policy, and limits even where execution remains local.
• Define thresholds for local authority, group approval, exception handling, and escalation.

---

63. Stress-Test Simulation Framework

Kael ran a quarterly simulation: a mock liquidity crisis caused by delayed collections, sudden FX loss, covenant pressure, and restricted bank lines.

The war-room tested response time, communication flow, decision hierarchy, bank messaging, and board escalation.

Post-mortem reviews converted panic into procedure.

The exercise revealed who waited for instruction, who took ownership, and which data arrived too late to be useful.

A stress test is not theatre. It is rehearsal for the day when hesitation becomes expensive.

CFO Practice Note:
• Run treasury stress simulations covering cash shortfall, customer default, FX shock, bank-line freeze, and covenant pressure.
• Measure response time, data quality, decision ownership, and communication sequence.
• Convert simulation gaps into SOP updates, not meeting notes.

---

64. Early Liquidity War-Room SOP

Kael formalised a Liquidity War-Room Standard Operating Procedure.

Roles were pre-defined: Treasury Lead for operations, Controller for data, CFO for communication, CEO for approval, and legal or communications support where external messaging was required.

Every scenario had a day-zero communication template for banks, board, auditors, and key internal stakeholders.

The objective was simple: in a crisis, no one should be searching for the playbook — they should be the playbook.

CFO Practice Note:
• Pre-define war-room roles, decision rights, approval limits, communication owners, and escalation triggers.
• Prepare crisis templates for banks, board, auditors, key vendors, and internal leadership before they are needed.

• Run at least one mock liquidity war-room annually to test whether the SOP works under pressure.

65. Treasury Reporting Discipline and Weekly CFO Review Cadence

Kael converted treasury reporting into a fixed weekly discipline.

Every Friday, the treasury team submitted a one-page **CFO Treasury Note** covering opening cash, closing cash, forecast variance, bank exposure, covenant status, unutilised credit lines, major expected receivables, statutory outflows, debt maturities, and any liquidity trigger requiring attention.

The weekly review was not designed to create another report. It was designed to create rhythm.

Kael insisted that treasury should never surprise the CFO, and the CFO should never surprise the CEO or the board.

In normal times, cash should be visible. In stressful times, cash should be actionable.

CFO Practice Note:

• Create a weekly treasury note covering cash, forecast variance, bank lines, covenant status, debt maturities, and liquidity triggers.
• Use the weekly review to make decisions, not merely receive updates.
• Escalate emerging pressure early; treasury discipline is measured by how few surprises reach the CEO and board.

30-Day Treasury Action Grid

1. Map all bank accounts and rationalise within 30 days.
2. Establish cash-pooling and daily liquidity dashboard.
3. Set accuracy metric for 13-week cash forecast (≤ 5% variance).
4. Publish Covenant Calendar and WACF tracker.
5. Pilot TMS integration and dual-authentication controls.
6. Conduct first Liquidity War-Room simulation.

Leadership Reflection

"Cash is truth in motion." — Kael Cipher

In his first audit, Kael learned that treasury discipline wasn't about hoarding liquidity but about commanding confidence.
By the end of the month, he could see the organisation's financial circulatory system as clearly as a surgeon sees a heartbeat.
The lesson was enduring: visibility precedes velocity, and trust is the most valuable currency on the balance sheet.

Practical Tool: The 13-Week Cash-Flow Visibility Table

A CFO does not need perfect certainty in cash management. He needs early visibility.

The 13-week cash-flow forecast is one of the simplest and most powerful instruments in a CFO's first-year toolkit. It does not replace the annual budget or the monthly MIS. Its purpose is sharper: to tell the CFO whether the organisation can breathe for the next quarter.

Kael Cipher treated the 13-week model as a truth instrument. Every Monday morning, the treasury team updated actual collections, committed payments, statutory dues, payroll, debt service, and expected bank movements. The model was not prepared for decoration. It was prepared to expose pressure before pressure became panic.

Illustrative: 13-Week Cash-Flow Table *(All figures are in ₹ crore / local currency equivalent)*

Particulars	**W1**	**W2**	**W3**	**W4**	**W5**	**W6**	**W7**	**W8**	**W9**	**W10**	**W11**	**W12**	**W13**
Opening Cash Balance	42	35	26	14	11	10	5	-1	-4	-8	-10	-17	-19
Customer Collections	16	20	15	27	24	22	18	26	22	28	20	34	26
Other Inflows	2	2	1	3	2	2	2	2	2	2	2	2	2
Total Inflows	**18**	**22**	**16**	**30**	**26**	**24**	**20**	**28**	**24**	**30**	**22**	**36**	**28**
Payroll	8	0	0	8	0	0	8	0	0	8	0	0	8
Vendor Payments	10	18	16	14	15	16	10	18	15	14	16	20	14
Statutory / Tax Payments	3	4	3	4	3	4	3	4	3	4	3	4	3
Debt Servicing	2	5	4	3	5	5	3	5	5	4	5	6	4
Committed Capex	2	4	5	4	4	4	2	4	5	2	5	6	2
Total Outflows	**25**	**31**	**28**	**33**	**27**	**29**	**26**	**31**	**28**	**32**	**29**	**38**	**31**
Net Cash Movement	**-7**	**-9**	**-12**	**-3**	**-1**	**-5**	**-6**	**-3**	**-4**	**-2**	**-7**	**-2**	**-3**
Closing Cash Before Action	35	26	14	11	10	5	-1	-4	-8	-10	-17	-19	-22
Minimum Liquidity Buffer	15	15	15	15	15	15	15	15	15	15	15	15	15
Surplus / Gap	**20**	**11**	**-1**	**-4**	**-5**	**-10**	**-16**	**-19**	**-23**	**-25**	**-32**	**-34**	**-37**

The table tells a simple story: the company does not run out of cash in Week 1. It runs out of comfort in Week 3.

That difference matters.

A CFO who sees the Week 3 gap in Week 1 still has choices. He can accelerate collections, defer non-critical capex, renegotiate vendor timing, draw unused credit lines, or prepare the board for a temporary liquidity bridge. A CFO who sees the gap in Week 3 has fewer choices and weaker negotiating power.

Kael's rule was clear:

"Cash forecasting is not accounting for the future. It is buying time before the future arrives."

The 13-week model must therefore show four things with brutal clarity:

1. What cash is available today.
2. What cash is expected to arrive.
3. What cash must legally or operationally leave.
4. When management action is required.

A CFO should not allow this table to become a clerical exercise. The first version may be imperfect, but it must be alive. Each week, forecast accuracy should be measured against actuals. Large variances should be investigated, not explained away.

The goal is not to predict every rupee. The goal is to remove surprise.

CHAPTER 5

WORKING CAPITAL SNAPSHOT: Receivables, Vendors & Conversion Cycle

Identify where value leaks before losses appear.

When Kael Cipher looked at the balance sheet of G Z Corporation's Asia-Pacific division, he didn't see assets and liabilities — he saw velocity and friction. The company's profit looked healthy on paper, yet liquidity felt strained in practice. That paradox, he knew, had only one culprit: **working capital.**

"Revenue is vanity, profit is sanity, but cash is reality." — **Sir Alan Miltz**

Working capital, Kael believed, was the hidden battlefield where efficiency, ethics, and enterprise value collided every day.

66. Cash Conversion Cycle Explained and Mapped

Kael began by teaching his direct reports that the cash conversion cycle was not merely a metric. It was a diagnosis.

He mapped the three arteries:

- **Days Sales Outstanding:** how long before the customer pays.
- **Days Payables Outstanding:** how long before the company pays.
- **Days Inventory Outstanding:** how long before stock becomes sale.

Then he overlaid these across business lines, countries, customer segments, and product categories. The results were revealing. Each country followed a different rhythm, and each rhythm exposed a different operating behaviour.

Some businesses sold fast but collected slowly. Some held inventory too long. Some paid vendors faster than they recovered cash from customers.

His mantra became operational gospel: "Standardise the tempo, not just the template."

CFO Practice Note:

- Map DSO, DPO, and DIO by business unit, geography, product line, and customer segment — not only at consolidated level.
- Identify where the cash cycle is stretched by customer behaviour, vendor terms, stock movement, or internal process delay.
- Convert the CCC into an operating discussion; every extra day in the cycle has a cash cost.

---

67. Receivable Ageing and DSO Measurement

Kael asked for a DSO report. It arrived with seven versions.

He restructured it by customer segment, sales channel, and region rather than by company code. Patterns emerged quickly. Older receivables were not random; they clustered around legacy customers with political protection, weak contract discipline, or low-margin business that received too much tolerance.

He enforced a DSO target per segment with executive ownership.

Every day lost in receivables, he explained, costs enterprise value.

Kael's rule was blunt: "If you cannot measure it in days, you do not really manage it."

CFO Practice Note:

- Standardise one official DSO definition across finance, sales, and business units.
- Review receivables by ageing, customer quality, margin, dispute reason, and collection owner.
- Assign DSO targets by segment; one common target may hide very different customer behaviours.

---

68. Credit Approval Matrix and Authority Limits

Kael redesigned the credit policy around judgement with accountability.

Credit limits were no longer approved purely by sales. They required cross-signoff from finance where exposure exceeded defined thresholds. Each request had to justify why credit was needed, how it aligned with risk appetite, what the customer's payment record indicated, and what margin justified the exposure.

Authority levels were pegged to value, tenure, overdue history, and concentration risk.

No single executive could override a limit without CFO visibility.

Discipline replaced discretion.

CFO Practice Note:

• Build a credit approval matrix based on exposure size, customer rating, payment history, margin, and strategic importance.
• Require finance sign-off for new credit limits, limit increases, overdue exceptions, and politically sensitive accounts.
• Track all overrides separately; repeated exceptions usually reveal weak policy or excessive commercial pressure.

---

69. Customer Creditworthiness Assessment

Kael introduced a structured credit evaluation system integrating financial health, payment behaviour, sector outlook, management reputation, contract quality, and dispute history.

He subscribed to regional credit bureaus and used predictive models to flag early risk. For the top twenty customers, treasury maintained living profiles updated quarterly.

These profiles did not merely store financial ratios. They recorded payment promises kept, disputes raised, delays explained, and changes in procurement behaviour.

When questioned about the time investment, Kael replied simply: "The cost of diligence is always lower than the cost of surprise."

CFO Practice Note:

• Maintain credit profiles for major customers covering financials, payment history, disputes, industry risk, and exposure trend.
• Update profiles periodically, not only when default risk becomes visible.

• Link customer credit limits to actual behaviour; past reputation should not override current payment discipline.

---

70. Receivables Automation and AI-Predictive Models

Legacy collections ran on Excel trackers and hope.

Kael implemented an AI-enabled collections dashboard that predicted payment delays based on historical patterns, invoice behaviour, dispute history, email sentiment, seasonality, and customer-response delays.

Collectors were alerted before defaults occurred. Automated reminders were sent in calibrated tones — courteous, firm, or legal — depending on account history and overdue stage.

By the second month, overdue accounts started falling, but Kael remained cautious. Automation was useful only when the underlying data was clean and the follow-up ownership was clear.

AI could predict delay. People still had to recover cash.

CFO Practice Note:

• Use automation to prioritise collection effort by risk, ageing, customer behaviour, and expected payment probability.

• Clean customer master data, invoice records, dispute coding, and contact details before trusting predictive models.

• Assign human owners for AI alerts; a dashboard without follow-up is only sophisticated decoration.

---

71. Designing Collection Targets and Dashboards

Kael redefined collection KPIs around velocity and predictability.

Instead of relying only on "percentage of collections achieved," he introduced two sharper measures: **average days to resolve overdue** and **promises-kept ratio**.

The first showed collection speed. The second showed customer reliability.

Dashboards were displayed in leadership reviews, creating healthy transparency among regional teams. Collections now felt less like chasing and more like closing the loop between sales promise, customer obligation, and cash discipline.

A sale was not complete when the invoice was raised. It was complete when cash entered the system.

CFO Practice Note:
• Measure collections by overdue resolution speed, promise-kept ratio, dispute closure, and cash collected against due date.
• Avoid rewarding only invoice booking or gross sales where cash quality is weak.
• Review collection dashboards with both finance and sales; receivables are a commercial outcome, not only a finance problem.

---

72. Escalation Procedures for Overdue Accounts

Kael established a clear three-tier escalation:

30 days: friendly reminder by finance.

45 days: sales notified; future orders reviewed or placed on hold.

60 days: CFO and legal review; settlement, collection agency, or legal trigger considered.

No exceptions. No silence.

He also introduced Weekly Ageing Calls — short, data-driven sessions focused only on red accounts.

The discipline changed behaviour. Customers learned that payment delay had a predictable response, and internal teams learned that relationship management did not mean ignoring cash risk.

CFO Practice Note:
• Define escalation stages by overdue age, amount, customer importance, dispute status, and risk rating.
• Involve sales early; collections fail when customer relationships and cash responsibility are separated.
• Document every major overdue action so legal, audit, and management have a clear trail.

---

73. Early Warning Indicators for Bad Debts

The best CFOs, Kael knew, do not wait for defaults. They read behaviour before the ledger confirms it.

He asked the analytics team to track indicators such as:

• Unusual order cancellations.
• Frequent credit-limit requests.
• Declining response rates.

• Repeated invoice disputes.
• Shifts in customer procurement personnel.
• Sudden requests for longer payment terms.

Each flag was reviewed weekly.

Preventive accounting became the new risk management. Bad debts were no longer treated as unfortunate surprises; they were treated as signals that should have been heard earlier.

CFO Practice Note:
• Build a bad-debt early-warning list combining financial, behavioural, contractual, and relationship indicators.
• Review warning signs before quarter-end provisioning discussions; prevention is cheaper than recognition.
• Link high-risk flags to credit holds, revised terms, collection escalation, or security requirements.

---

74. Vendor Segmentation — Critical, Routine, Opportunistic

On the payables side, Kael launched a vendor segmentation matrix:

• **Critical vendors:** whose stoppage could halt operations.
• **Routine vendors:** easily replaceable or negotiable.
• **Opportunistic vendors:** useful during growth, dispensable during contraction.

This classification informed payment priority, negotiation strategy, continuity planning, and supplier-risk review.

He ensured critical vendors were paid on time because supplier trust sustains production when capital markets do not.

The cheapest payment delay can become the most expensive operational disruption.

CFO Practice Note:
• Segment vendors by operational criticality, substitutability, payment sensitivity, contract strength, and supply-chain dependency.
• Protect critical vendors from arbitrary payment delays; liquidity management should not damage production continuity.
• Use segmentation to negotiate terms intelligently rather than applying one blanket payment policy to all vendors.

---

75. Payables Discipline and Approval Hierarchy

Payment delays, Kael argued, were not cash strategies. They were reputation risks when used carelessly.

He tightened approval hierarchies and automated payment authorisation through ERP. Material payments required system-based approval, maker-checker validation, budget reference, vendor verification, and treasury scheduling.

Treasury timing was optimised, not weaponised.

The goal was not to pay late. The goal was to pay with discipline — neither earlier than necessary nor later than trust allowed.

CFO Practice Note:
• Define approval limits by amount, vendor type, payment urgency, statutory nature, and business criticality.
• Separate invoice approval, payment approval, vendor-master changes, and treasury release authority.
• Track delayed payments by reason; unexplained delays may indicate process weakness, cash stress, or control failure.

---

76. Vendor Financing and Supply-Chain Finance Models

Kael partnered with banks to introduce supply-chain finance, enabling approved vendors to access early payment at discounted rates.

The arrangement improved vendor liquidity without immediately burdening the company's own cash position. Critical suppliers gained predictability, while the company strengthened ecosystem resilience.

By integrating supply-chain finance dashboards, finance became a value creator for the operating network.

Kael reminded the team that a CFO's cash responsibility did not end at the company's bank account. A fragile vendor base could become the company's next liquidity crisis.

"A great CFO does not merely manage his cash — he protects the cash rhythm of the ecosystem."

CFO Practice Note:
• Identify vendors suitable for supply-chain finance based on criticality, volume, invoice reliability, and bank eligibility.
• Ensure SCF terms are transparent and do not hide supplier distress or create

undisclosed obligations.
• Monitor supplier participation, cost, payment timing, and working-capital impact through a dedicated dashboard.

---

77. Dynamic Discounting and Cost of Delay

Kael introduced dynamic discounting.

Vendors could choose early payment in exchange for small, time-linked discounts. The system calculated implied annualised yield, ensuring every rupee accelerated or deferred had an economic logic.

Treasury evolved from gatekeeping to yield generation.

But Kael imposed discipline: discounts could not be chased at the cost of liquidity buffer, critical payments, or supplier fairness.

Dynamic discounting was not about squeezing vendors. It was about converting payment timing into mutual value.

CFO Practice Note:
• Use dynamic discounting only after comparing discount yield with cash availability, borrowing cost, and liquidity buffer.
• Offer early-payment options transparently, especially to vendors who benefit from faster cash.
• Track whether discount gains are real after considering bank charges, process cost, and supplier relationship impact.

---

78. Inventory Analytics — ABC / XYZ / Ageing Reports

Kael demanded inventory data not in volume, but in velocity.

He used ABC and XYZ analysis to identify high-value stock, volatile-demand items, slow-moving inventory, obsolete stock, and items held only because no one wanted to write them off.

Ageing reports were colour-coded for immediate visibility.

He instructed finance to participate in monthly stock counts — not as auditors looking for fault, but as observers of operational discipline.

Inventory, he believed, was not sitting material. It was cash waiting for permission to move.

CFO Practice Note:
• Analyse inventory by value, movement, demand predictability, ageing,

obsolescence risk, and business criticality.
• Review slow-moving and obsolete stock with operations, sales, and procurement — not finance alone.
• Link inventory ageing to provisioning, purchasing discipline, sales planning, and warehouse accountability.

---

79. Inventory Valuation Methods — FIFO, Weighted Average

Kael reviewed inventory valuation methods across countries.

While accounting standards allowed certain flexibility, he insisted on consistency where comparability mattered. Different valuation methods across similar businesses were distorting margin analysis and making regional performance difficult to compare.

He standardised valuation using weighted average where appropriate, reducing P&L distortion caused by inflationary swings and inconsistent local practice.

The issue was not merely technical accounting. It was leadership comparability.

A CFO cannot allocate capital intelligently if inventory profits are measured differently across the map.

CFO Practice Note:
• Review whether inventory valuation methods are consistent across comparable entities, product lines, and reporting units.
• Assess how valuation choices affect gross margin, inventory value, tax, provisions, and management incentives.
• Document any method changes carefully with auditor consultation, board awareness, and clear transition logic.

---

80. Inventory Reduction Programmes and JIT Relevance

Kael collaborated with operations to explore Just-in-Time initiatives, but he refused to treat lean inventory as a slogan.

Working-capital efficiency had to be balanced with supply-chain resilience.

Safety-stock policies were recalibrated using supplier reliability, lead times, demand volatility, geopolitical exposure, and criticality of components.

Within 90 days, the division released cash from tied-up stock without weakening service continuity.

Kael's approach was balanced: reduce excess, not resilience.

CFO Practice Note:

• Review inventory reduction opportunities alongside service-level risk, supplier reliability, and demand volatility.
• Avoid aggressive cuts to safety stock where disruption risk is high or replacement time is uncertain.
• Measure inventory programmes by cash released, stockout incidents, obsolete reduction, and customer-service impact.

---

81. Interdepartmental Collaboration Between Finance and SCM

Kael institutionalised a joint Finance–Supply Chain Council, meeting fortnightly.

The agenda was practical: demand planning, supplier terms, inventory turnover, capacity forecasting, purchase commitments, logistics cost, and working-capital exposure.

Finance moved from being the last to know to being the first to anticipate.

The council changed the conversation. Supply chain stopped seeing finance as a brake, and finance stopped seeing inventory as a static number.

Working capital became a shared operating responsibility.

CFO Practice Note:

• Create a recurring finance–supply chain review covering demand, inventory, supplier terms, logistics, and purchase commitments.
• Use the meeting to anticipate cash impact before purchase orders, imports, or production decisions lock capital.
• Assign joint owners for inventory days, supplier terms, and forecast accuracy.

---

82. Working Capital Stress Scenario Testing

Kael conducted scenario tests on DSO, DPO, and DIO.

"What happens," he asked, "if collections slow by 15%, vendors demand faster payment, and inventory turns stretch by ten days?"

The sensitivity analysis helped determine the division's liquidity cliff — the point at which operations would require emergency funding.

The exercise made working capital visible as risk, not merely efficiency.

In calm periods, ratios look academic. Under stress, they become survival indicators.

CFO Practice Note:
• Stress-test working capital using realistic shocks: slower collections, shorter vendor terms, excess inventory, customer default, or import delay.
• Quantify the cash gap created by each scenario and identify when emergency funding becomes necessary.
• Use stress results to set liquidity buffers, credit limits, inventory policy, and vendor-negotiation priorities.

83. AI-Assisted Forecasting for Working Capital Needs

An AI forecasting tool projected future working-capital requirements based on seasonality, historical variance, customer behaviour, purchase cycles, inventory velocity, and macroeconomic trends.

It helped treasury anticipate cash needs rather than react to them.

But Kael did not allow the model to become an oracle. Forecasts were reviewed with business context, challenged against known events, and compared with actual cash movement.

Automation created foresight — but only disciplined review converted foresight into action.

CFO Practice Note:
• Use AI forecasting to identify working-capital pressure early, especially around seasonality, customer delay, and inventory build-up.
• Validate model outputs with sales, supply chain, treasury, and FP&A before acting on them.
• Track forecast accuracy regularly; AI is useful only when the organisation learns from variance.

84. Designing Working Capital KPIs for Dashboard Integration

The final step was visualisation.

Kael designed a **Working Capital Performance Cockpit** with metrics such as:

• DSO vs. DPO vs. DIO trendlines.
• Cash conversion movement by business unit.
• Ageing buckets and high-risk customers.
• Forecast accuracy ratio.
• Cash-in-hand per operational day.
• Inventory ageing and vendor criticality.

It made CFO discussions visible and actionable across leadership meetings.

The cockpit turned working capital from a finance review topic into an enterprise operating discipline.

CFO Practice Note:
• Build a dashboard that shows trend, owner, threshold, and action — not only ratios.
• Include receivables, payables, inventory, forecast accuracy, customer risk, and supplier risk in one view.
• Use the dashboard in cross-functional meetings so working capital is owned beyond finance.

---

85. Final Working Capital Improvement Plan

Kael's 90-day plan summarised improvement targets:

• Reduce DSO by five days.
• Extend DPO by three days without supplier distress.
• Trim inventory days by seven days.
• Improve forecast accuracy and overdue escalation discipline.
• Release trapped cash without weakening relationships.

Together, these efforts unlocked meaningful operational cash without new funding.

Kael closed the plan with a sentence that later became a team refrain: "Most liquidity crises are not from lack of money, but from lack of motion."

Working capital is motion. The CFO's job is to keep that motion visible, disciplined, and honest.

CFO Practice Note:
• Set quantified working-capital targets by DSO, DPO, DIO, forecast accuracy, and overdue closure.
• Ensure each target has a business owner, finance owner, timeline, and cash-impact estimate.
• Review progress weekly for the first 90 days; working capital improves through cadence, not announcements.

30-Day Working Capital Action Grid

1. Redefine DSO/DPO/DIO benchmarks by segment and geography.
2. Launch predictive collection models and escalation protocols.

3. Implement vendor segmentation and SCF platform integration.
4. Standardise inventory valuation methods regionally.
5. Conduct working capital stress simulation (DSO + DPO + DIO).
6. Publish Working Capital Cockpit with target-linked metrics.

Leadership Reflection

Kael Cipher learned that the real strength of a balance sheet lies not in its totals, but in its *turns.*

Working capital, he discovered, is not a department's responsibility — it's a reflection of an organisation's discipline.

By the time his first quarter closed, G Z Corporation's Asia–Pacific division had reduced idle capital, rebuilt vendor trust, and installed a new rhythm of liquidity.
The lesson was timeless: **cash flow is culture in numeric form.**

Practical Tool: DSO, DPO, DIO and the Cash Conversion Cycle

Working capital is not a finance department statistic. It is the daily behaviour of the entire organisation expressed in cash.

Three numbers help the CFO read that behaviour quickly: DSO, DIO, and DPO.

DSO — Days Sales Outstanding
How long customers take to pay.

DIO — Days Inventory Outstanding
How long inventory remains locked before conversion into sales.

DPO — Days Payable Outstanding
How long the company takes to pay suppliers.

Together, they create the Cash Conversion Cycle.

Cash Conversion Cycle = DSO + DIO – DPO

A shorter cycle usually means that the company converts operations into cash faster. A longer cycle means cash is trapped in receivables, inventory, or poor payment discipline.

Illustrative Working Capital Calculation

Particulars	Amount / Formula	Result
Annual Revenue	₹3,650 crore	—
Average Trade Receivables	₹600 crore	—
Annual Cost of Goods Sold	₹2,555 crore	—
Average Inventory	₹420 crore	—
Average Trade Payables	₹350 crore	—
DSO	Receivables ÷ Revenue × 365	60 days
DIO	Inventory ÷ COGS × 365	60 days
DPO	Payables ÷ COGS × 365	50 days
Cash Conversion Cycle	**60 + 60 – 50**	**70 days**

A 70-day cash conversion cycle means the company's operating cash is locked for more than two months before it comes back into the system.

Kael Cipher never treated this as a mere ratio. He converted it into cash language.

If the company reduces DSO from 60 days to 52 days, it releases nearly eight days of sales cash. At daily sales of ₹10 crore, that is approximately ₹80 crore released from receivables.

If inventory holding falls from 60 days to 55 days, and daily COGS is ₹7 crore, nearly ₹35 crore is released from inventory.

If vendor terms improve from 50 days to 55 days without damaging supplier trust, another ₹35 crore of cash support is created.

Illustrative Cash Release

Improvement Area	Movement	Cash Impact
DSO reduction	60 days to 52 days	₹80 crore
DIO reduction	60 days to 55 days	₹35 crore
DPO improvement	50 days to 55 days	₹35 crore
Total Potential Cash Release	—	**₹150 crore**

This is why working capital discipline is often cheaper than borrowing.

A company may spend months negotiating fresh bank limits while ignoring cash already trapped inside its own operating cycle. The CFO's role is to reveal that trapped liquidity and convert it into usable strength.

Kael's instruction to his team was simple:

"Do not tell me working capital is improving. Show me which behaviour changed."

A DSO reduction must be linked to stronger collection discipline. A DIO reduction must be linked to better demand planning. A DPO improvement must be linked to negotiated trust, not delayed payments disguised as strategy.

Working capital is healthy only when cash improves without damaging customers, suppliers, or operations.

CHAPTER 6

QUICK LIQUIDITY & GOING-CONCERN CHECK: Silent Solvency Tests to Safeguard Reputation

In the hierarchy of CFO responsibilities, liquidity is the first covenant with trust.

Revenue earns applause; solvency earns survival. The moment Kael Cipher assumed the CFO chair, he knew that before talking strategy, he must know if the company could breathe next quarter without external oxygen.

Liquidity management is not about cash alone—it's about **continuity**. A CFO must know whether the enterprise can meet obligations, sustain shocks, and still protect its credibility in the markets.

86 · Building a 13-Week Rolling Cash-Flow Model

A first-time CFO's most truthful mirror is a 13-week cash-flow model.

It compresses complexity into discipline — forcing the organisation to visualise liquidity, not profit.

Kael began by converting static budgets into a rolling weekly horizon: every Friday, forecasts extended one week forward, maintaining a perpetual 90-day view.

This rhythm separated perception from precision — showing when inflows truly arrived, not when they were booked.

Kael treated *liquidity not as a balance-sheet line, but as a rhythm the CFO had to conduct.*

CFO Practice Note:
• Use direct-method forecasting, not indirect accrual adjustments.
• Align treasury, FP&A, operations, collections, and vendor-payment data into one weekly model.
• Present the 13-week model at every Executive Committee until liquidity discipline becomes part of decision cadence.

---

87 · Scenario Planning — Base, Stress, and Severe Cases

The difference between good finance and great finance is imagination.

Kael built three layered scenarios:

• **Base Case** — the business as planned.
• **Stress Case** — one major revenue delay or cost spike.
• **Severe Case** — simultaneous market contraction, rate hike, and default event.

Each case answered one question: how long can we last before we breach covenants?

The model was less about prediction and more about reaction time — the early window to pivot before liquidity eroded.

Kael knew *the CFO could not predict every storm, but he still had to build the breakwater before the sky changed.*

CFO Practice Note:
• Simulate base, stress, and severe cases quarterly using sales, payables, inventory, FX, interest rates, and customer collections as stress levers.
• Define the trigger point for each scenario — when to freeze spend, accelerate collections, draw lines, or escalate to the CEO and Board.
• Treat scenario planning as an agility tool, not a prediction contest; the goal is response time, not perfect forecasting.

---

88 · Early-Warning Liquidity Triggers and Tolerance Bands

Liquidity crises never arrive announced; they echo in the margins first.

Kael institutionalised triggers — quantitative signals that warned when comfort turned to caution:

• Cash-to-expense coverage below 1.5×
• DSO rising more than 10% month-over-month
• Unutilised credit lines below 30% of headroom
• Daily bank balance volatility above 20%

Each was coded into the dashboard with colour bands: green for stable, amber for watch, red for action.

This system shifted treasury from reactive firefighting to proactive surveillance.

Kael's view was simple: *the worst liquidity crisis is the one the dashboard never saw coming.*

CFO Practice Note:
• Design a tolerance matrix covering cash coverage, DSO, bank headroom, covenant proximity, and daily balance volatility.
• Share amber and red triggers with the CEO and Audit Committee before pressure becomes panic.
• Review trigger breaches with owner, cause, corrective action, and expected closure date.

---

89 · Assessing Funding Gaps vs. Available Lines

A CFO's credibility is tested when lines of credit become lines of defence.

Kael reviewed every facility — working-capital limits, overdrafts, supplier financing, commercial paper programmes, and standby lines — and overlaid them on the 13-week forecast to identify funding gaps before they materialised.

He built a **Liquidity Gap Bridge** that displayed:

• Forecast deficit by week
• Available headroom
• Speed of drawdown
• Alternate funding options

When presented to the global CFO, it turned anxiety into confidence.

No surprises; only signals.

CFO Practice Note:
• Maintain real-time visibility of credit utilisation, sanctioned limits, available headroom, maturity dates, and drawdown conditions.
• Negotiate renewals, extensions, or backup facilities at least 90 days before maturity.
• Use the funding-gap bridge to convert liquidity concern into specific action:

draw, defer, collect, refinance, or escalate.

---

90 · Contingency-Liquidity Hierarchy — Cash > Credit > Assets

In liquidity management, sequence defines survival.

Cash is king, credit is counsel, and assets are the last resort.

Kael categorised every option in a contingency-liquidity hierarchy:

1. **Immediate** — on-hand cash and overnight sweep accounts.
2. **Near-term** — unutilised lines and re-discountable instruments.
3. **Medium-term** — sale of non-core investments or inventory.
4. **Last resort** — secured asset pledges or strategic equity infusion.

This hierarchy formed the foundation of his CFO Liquidity Playbook — a living document reviewed every quarter with the CEO.

Kael treated *the liquidity hierarchy like the balance sheet's seat belt: rarely celebrated, but essential before impact.*

CFO Practice Note:
• Define clear thresholds for activating each liquidity tier.
• Document approval authorities for emergency drawdowns, asset sales, pledges, or strategic funding decisions.
• Ensure treasury, FP&A, CEO, and legal understand the first move when cash tightens.

---

91 · Emergency Funding Options — Bridge Loans, Factoring, Commercial Paper

When the tide recedes, speed matters more than pride.

Kael built a contingency catalogue of short-term instruments — bridge loans, factoring, and commercial paper — each chosen not for glamour but for liquidity velocity.

• Bridge loans offered immediate oxygen but demanded strong banker credibility.
• Factoring unlocked trapped receivables, converting paper promises into survival capital.
• Commercial paper issuance, though efficient, demanded timing — entering markets before volatility raised the price of urgency.

The goal was not to borrow. It was to signal preparedness.

He presented the liquidity readiness deck at the regional CEO meeting, ending with one idea: *liquidity is not merely cash; it is confidence in motion.*

CFO Practice Note:

• Maintain pre-approved bridge-funding options and refresh them periodically with banks.

• Negotiate factoring or receivable-discounting limits before urgent need arises.

• Review commercial paper or short-term market eligibility annually to preserve access even when unused.

---

92 · Analysing Short-Term Debt Maturity Ladders

Maturity ladders reveal timing — the CFO's hidden calendar of risk.

Kael reconstructed the entire debt maturity profile for the Asia–Pacific region, line by line and instrument by instrument, visualising repayments by month and year.

He used three colours on his confidential dashboard:

• **Green** for maturities within revolving facilities.

• **Amber** for debts rolling within six months.

• **Red** for any cluster of repayments exceeding projected inflows.

The exercise uncovered an uncomfortable truth: two subsidiaries were heading into overlapping debt redemptions within 45 days, unnoticed because of fragmented local reporting.

Within a week, Kael restructured the sequencing.

Crisis averted.

Kael knew *maturity concentration could kill quietly; one refinancing delay was enough to start the dominoes.*

CFO Practice Note:

• Consolidate all short-term maturities into one group-level view by entity, lender, currency, and due date.

• Run monthly ladder simulations to identify repayment clusters and refinancing peaks.

• Stagger redemptions wherever possible to avoid liquidity cliffs.

---

93 · Going-Concern Self-Assessment Framework

A CFO does not wait for the auditor to ask, "Are you a going concern?" He proves it before the question becomes uncomfortable.

Kael implemented a self-assessment framework built around five tests:

1. **Liquidity adequacy** — 13-week cash-flow sufficiency.
2. **Funding continuity** — committed versus uncommitted lines.
3. **Covenant integrity** — stress impact on compliance.
4. **Operational dependency** — supplier continuity and working-capital rotation.
5. **Management intent** — capital-raising or restructuring readiness.

He formalised it as a quarterly declaration signed jointly by the CFO, CEO, and regional controller — not as compliance theatre, but as a credibility ritual.

Kael treated *going concern not as a checkbox, but as a character test for leadership.*

CFO Practice Note:

• Embed going-concern assessment into quarterly business reviews, not only audit season.

• Document mitigation plans for any material liquidity shortfall, covenant stress, or funding uncertainty.

• Use the framework as pre-audit assurance for the Board Audit Committee.

---

94 · Asset-Pledge Mapping and Collateral Utilisation

Every pledge made in haste becomes a constraint in crisis.

Kael ordered an asset-pledge audit, identifying every fixed asset, current asset, financial asset, and receivable already encumbered with lenders or counterparties.

He discovered overlapping liens — two banks unknowingly holding charges over the same export receivables.

Such errors do not always cause immediate loss, but in a liquidity crunch they erase optionality.

He then implemented a **Collateral Register**: a dynamic system tracking asset status as free, pledged, conditional, disputed, or restricted.

By quarter-end, collateral utilisation dropped from 91% to 73%, expanding real borrowing headroom without raising a rupee.

Unused collateral became Kael's silent buffer against panic.

CFO Practice Note:

• Digitise the collateral register with asset status, lender charge, value, renewal date, and release conditions.

• Reconcile pledged assets across banks to avoid duplicate charges, outdated liens, or unavailable security.

• Set a collateral utilisation ceiling; when too many assets are pledged, borrowing capacity becomes illusionary.

---

95 · Working-Capital Loan Covenant Monitoring

In the world of credit, breach precedes blame.

Kael designed an automated covenant-monitoring dashboard that converted legal terms into live alerts — EBITDA coverage, DSCR, leverage ratio, current ratio, and borrowing-base conditions.

Every Friday, treasury and FP&A received an email titled **Covenant Pulse**.

Green meant business as usual. Amber demanded discussion. Red meant escalation.

When one subsidiary missed a covenant threshold due to temporary forex loss, Kael's pre-alert note to the lender preserved trust. The bank appreciated transparency more than mechanical compliance and later enhanced the company's credit line.

Kael understood that *honesty with lenders was often the cheapest capital a CFO could raise.*

CFO Practice Note:

• Maintain covenant definitions, ratio formulas, thresholds, and reporting dates in one controlled repository.

• Automate variance alerts with green, amber, and red tolerance bands.

• Engage lenders quarterly even when there is nothing urgent to explain.

---

96 · Building a CFO Liquidity War-Room Protocol

When liquidity trembles, governance must harden.

Kael established a Liquidity War-Room Protocol — a clear, cross-functional chain of command triggered whenever the rolling forecast breached its amber band.

The rule was simple: three calls within three hours.

Treasury to CFO. CFO to CEO. CEO to Chair.

No blame, only data.

Every meeting began with two dashboards: cash-on-hand versus forecast, and counterparty exposures.

He treated the war-room not as a crisis bunker but as a decision accelerator, where speed met sanity.

When interest rates spiked overnight in Singapore, this rhythm helped the group avoid an expensive refinancing mistake.

Kael's lesson was clear: *in liquidity turbulence, hierarchy must become choreography.*

CFO Practice Note:

• Define war-room triggers in advance through cash, covenant, funding, or counterparty thresholds.
• Keep a pre-approved action playbook covering drawdowns, term extensions, expense freezes, collection pushes, and lender communication.
• Run simulation drills at least twice a year; crisis rewards rehearsal.

---

97 · Stress-Testing Customer Collections under Macro Shock

A CFO who monitors cash without testing its origin is only half-prepared.

Kael ran macro-shock simulations — a revenue drop, a DSO spike, currency volatility, and customer-payment delays.

The outcome was not prediction. It was prioritisation.

Which customers would still pay on time?

Which distributors would need credit relief before defaulting?

Which contracts looked profitable only because risk had not yet arrived?

This forward lens allowed sales and finance to craft differentiated terms — rewarding reliability, cushioning the vulnerable, and protecting liquidity.

Kael recognised that *liquidity risk was often credit risk in disguise.*

CFO Practice Note:

• Integrate collection stress tests into customer credit-policy reviews.
• Model cascading effects; one delayed major payment may weaken vendor trust, bank confidence, and operating continuity..
• Share results with business heads so prevention becomes partnership, not finance enforcement.

98 · Crisis-Communication Plan with Banks and Board

In every liquidity event, the message is half the solution.

Kael scripted a Crisis Communication Plan long before it was needed.

It defined who speaks, what is shared, when escalation occurs, and which facts must be verified before communication leaves the CFO office.

Lenders received early heads-up memos with factual metrics, not defensive narratives.

The Board received two-tier updates: a brief data note within 24 hours and a strategic remediation plan within 72.

Transparency during turbulence built Kael's credibility faster than any financial ratio could.

Kael knew that ***early communication borrowed time — the only capital that compounds under stress.***

CFO Practice Note:

• Prepare draft emails, lender notes, and board-slide templates before a liquidity event occurs.
• Maintain one voice per channel; silence creates confusion, while over-talking erodes trust.
• Document every external and board communication for post-event review and governance continuity.

---

99 · AI-Enabled Anomaly Detection for Cash Movements

The modern treasury's superpower is pattern recognition.

Kael deployed an AI-driven anomaly-detection system across bank accounts, flagging unusual transfers by amount, frequency, timing, geography, or counterparty.

Within a month, the system identified a repeated offset entry — benign, but proof that the machine's vigilance worked.

This shifted treasury review from post-mortem to real-time prevention.

Kael did not see AI as a replacement for judgement. He saw it as a guardrail that gave judgement more time to act.

CFO Practice Note:

• Integrate anomaly dashboards with ERP logs, bank feeds, vendor-master changes, and payment approvals.

• Classify alerts as informational, review-required, or action-required to avoid alert fatigue.
• Track false positives and missed exceptions so audit committees trust the system's usefulness.

---

100 · Designing a 5-Day Liquidity-Visibility Dashboard

Visibility is the antidote to panic.

Kael's final instrument in his first quarter was a five-day rolling liquidity dashboard — an at-a-glance fusion of:

• Current cash and headroom.
• Expected inflows and outflows.
• Top counterparty exposures.
• Alert matrix linked to liquidity tolerance bands.
• Country and currency-level drill-down.

Displayed on a single screen in the CFO suite, it made liquidity tangible.

The Board began calling it **The Heartbeat Chart**.

When questions arose in meetings, Kael no longer said, "I'll get back to you." He pointed to the chart.

For him, clarity itself had become a form of liquidity.

CFO Practice Note:
• Update the five-day dashboard daily before leadership decisions begin.
• Ensure drill-down capability by region, currency, bank, entity, and counterparty.
• Review anomalies jointly with treasury and FP&A every week so visibility turns into action.

30-Day Liquidity Action Grid — Executive Checklist

In the first month, a new CFO must silently earn the title of *financial first responder.*
Kael's disciplined 30-day framework is replicable for any enterprise — from mid-market to Fortune 500.

Week 1 — See Clearly

- Compile daily bank balances; reconcile all entities.
- Launch 13-week rolling cash-flow model.
- Identify pledged vs. free assets.

Week 2 — Simulate Reality

- Build base/stress/severe scenarios.
- Map debt-maturity ladder.
- Initiate AI anomaly monitoring.

Week 3 — Secure Confidence

- Meet top three banks; confirm credit headroom.
- Prepare war-room protocol and communication plan.
- Design early-warning tolerance bands.

Week 4 — Institutionalise Discipline

- Publish liquidity dashboard to CEO and Audit Committee.
- Document go-forward CFO Liquidity Playbook.
- Review team roles for future crisis rehearsal.

By Day 30, the CFO's mission is simple: **replace surprise with sight**.
When the enterprise knows its breathing space, strategy can finally begin.

CHAPTER 7

CULTURE AND GOVERNANCE TEMPERATURE: The Unwritten Ledger of Behaviour

Measure ethics as carefully as earnings.

When Kael Cipher completed his first liquidity review, he realized numbers could buy stability, not integrity.
A balance sheet may stay solvent while a culture quietly decays.
Hence began his second audit — not of accounts, but of **behaviour**.

The CFO's unseen duty is to read the organisation's moral pulse: how decisions are really made, how power flows, and how truth travels. Every enterprise leaves two ledgers — one financial, one ethical. Only the second defines legacy.

"Culture is not what we say in meetings; it's what people do when the meeting ends."
— Paul Polman, Former CEO, Unilever

101 · Identifying Implicit Decision-Making Hierarchies

Formal charts show who reports to whom; informal ones show who truly decides.

Kael spent his first fortnight quietly mapping influence — whose emails got instant replies, whose opinions silenced a room.

He noted that approval rarely followed structure; it followed trust networks.

Understanding these unwritten lines helped him predict resistance points long before policy conflicts surfaced.

The finance transformation that ignored these dynamics would fail before the first budget cycle closed. Kael understood that *authority was official; influence was earned.*

CFO Practice Note:
• Observe conversations, response patterns, and meeting behaviour — not only minutes, designations, and approval charts.
• Identify shadow influencers who shape fiscal priorities, budget resistance, and execution speed.
• Use informal hierarchy maps to plan stakeholder alignment before introducing policy, process, or reporting changes.

---

102 · Reading Board Minutes for Tone and Alignment

Kael reread five years of board and audit-committee minutes — not for numbers, but for language. *Were discussions exploratory or defensive? Did the minutes capture curiosity or compliance?*

He underlined phrases like "noted with concern" and "management assured" — signals of cultural strain between oversight and execution.

Boards that accept comfort over candour breed governance fatigue.

By quantifying tone shifts over time, Kael identified the precise moment when open dialogue had turned into performance theatre. Kael realized that *when minutes begin to sound polished instead of honest, governance has already started losing its nerve.*

CFO Practice Note:
• Establish a quarterly review of board-minute language to detect sentiment drift, recurring concerns, and repeated management assurances.
• Invite independent directors or committee chairs to give candid feedback on whether finance communication feels transparent or defensive.
• Train finance leaders to answer board questions with clarity, evidence, and limitation notes — not optimism dressed as certainty.

---

103 · Governance Maturity Assessment — Level 1 to 5

Numbers reveal competence; governance reveals character.

Kael implemented a **Governance Maturity Index**, rating each subsidiary on five progressive levels:

Reactive — compliance after issue.

Controlled — documented processes, limited ownership.

Integrated — governance embedded in management rhythm.

Proactive — self-auditing, risk-anticipating.

Purpose-Led — governance aligned with values and long-term trust.

Every quarter, he published the heat map to the regional CEO, sparking constructive competition across countries.

Within six months, two markets moved from Level 2 to Level 4 — not through fear, but through visibility.

Kael believed that *governance proved its worth most clearly when pressure arrived; what looked invisible in calm periods became invaluable in crisis.*

CFO Practice Note:

- Use governance-maturity scoring to guide audit planning, leadership reviews, and subsidiary-level improvement priorities.
- Reward early escalation, self-auditing, and issue closure — not merely clean-looking compliance reports.
- Link part of leadership evaluation to governance progress, control discipline, and transparency, not only profit delivery.

---

104 · Evaluating Ethics-Compliance Infrastructure

Policies exist everywhere; culture enforcement exists rarely.

Kael ordered a forensic review of ethics infrastructure — code of conduct, whistle-blower hotlines, third-party compliance portals, vendor declarations, employee disclosures, and investigation logs.

He discovered fragmentation: three ethics inboxes, none monitored weekly; vendor declarations filed but never validated; complaint ownership unclear between HR, legal, and internal audit.

He merged everything into one digital **Ethics Hub**, routing every complaint directly to internal audit with timestamped transparency and defined escalation trails.

He presented it to the Board as the company's **Moral ERP**.

Kael understood that *a code of conduct meant little unless the organisation also had the courage to enforce consequence.*

CFO Practice Note:
• Centralise all ethics and compliance channels into one monitored system with clear ownership, timestamps, and escalation routes.
• Automate complaint routing to an independent ethics officer, internal audit, or board committee where sensitivity requires independence.
• Report quarterly closure rates, ageing of complaints, repeat themes, and unresolved high-risk matters to the Audit Committee — silence is not success.

---

105 · Detecting Red Flags in Approval Chains

Fraud rarely begins with theft; it begins with tolerance.

Kael scrutinised approval trails for patterns — same approver pairs, repeated threshold-limit transactions, last-minute vendor creations, sudden approval bursts before month-end, and frequent manual overrides. He flagged these as behavioural anomalies, not merely control breaches.

He understood that risk lives where routine hides. A ₹10-crore fraud often begins as a ₹10,000 exception nobody questioned. By cross-mapping digital signatures with behavioural logs, he reduced override frequency in one quarter and turned approval analytics into an early-warning control.

Kael believed that *internal control was not merely a process; it was a culture of pause before approval.*

CFO Practice Note:
• Integrate approval analytics with vendor-master changes, HR data, user-access logs, and threshold-breach reports.
• Audit for consistency, not just completion; repeated exceptions often reveal collusion, pressure, or weak design.
• Reinforce the four-eyes principle even for low-value spends where patterns may matter more than amount.

---

106 · Finance Team Integrity-Risk Mapping

Numbers can be audited; intent cannot — unless the CFO learns to map exposure.

Kael introduced a quarterly **Integrity-Risk Matrix** for his finance leadership bench. It was not about suspicion; it was about awareness. Each team member was assessed across three dimensions:

• **Access risk** — who can move money or override controls?
• **Pressure risk** — who faces personal, performance, or role-related stress that may blur judgement?
• **Opportunity risk** — where do segregation gaps, system overrides, or approval shortcuts exist?

The matrix remained confidential, reviewed only with HR and Internal Audit. Its purpose was preventive empathy, not policing. Kael understood that *integrity weakens quietly when pressure becomes stronger than purpose.*

CFO Practice Note:
• Combine qualitative HR inputs with quantitative system logs, access rights, override history, and role concentration.
• Review integrity-risk exposure quarterly, especially around high-pressure periods such as year-end, audits, restructuring, or liquidity stress.
• Link audit rotation and leave-rotation cycles to high-exposure roles without making the process feel punitive.

---

107 · Role of the CFO as Moral Compass

The CEO drives ambition; the CFO defines its boundary.

When business heads pressed for aggressive revenue recognition in Q3, Kael reminded the room that recognition without realization was fiction. He explained that a CFO's real KPI was trust capital — how many stakeholders still believed the numbers when the numbers were not comfortable.

In that moment, he was not just managing finance. He was preserving the organisation's reputation equity.

Kael knew that *the CFO had to become the conscience that spoke clearly when numbers tried to whisper comfort.*

CFO Practice Note:
• Attend key commercial reviews where revenue recognition, discounting, provisioning, or target pressure may create ethical tension.
• Record professional dissent formally when principles, standards, or disclosure integrity are tested.
• Frame dissent as protection of trust, not opposition to growth.

---

108 · Whistle-Blower and Speak-Up Mechanisms

Fear is the tax on silence.

Kael restructured the **Speak-Up Framework** into a simple triage model — **Receive, Review, Respond**. He ensured anonymity through encrypted reporting channels hosted by a third-party ethics platform.

Each quarter, an **Ethics Pulse Dashboard** went to the Audit Committee, showing case type, closure time, ageing, corrective action, and repeat themes. When one mid-manager reported procurement coercion, Kael personally ensured the matter was handled with dignity and protection. The story circulated quietly; participation rose because people saw that the system had spine.

Kael understood that *employees rarely trust a speak-up system because it exists; they trust it when it protects truth from retaliation.*

CFO Practice Note:

• Publicise the speak-up process clearly, but protect the identity and dignity of people who use it.
• Route sensitive complaints to independent reviewers where HR, finance, legal, or management conflict may exist.
• Audit closure rates, ageing, retaliation risk, and repeated themes; silence is not proof of ethical health.

---

109 · Aligning Incentives with Governance Outcomes

If bonuses reward revenue without responsibility, culture will mirror the metric.

Kael partnered with HR to link governance KPIs — audit-finding closure, control compliance, ethics training completion, policy adherence, and timely escalation — to variable pay. The first year saw quiet resistance; the second saw pride.

Finance managers began treating control remediation as a leadership act, not an administrative task. Governance stopped being a compliance lecture and became part of performance language.

Kael believed that *what the company measured influenced performance, but what it rewarded shaped behaviour.*

CFO Practice Note:

• Include a modest governance weightage in annual scorecards for finance

leaders and control-sensitive business roles.
• Communicate the purpose clearly: integrity, control closure, and timely escalation protect enterprise value.
• Celebrate clean audits, early escalations, and closure discipline as visibly as financial wins.

---

110 · Cross-Cultural Ethics Calibration in Multi-Country Operations

What feels customary in one market may be unacceptable in another — but standards must converge upward, not downward.

Kael led **Ethics Across Borders** workshops, contextualising global policy through local examples: gift-giving in Japan, facilitation expectations in certain markets, hospitality norms in India, and procurement relationship practices across Southeast Asia. Instead of imposing rules mechanically, he built shared interpretation.

Local CFOs began documenting cultural exceptions with rationale, creating transparency instead of evasion. The objective was not cultural arrogance; it was ethical consistency.

Kael understood that *global integrity was local behaviour placed under enough sunlight.*

CFO Practice Note:
• Maintain a country-wise registry of ethical clarifications, sensitive practices, gift limits, and approval requirements.
• Train local leadership to challenge questionable traditions diplomatically but firmly.
• Escalate grey-zone cases to a regional ethics council so precedents are documented and applied consistently.

---

111 · Designing Periodic Culture-Temperature Surveys

Kael believed culture could be measured — not by slogans, but by signals.

He commissioned an anonymous **Culture-Temperature Survey** twice a year across finance and business teams. The questions were precise: Do you feel safe to disagree? Does the system punish transparency? Are control concerns heard before they become audit findings?

Results were plotted on a heat map and reviewed by the Board CSR and Audit Committees. Patterns emerged: regions with high profitability but low psychological safety also carried higher audit exceptions.

Kael understood that *culture revealed itself most clearly when controls were not watching.*

CFO Practice Note:

• Keep the survey short, consistent, and repeatable; trend matters more than novelty.
• Track shifts in trust, openness, fairness, escalation comfort, and fear of retaliation by geography and function.
• Discuss findings personally with functional heads; culture data without dialogue becomes decoration.

---

112 · Shadow Audits for Behavioural Compliance

Kael introduced **Shadow Audits** — unannounced deep-dives led by independent reviewers into approvals, reimbursements, vendor onboarding, travel claims, exception handling, and policy adherence.

Unlike statutory audits, these examined behaviour, not only balance sheets. They revealed small cultural fractures: pressure to pre-date invoices, habitual manager overrides, informal reimbursement norms, and emotional fatigue from constant firefighting.

He treated these not merely as violations, but as vital signs. Shadow Audits became mirrors that restored self-awareness.

Kael believed that *true compliance was visible when people chose discipline without being watched.*

CFO Practice Note:

• Schedule limited-scope surprise audits twice a year in high-risk or high-volume areas.
• Rotate reviewers and sample periods to avoid predictability.
• Share thematic lessons with leadership while protecting dignity; correct behaviour without creating fear theatre.

---

113 · Integrating ESG Oversight into Finance Routines

ESG was not a separate committee; it was a CFO lens.

Kael embedded Environmental, Social and Governance metrics directly into monthly management reports — carbon cost per unit of revenue, gender balance in treasury, vendor-ethics grading, safety-linked cost exposure, and compliance exceptions.

He understood that capital markets increasingly rewarded credibility, not cosmetics. When the Asia–Pacific division published its first integrated report, the achievement mattered less as a document and more as a signal: non-financial data now carried financial consequence.

Kael believed that *ESG was not a disclosure exercise; it was an accountability audit.*

CFO Practice Note:

• Merge sustainability, social, and governance metrics into regular finance dashboards instead of treating them as annual-report decoration.
• Validate ESG data through ownership, controls, and external assurance where required.
• Build CFO accountability over non-financial reporting accuracy because markets increasingly price trust beyond profit.

---

114 · Governance Reporting to Audit Committee

Kael reframed the quarterly Audit Committee meeting as a conversation on trust.

Instead of long slide decks, he presented five dashboards:

1. Integrity Index by country
2. Audit-finding closure rate
3. Ethics-case resolution cycle time
4. Compliance calendar adherence
5. Culture-temperature trend

The result was less time defending and more time improving. The Committee began describing finance as a line of defence that listened.

Kael understood that *boards trusted CFOs who could make governance visible without burying judgement under slides.*

CFO Practice Note:

• Send governance dashboards at least 48 hours before the Audit Committee meeting.
• Quantify red flags with clear owners, timelines, and escalation status.

• Record committee feedback as actionable items within seven days and track closure visibly.

---

115 · Creating a Tone-at-the-Top Scorecard

Tone is the balance sheet of leadership.

Kael built a **Tone-at-the-Top Scorecard**, rating senior leaders on visibility, communication frequency, ethical modelling, escalation behaviour, and consistency between words and decisions. It included data points such as town-hall mentions of integrity, employee-survey credibility ratings, whistle-blower closure tone, and escalation timeliness.

The Board used it not for punishment, but for pattern recognition. The insight was profound: regions where leaders spoke openly about values saw higher retention and lower control incidents.

Kael understood that *what leaders ignore, culture eventually adopts.*

CFO Practice Note:

• Review tone metrics semi-annually across leadership visibility, ethical messaging, escalation behaviour, and employee trust indicators.
• Share composite results with the Executive Committee and Board without turning the scorecard into a public shaming tool.
• Treat every ethical lapse as a signal of leadership tone, not merely an isolated scandal.

30-Day Action Framework — Culture & Governance Stability Plan — Foundation of the CFO Office

Week	Focus Theme	Key Actions / Diagnostics	Observable Indicators / Outputs
Week 1 – Orient and Observe	Understand the Mandate (Ch. 1 & 2)	• Clarify enterprise purpose with CEO & Chair • Self-audit values & blind spots • Review strategy decks & vision statements • Identify first 100-hour listening touchpoints	Alignment of CFO mandate with board expectations "CFO Strategy Interpretation Memo v1"
Week 2 – Map Reality	Decode Culture & Finance DNA (Ch. 2 & 3)	• Stakeholder interviews and listening audits • Create "financial anatomy chart" of business • Review 3-year trends & audit letters • Identify decision hierarchies & informal power centres	"Organisational Intent Map" ready Top 10 process dependencies listed
Week 3 – Assess Liquidity and Controls	Early Financial Reality Check (Ch. 4 & 5 & 6)	• Build 13-week cash-flow model • Review working-capital conversion cycle • Stress-test customer collections • Review bank covenants & funding lines • Identify liquidity early-warning triggers	5-Day Liquidity Dashboard active Cash-flow variance baseline set Early Liquidity War-Room protocol drafted
Week 4 – Diagnose Culture & Governance Tone	Measure the Unwritten Ledger of Behaviour (Ch. 7)	• Conduct Culture-Temperature Survey v1 • Launch Governance-Maturity Assessment (Level 1–5) • Map ethics-risk clusters & approval-chain red flags • Draft Tone-at-the-Top Scorecard • Present Governance Heat-Map to CEO and Audit Committee	Culture Score Baseline captured Ethics Hub & Speak-Up Dashboard soft-launched Board endorsement of governance framework

PART II

The First 90 Days: Taking Control of the Cockpit

Theme: Stabilise | Earn Trust | Deliver Early Wins

Deliverable: 90-Day CFO Credibility Index — Visible Control Improvements

Introduction

The first 90 days define whether a CFO becomes a *steady hand* or a *symbolic signature.*
After the initial orientation and listening phase, Kael steps into a cockpit that demands clarity, speed, and authority.
The numbers now speak daily — liquidity, collections, compliance, and board trust are all visible signals of control.

This is the phase where the organisation learns whether it has hired a **scorekeeper or a strategist**.
The finance function must move from reports to reliability, from dashboards to decisions.
Kael's mission is to demonstrate that discipline can coexist with optimism — that transparency is not a threat but a foundation of confidence.

"In your first 90 days, control is communication — every accurate number tells the organisation it's safe to move forward."
— **Luca Maestri, CFO Apple Inc.**

Purpose of the First 90 Days

- **Stabilise the Core:** Secure liquidity, enforce working-capital discipline, and plug control gaps.
- **Earn Trust:** Deliver facts before forecasts; integrity before innovation.
- **Deliver Early Wins:** Visible, measurable improvements that build credibility.
- **Strengthen Governance:** Embed ethical rigor and compliance cadence.
- **Build Relationships:** Position finance as a trusted voice in board and business conversations.

By Day 90, a CFO must prove that the organisation's financial architecture is no longer fragile.

Kael's visibility rises not through grand announcements, but through **quiet precision** — reconciled numbers, predictable cash cycles, and confident boardrooms.

"Trust in a CFO is not earned by optimism; it's earned by accuracy."

— **Ruth Porat, CFO Alphabet Inc.**

Structural Journey

Phase	Focus Area	Expected Outcome
Days 1 – 30	Assess the financial terrain — cash, controls, compliance	Baseline visibility · Liquidity map · Governance pulse
Days 31 – 60	Tighten execution — collections, capex discipline, early dashboards	Reduced cash leakage · Predictable outflows · Faster reporting
Days 61 – 90	Institutionalise trust — Board credibility and team alignment	Reliable MIS · Compliance cadence · Cross-functional trust

Each chapter in Part II ends with a **90-Day Dashboard** — a concise visual of measurable shifts in liquidity, governance, and credibility.

Together, these dashboards create the **CFO Credibility Index**, the organisation's first tangible indicator that finance is in steady, transparent hands.

"Control is not rigidity — it's rhythm." — **Soumen Ray, CFO L&T Finance Holdings**

Bridge to Action

With stability restored and trust visibly earned, Kael's next horizon is to **build permanence** — to translate control into capability.

Part III will take him from managing numbers to designing systems that generate them.

CHAPTER 8

Cash-Flow Redesign & Receivables Discipline

Rebuild rhythm, predictability, and confidence.

116 · Mapping Inflow–Outflow Mismatches by Week

Kael's first instinct as CFO was to see time, not numbers. He spent his opening weekend at the regional treasury hub, manually mapping every inflow and outflow by week for the past quarter. The result was unsettling — cash peaks and troughs formed chaotic waves rather than predictable patterns.

Customer receipts came in bursts; vendor payments dribbled out on instinct. Payroll dates shifted subtly across countries, tax remittances bunched at quarter-end, and no one could predict when liquidity would tighten. Kael pinned a **13-week rolling liquidity chart** beside his desk — red for outflows, green for inflows — and stared at it each morning until patterns began to speak.

He realized that cash volatility was not caused by markets alone; it was also caused by management rhythm. Every delay, exception, and manual override was a symptom of institutional impatience. By restoring rhythm, he could restore credibility. Kael understood that *liquidity was the enterprise's pulse; a CFO who could not hear it could not heal it.*

CFO Practice Note:

• Build a 13-week rolling liquidity chart with weekly inflow, outflow, headroom, and variance visibility.
• Separate predictable flows from discretionary or exception-driven flows.
• Treat rhythm variance as a risk metric, not a reporting detail.

---

117 · Restructuring Payment Calendars with Predictability

When Kael joined, disbursements were driven by persuasion, not policy. Vendors waited for signatures; employees waited for mood. To fix trust before fixing cash, he rebuilt the **payment calendar** into two weekly cycles approved ten days in advance.

Every Monday at 9 a.m., treasury confirmed available cash. Every Thursday at 2 p.m., approved vendor payments went out globally. No exceptions, no inbox lobbying. The ritual reduced negotiation noise and forced functions to plan ahead.

Within eight weeks, disputes over payment timing dropped sharply. Treasury staff began leaving office earlier, and even suppliers remarked that finance finally ran like a clock. Kael learned that *a reliable payment rhythm could become more valuable than an emergency overdraft.*

CFO Practice Note:

• Define fixed pay-out windows and restrict deviations to approved emergency cases.
• Publish a 90-day payment calendar across the organisation.
• Align vendor terms, statutory outflows, payroll, and cash peaks before releasing payment cycles.

---

118 · Receivables Risk Clustering by Customer Type

The first receivables report Kael reviewed was 47 pages long — numbers, not insight. He asked FP&A to rebuild it as a **receivables risk heat map**, clustering customers by payment discipline, credit exposure, margin quality, and contract dependency.

The results were revealing. Ten key accounts, though profitable, created half the overdue value. Another set paid precisely on time because account managers maintained close personal rapport. Kael reframed it as behavioural risk: finance did not merely collect invoices; relationships influenced cash.

He convened Sales and Treasury into a single review room. Each red-flagged client was assigned a joint action plan — escalation, renegotiation, revised terms, or phased withdrawal. Collections improved within one quarter, not because of threats but because accountability had a face. Kael understood that *receivables aged faster when ownership aged slower.*

CFO Practice Note:

• Cluster receivables by customer type, payment behaviour, margin, exposure, and relationship dependency.

• Link sales incentives partly to collection performance, not only booked revenue.

• Publish receivable heat maps monthly for executive visibility and joint ownership.

---

119 · Redesigning Approval Flow for Disbursements

Kael's second discovery was procedural — ten approval layers for a single rupee outflow. Everyone could block a payment; no one truly owned it. He dismantled the legacy hierarchy and created a three-layer digital flow: initiator, approver, releaser. Each stage carried timestamps, document references, and ERP escalation triggers.

He coined the rule **one reason, one record** — if an expense could not be justified in one clear line, it did not deserve approval. The clarity changed behaviour quickly. Finance teams stopped hiding behind circular emails, and policy became permission with evidence rather than bureaucracy with excuses.

Kael understood that *controls should guide decisions without becoming a maze where accountability disappears.*

CFO Practice Note:

• Simplify disbursement approvals into clear accountable roles: initiator, approver, releaser.

• Automate approval trails and remove dependency on email-based clearance.

• Review all exceptions quarterly for behavioural trends, repeat approvers, and process weakness.

---

120 · Dynamic Cash-Flow Forecasting Using AI Models

Forecasting had long been a ritual of guesses and revisions. Kael replaced that ritual with data discipline — linking ERP, CRM, banking APIs, collection trackers, and regional calendars into a live predictive model. The algorithm learned from seasonality, invoice terms, payment behaviour, holidays, and historical variance.

The forecast was not perfect, but it was honest. It gave management early sight of pressure points and allowed treasury to pre-arrange bridge facilities instead of borrowing under panic. Within three months, forecast accuracy tightened materially.

Kael refused to worship the model. He used it to ask better questions. Kael believed that *forecasting was not prophecy; it was disciplined curiosity applied before cash became scarce.*

CFO Practice Note:

• Integrate ERP, CRM, bank, collection, and payment data into one forecasting model.
• Monitor forecast accuracy variance and investigate repeated misses by owner and source.
• Use base, stress, and severe scenarios for board readiness, not only treasury planning.

---

121 · Cash-Flow Variance Analysis vs. Budget vs. Actual

Kael believed numbers meant little until compared against reality. He instituted a three-way variance discipline — **Budget | Forecast | Actual**. Every Friday, FP&A produced a one-page bridge that exposed gaps, not stories. The rule was clear: explain the variance, not the weather.

Early sessions were uncomfortable. Sales blamed timing; operations blamed unforeseen logistics. Kael stopped the blame chain with one question: "Was it predictable?" If yes, it was controllable. Within a quarter, teams started submitting explanations before being asked.

The biggest shift was not accuracy alone; it was accountability. Forecast credibility became reputation currency inside finance, and Kael quietly started tracking it in performance reviews. Kael understood that *precision became the language of trust only when variance created learning, not excuses.*

CFO Practice Note:

• Run weekly budget–forecast–actual reviews with concise visual bridges.
• Separate variance type clearly — timing, volume, pricing, valuation, judgement, or execution.
• Track forecast accuracy by function to create peer learning and accountability.

---

122 · Reconciliation Frequency Standards and RACI Matrix

The root of every cash shock, Kael observed, was often a forgotten reconciliation. Bank statements were matched in bulk at month-end, allowing small discrepancies to snowball. He changed the rhythm — daily reconciliation for high-volume accounts, weekly for the rest.

He formalised a **Reconciliation RACI Matrix**: Preparer, Reviewer, Approver. Each role carried a signature, timestamp, SLA, and escalation path. For the first time, every open item had an owner. Controllers began competing on reconciliation timeliness, and unresolved differences fell sharply.

What improved was not just accounting hygiene, but management reflex. Errors surfaced early; corrections became routine instead of dramatic. Kael believed that *the strength of the close depended on the speed of reconciliation.*

CFO Practice Note:

- Standardise reconciliation frequency by transaction volume, risk, and account sensitivity.
- Use dashboards to track pending items, ageing, owners, and escalation status.
- Treat reconciliation delays as internal-control exceptions, not clerical lapses.

---

123 · Cross-Functional Cash Councils — Sales + Treasury

Kael knew cash discipline could not live in finance alone. He formed a **Cross-Functional Cash Council** with Sales, Treasury, Supply Chain, and Operations, meeting every second Monday. The agenda was simple: inflows, outflows, bottlenecks, customer behaviour, supplier pressure, and working-capital commitments.

At first, the meetings were tense. Sales feared exposure; Treasury spoke in acronyms. But over coffee and data, teams began connecting liquidity to credibility. A delayed collection now meant a delayed campaign. A supplier prepayment now required joint justification.

The council soon became a mini-boardroom for working-capital strategy. When regions hit their DSO targets, Kael had them present learnings company-wide; peer recognition replaced policing. Kael realized that *liquidity improved fastest when sales and finance learned to speak the same language.*

CFO Practice Note:

- Charter a monthly cash-council forum chaired by the CFO or treasury head.
- Track joint KPIs such as DSO, DPO, inventory days, and cash-conversion cycle.

• Document decisions and circulate action summaries within 48 hours.

124 · Early-Payment Incentive Programmes for Clients

Instead of chasing slow-paying customers, Kael designed a carrot economy. Treasury computed the company's average borrowing cost and approved a selective early-payment discount for clients settling within the agreed accelerated window.

Sales doubted the uptake, but within two months a meaningful share of customers opted in. Average DSO fell, short-term borrowing needs reduced, and early payers became reference clients because their predictability lowered operational stress.

Kael presented the initiative to the Audit Committee not as finance ingenuity but as trust engineering — rewarding reliability instead of punishing delay. Kael understood that *working capital often responded faster to respect than to reminders.*

CFO Practice Note:

• Compute early-payment incentive ROI against weighted cost of borrowing and liquidity benefit.

• Embed discount logic in invoicing and ERP workflows to avoid manual errors.

• Publicise results internally so cash discipline becomes visible and repeatable.

125 · Vendor Term Negotiations — Balancing Ecosystem Health

Kael refused to squeeze suppliers for optics. He launched a **Vendor Health Program**, categorising partners into strategic, critical, and transactional. Strategic vendors received transparent forecasts and prompt payment discipline; transactional vendors were offered digital invoice-discounting through partner banks.

The philosophy was mutual liquidity. By giving visibility, Kael reduced panic pricing and supply disruption. In turn, vendors offered better rates, priority delivery, and fewer emergency escalations. Vendor trust improved because payment terms became predictable rather than tactical.

Kael understood that *healthy suppliers created sustainable margins; weak vendors eventually became the company's own operating risk.*

CFO Practice Note:

• Map vendor tiers by spend, criticality, substitutability, and operational dependency.

• Introduce supply-chain financing or invoice-discounting channels where they strengthen ecosystem resilience.

• Measure vendor health and payment trust periodically as a working-capital risk indicator.

---

126 · Automating Cash-Flow Reports via ERP Integration

For years, treasury teams at Kael's division spent Mondays reconciling spreadsheets from eight countries. By the time the report reached the CFO, reality had already changed. Kael's instruction was blunt: "If the system knows, I must know."

He led a rapid automation sprint connecting bank APIs, ERP ledgers, and collection trackers into a single live cash-visibility dashboard. Data refreshed every few hours, flagging discrepancies automatically. Controllers could drill down by country, currency, entity, and bank.

The result was not just speed — it was trust. Executives no longer asked, "Is this the latest data?" They asked, "What does it tell us?" Kael believed that *automation was not merely about efficiency; it was about credibility.*

CFO Practice Note:

• Integrate ERP with real-time banking APIs and collection data sources.

• Automate cash-flow updates and eliminate manual consolidation wherever controls allow.

• Archive daily system snapshots for audit trail, variance review, and governance readiness.

---

127 · Cash-Velocity KPIs — CFO Dashboard Essentials

Once visibility stabilised, Kael defined what mattered most — velocity, not volume. He redesigned the **CFO Dashboard** to measure the speed of cash movement through the enterprise.

Core KPIs included:

• Days Sales Outstanding

• Days Payable Outstanding

• Cash Conversion Cycle

- Liquidity Coverage Ratio
- Forecast Accuracy

Every Monday, leaders viewed these metrics in red–amber–green status, not in long slide decks. A five-minute glance replaced a two-hour review. Within two months, velocity became language: "We are running at a 58-day cycle, aiming for 50."

Kael understood that *cash velocity was the enterprise's heartbeat; if ignored, the pulse faded silently.*

CFO Practice Note:

- Restrict the dashboard to a small set of cash-velocity indicators that drive decisions.
- Refresh metrics regularly and review trend movement weekly.
- Make velocity ownership cross-functional — treasury can measure it, but the business must move it.

---

128 · Establishing Weekly Cash Governance Meetings

Kael institutionalised rhythm. Every Monday at 8:00 a.m., his leadership team gathered for the **Cash Governance Meeting** — 30 minutes sharp, no slides, no storytelling. Each region presented four numbers: opening cash, expected cash, actual cash, and variance.

If variance exceeded the tolerance band, the conversation shifted to why, not who. Over time, this ritual became sacred. People arrived prepared because unpreparedness was visible. Teams learned that liquidity discipline starts with punctuality.

Even the CEO began dropping by, noting that the meeting saved the organisation from expensive surprises. Kael understood that *cadence was culture expressed in numbers.*

CFO Practice Note:

- Fix the meeting cadence and avoid rescheduling liquidity reviews casually.
- Use a one-page template with traffic-light variance reporting.
- Document action points with owners, deadlines, and next-review status.

---

129 · Designing a Liquidity Buffer Policy

Predictability without protection is illusion. Kael framed a **Liquidity Buffer Policy** approved by the Audit Committee, maintaining a minimum operating cash cushion based on market volatility, payroll dependency, supplier sensitivity, and access to credit lines.

He defined clear trigger rules: below threshold activated credit-line review; volatility beyond trend triggered CFO notification; repeated breaches required board awareness. The buffer was not treated as idle capital, but as an insurance premium for continuity.

During a supplier disruption, the policy protected payroll continuity and prevented public embarrassment. Kael understood that *liquidity buffers did not weaken returns; they protected reputation when timing turned hostile.*

CFO Practice Note:
• Quantify buffer requirements based on business volatility, payroll cycle, supplier risk, and credit access.
• Align the funding hierarchy clearly — cash, credit, asset liquidation, strategic funding.
• Review buffer adequacy quarterly with treasury, CEO, and board committee where appropriate.

---

130 · Root-Cause Analysis of Cash Leakages

By the end of Quarter 1, Kael ordered a **Cash Integrity Audit** — not to assign blame but to uncover behavioural leaks. The task force traced anomalies in collections, price adjustments, unclaimed rebates, unapproved discounts, delayed invoicing, vendor rounding-offs, and idle cash balances.

Patterns emerged: habitual early discounts offered without CFO review, service invoices delayed due to missing internal approvals, and cash left uninvested because no one owned the float. Each leakage had a human fingerprint.

Kael reframed the findings into a **Cash Integrity Playbook**, turning each error into a preventive control. Within 90 days, leakages fell and unaccounted deductions reduced materially. Kael understood that *cash did not leak from ledgers; it leaked from habits.*

CFO Practice Note:
• Conduct quarterly root-cause sessions on major cash variances, deductions, delays, and unexplained adjustments.
• Classify findings as process, policy, system, ownership, or behaviour failures.
• Convert recurring leakages into automated controls, approval triggers, or dashboard alerts.

Each chapter in Part II culminates in a 90-Day Dashboard — the CFO's instrument panel to measure early credibility.

90-Day Dashboard — Cash-Flow Credibility Index

Metric	Baseline (Day 0)	Target (Day 90)	Outcome Owner
Forecast Accuracy (±%)	±22%	±5%	FP&A
Average DSO	72 days	60 days	Sales + Treasury
Cash Conversion Cycle	66 days	52 days	CFO Office
Bank Reconciliation Lag	12 days	0 days	Controllers
Variance Reporting Compliance	45%	100%	Finance Heads
Liquidity Buffer Coverage	8 days	15 days	Treasury
Leakage Recovery Rate	—	≥25% reduction	CFO Audit Cell

By Day 90, Kael's liquidity rhythm turned finance from a reporting centre into a reflex system.
"Cash credibility is the CFO's first language — the faster it speaks, the deeper the trust." **— Scott Herren, CFO Cisco Systems *(CFO Roundtable 2023)***

The Asia–Pacific division's reputation in group boardrooms changed from "tight on cash" to "tight in control."

CHAPTER 9

Capex Pause and Rationalization

Saying "no" with numbers and clarity.

131 · Creating a Capex Evaluation Matrix — Strategic vs. Sustenance

Kael halted all new Capex approvals and drew a two-by-two grid — **Strategic vs. Sustenance** on one axis, **Return Certainty vs. Risk** on the other. It forced business heads to admit whether they were building tomorrow or maintaining yesterday.

What emerged shocked the executive team: two-thirds of open proposals were operational maintenance dressed up as strategic growth. Kael's quiet remark during the board call stayed with everyone — capital was loyal only to purpose.

Kael understood that *strategy could describe where the company wanted to go, but capital proved whether the company truly meant it.*

CFO Practice Note:

- Classify every Capex proposal by purpose, return certainty, risk, and strategic relevance — not by department.
- Approve projects only after comparing them visually against the full capital portfolio.
- Treat Capex as a narrative of priorities, not merely a procurement request.

132 · Building Hurdle-Rate Guidelines and WACC Integration

Kael brought back financial gravity. He tied every project to the region's **Weighted Average Cost of Capital** plus a defined market-risk premium. "If it cannot beat the cost of our own money, it should not use our money," he told his team.

When markets softened, some executives lobbied to relax the rate. Kael resisted, reminding them that cheap optimism often becomes the most expensive debt. Within one quarter, capital requests reduced, but the approved projects carried stronger assumptions and cleaner ownership.

Kael believed that *capital was one of the most expensive promises a CFO could make; it had to be priced with respect.*

CFO Practice Note:

• Anchor hurdle rates to dynamic WACC, project risk, market volatility, and strategic importance.
• Review hurdle rates semi-annually and communicate the logic transparently to business heads.
• Publish a one-page guide linking return thresholds to funding capacity and capital discipline.

---

133 · Payback, NPV, and IRR Triangulation Method

Different metrics told different stories; Kael demanded harmony. He enforced a **Triangulation Discipline** — **Payback** for liquidity, **NPV** for value, and **IRR** for ranking.

Finance became a referee of truth. Business heads learned to pre-test projects on all three metrics before submission, and board debates slowly shifted from excitement to evidence. A project that looked attractive on IRR but weak on payback could no longer hide behind one elegant number.

Kael understood that *one number could seduce; three numbers together created perspective.*

CFO Practice Note:

• Use Payback, NPV, and IRR as a triple-gate review for major capital proposals.
• Revalidate assumptions when macro conditions, demand, cost, or FX assumptions move materially.
• Maintain a Capex log linking original approval, revised assumptions, actual spend, and final outcome.

134 · Post-Completion Audit of Projects

Kael believed governance ended where memory began. He introduced **Post-Completion Audits** for every project above the approved threshold, comparing forecast ROI, project cost, timeline, utilisation, and realized benefit.

Instead of punishment, Kael used the audits as mirrors: what did the company learn about timing, people, vendors, pricing, or execution discipline? The reflections became institutional memory, and future business cases began improving because past promises were no longer forgotten.

Kael understood that *accountability meant remembering what the company once promised in front of numbers.*

CFO Practice Note:

• Make post-completion audit mandatory within a defined period after commissioning or benefit start date.

• Track benefit-realisation variance, cost overrun, timeline slippage, and owner response.

• Feed lessons into the next-cycle business-case template so mistakes become institutional learning.

---

135 · ROI Communication to Non-Financial Executives

Kael noticed non-finance leaders glazing over when ROI graphs appeared. He reframed returns in human terms: "This system saves forty hours a week — that is one new employee without hiring."

ROI storytelling bridged empathy and evidence. When marketing leaders began presenting their own investment returns in quarterly reviews, Kael knew finance had earned its seat as a translator, not a gatekeeper.

Kael understood that *if people could not feel the numbers, they would rarely follow the math.*

CFO Practice Note:

• Translate ROI into time saved, quality improved, risk reduced, customer benefit, or capacity created.

• Use simple visuals to connect Capex spend with business outcomes.

• Train business heads to narrate ROI in their own operating language before presenting to leadership.

---

136 · Capex Prioritisation During Downturns

The first macro shock of Kael's tenure arrived six months in — commodity prices spiked, and the Group CFO ordered all regions to cut discretionary Capex. Panic meetings followed. Kael did not freeze; he filtered.

He convened a 48-hour **Capital Prioritisation War Room**, where every project was placed into one of three buckets: **Protect, Postpone, or Purge**. Projects that improved cash velocity, digital capability, safety, compliance, or strategic continuity survived; vanity expansions did not.

In a follow-up note to the CEO, Kael wrote: "We cannot stop investing, but we can stop guessing." Kael understood that *tough cycles did not cancel ambition; they clarified which ambition deserved capital.*

CFO Practice Note:

• Use downturns to re-rank projects instead of applying blanket freezes.
• Define survival rules: cash impact, strategic continuity, compliance need, resilience, and digital leverage.
• Maintain an emergency Capex reserve for mission-critical interventions.

---

137 · Leasing vs. Buy Decision Framework

Kael discovered the company owned dozens of depreciating assets — forklifts, servers, vehicles, and support equipment — that could have been leased at lower lifecycle cost and with greater flexibility. He launched a **Lease-or-Buy Diagnostic** across all units, evaluating net present cost, tax treatment, asset utilisation, maintenance burden, and exit flexibility.

The result released trapped capital. But the deeper change was philosophical: ownership gave way to stewardship. His finance brief to the board was clear — the company did not need to own everything it could control.

Kael understood that *balance sheets became lighter when ego stopped pretending ownership was strategy.*

CFO Practice Note:

• Apply lease-versus-buy tests for every capital request above the approved threshold.
• Consider asset volatility, utilisation rate, maintenance risk, tax treatment, and exit cost.
• Use leasing where it preserves flexibility, protects cash cycles, and avoids unnecessary balance-sheet weight.

---

138 · Divestiture and Asset Reallocation Criteria

Kael believed pruning was part of growth. He introduced a **Divestiture Readiness Framework** — a scoring grid combining asset performance, synergy value, market liquidity, maintenance burden, and strategic relevance.

Assets scoring below the acceptable threshold were reviewed for sale, redeployment, or restructuring. He briefed his team: "Dead assets consume more than they depreciate." Proceeds from underperforming assets were redirected into digital finance systems and higher-return capabilities.

The division improved returns not by addition, but by subtraction.

Kael understood that *selling well demanded detachment; not every asset deserved emotional protection.*

CFO Practice Note:

• Create a performance–potential matrix for fixed assets, investments, facilities, and non-core operations.

• Reinvest sale proceeds only into strategic capabilities or balance-sheet strengthening.

• Position divestitures as portfolio upgrades, not as signs of retreat.

---

139 · Automation of Capex Approvals in ERP

Every Capex approval once required too many signatures and countless emails. Kael replaced it with a fully automated workflow embedded in ERP. Each proposal carried ROI metrics, risk rating, budget reference, supporting documents, digital approval history, and exception notes.

Turnaround time reduced sharply because accountability became visible. Audit compliance improved because every exception left a timestamped footprint. Transparency replaced persuasion.

Kael noted in his next board presentation that automation was not merely about speed; it was about removing excuses from decision-making.

Kael understood that *good systems reduced drama by making responsibility impossible to hide.*

CFO Practice Note:

• Digitise Capex workflows with embedded thresholds, approval limits, supporting documents, and ROI fields.

• Use dashboards to track approval ageing, exception frequency, and pending decision owners.

• Enable real-time visibility for leadership through ERP-linked reports.

---

140 · Sustainability Lens in Capital Allocation

Kael saw sustainability not as CSR, but as the future cost of access to capital. He made it mandatory that all Capex proposals include an **ESG Impact Statement** covering carbon footprint, energy efficiency, resource use, safety impact, compliance exposure, and community value.

When challenged by an operations VP — "Why must finance care about emissions?" — Kael replied calmly, "Because lenders already do." Sustainability shifted from a compliance checkbox to a design principle, and capital discussions began including future funding cost, reputation, and regulatory resilience.

Kael understood that *capital increasingly flowed toward conscience when conscience could be measured.*

CFO Practice Note:

• Embed ESG scoring into Capex templates for major projects.

• Prioritise investments that reduce future regulatory, energy, safety, or reputational risk.

• Quantify sustainability ROI through cost savings, funding advantage, risk reduction, and brand trust.

---

141 · Creating a Capex Review Committee Charter

Kael formalised what had earlier been chaos. He drafted a **Capex Review Committee Charter**, co-chaired by Operations and Finance, with fixed quarterly cadence, defined thresholds, voting rules, documentation requirements, and published minutes.

Every proposal faced three questions before numbers appeared: does it fit strategic direction, does it build productivity or prestige, and can it survive the next downturn? By institutionalising the filter, Kael took emotion out of approval.

The charter became the invisible firewall between ambition and excess.

Kael understood that *committees did not slow good decisions; they slowed expensive mistakes.*

CFO Practice Note:

• Constitute a cross-functional Capex Review Committee with finance,

operations, strategy, procurement, and risk representation.
• Fix meeting cadence and publish decisions, conditions, and action owners within 48 hours.
• Rotate independent reviewers to reduce familiarity bias and political influence.

---

142 · Use of Throughput Costing for Make-or-Buy Decisions

When plants argued for in-house production, Kael replaced emotion with data. He introduced **Throughput Costing**, measuring margin per constrained resource hour instead of relying only on unit cost averages.

The analysis revealed that some in-house pride projects were destroying throughput value compared to outsourcing. His message to the manufacturing head was polite but firm: sentiment was not a cost centre, but it often behaved like one. The shift freed machine-hours for higher-margin lines.

Kael understood that *a business could not fix what it refused to measure in time, capacity, and constraint.*

CFO Practice Note:
• Apply throughput costing to make-or-buy decisions and capacity trade-offs.
• Evaluate margin contribution per constrained resource hour, not only per-unit averages.
• Present findings jointly with operations so the decision carries shared credibility.

---

143 · High-Volume / Low-Price Sale Scenarios — Throughput Impact

Sales once celebrated volume without calculating velocity loss. Kael's throughput dashboards showed that low-margin bulk orders consumed scarce production slots that could earn stronger contribution elsewhere.

He reframed success: revenue that slowed cash was not necessarily good revenue. After tough dialogue with sales leadership, the company walked away from a large but inefficient contract, and overall working-capital turn improved.

The decision hurt pride, but protected value.

Kael understood that *sometimes the bravest number was zero — the revenue the company refused because it trapped cash.*

CFO Practice Note:
• Link throughput data with sales incentive design and contract approval.
• Simulate how volume mix affects capacity, margin, inventory, and cash conversion.
• Use contribution-per-constraint dashboards to challenge revenue that looks impressive but weakens cash.

---

144 · Sensitivity Analysis on Major Capex Projects

Kael demanded that every major proposal carry a one-page **Sensitivity Matrix** — base, optimistic, and stressed cases for cost, volume, demand, timing, interest rate, and foreign-exchange impact. He called it rehearsing uncertainty.

When an automation project later faced cost pressure due to supply-chain disruption, finance already had its contingency plan. There was no panic, only pivot. Board members appreciated that foresight often looked like luck from the outside.

Kael understood that *anticipating risk was not paranoia; it was professionalism before pressure arrived.*

CFO Practice Note:
• Require three-case sensitivity analysis for all high-value or strategically critical Capex proposals.
• Highlight breakeven shift for key variables such as cost, volume, price, FX, and delay.
• Document mitigations alongside assumptions so stress cases create action, not anxiety.

---

145 · Linking Capex ROI to Shareholder Value

Kael's final reform was conceptual — linking every unit of capital deployed to its effect on **Economic Value Added** and long-term enterprise value. FP&A built a dashboard translating ROI gains into return improvement, capital productivity, and valuation logic.

When Kael presented the model to the global board, the Chairman paused and said, "You have connected Capex to market cap — that is financial storytelling at its finest." Business heads finally saw that capital approval was not only about project success; it was about investor confidence.

Kael understood that *shareholder value was not a slide at year-end; it was a lens for every rupee committed.*

CFO Practice Note:
• Embed EVA or value-accretion metrics into major Capex reviews.
• Report cumulative impact of capital spend on ROIC, equity returns, and capital productivity.
• Use this linkage to educate business heads on cost of capital and enterprise value.

90-Day Dashboard — Capital Discipline Index

Metric	Baseline (Day 0)	Target (Day 90)	Outcome Owner
Strategic vs. Sustenance Project Ratio	32 : 68	55 : 45	CFO Office + FP&A
Average Project ROI Variance (Post-Completion)	+17 % over-forecast	< ±5 % variance	Capex Review Committee
Average Approval Cycle Time	21 days	≤ 7 days	Finance Operations
Divestiture Proceeds Re-invested in Digital Assets	0 %	≥ 75 %	Group Treasury
Throughput Gain per Machine Hour	Baseline 1.0	≥ 1.25	Operations Finance
ESG-Compliant Capex Share of Total Spend	18 %	≥ 35 %	Sustainability Council

By Day 90, capital allocation had evolved from permission to principle.

Board minutes began referring to finance not as *"the cost police,"* but as *"the conscience of investment."*

"The CFO's first 90 days are remembered not for restraint, but for rationalization — proving that stewardship creates speed."
— **Ajay Banga**, former CFO Mastercard

Practical Tool: Mini Capex Evaluation — NPV, IRR and Payback Sensitivity

Capex decisions are dangerous because they usually look most attractive before the money is spent.

A CFO must therefore test capital proposals under several conditions before recommending approval. The first question is not, "Can we afford the project?" The better question is, "Will this project still deserve capital if reality is less generous than the presentation?"

Kael Cipher insisted that every major capex proposal carry at least three views: base case, upside case, and stress case. Optimism could be presented, but it could not be the only basis for approval.

Illustrative Capex Proposal

Particulars	Assumption
Project Cost	₹100 crore
Project Life Considered	6 years
Discount Rate / WACC	11%
Base Case Annual Free Cash Flow	₹24 crore
Strategic Purpose	Capacity expansion and margin improvement

Please refer sensitivity evaluation on the next page.

The CFO's role is not to kill ambition. It is to protect ambition from weak assumptions.

A good capex proposal answers three questions:

1. What return does the project promise?
2. What assumptions can break that return?
3. What controls will protect the company if those assumptions fail?

Capital is patient only when governance is strict.

Sensitivity Evaluation

Scenario	Annual / Patterned Cash Flow	NPV @ 11%	Approx. IRR	Payback Period	CFO View
Stress Case	₹18 crore per year	-₹23.9 crore	2.20%	5.6 years	Reject / redesign
Base Case	₹24 crore per year	₹1.5 crore	11.50%	4.2 years	Marginal approval
Upside Case	₹30 crore per year	₹26.9 crore	19.90%	3.3 years	Attractive
Delayed Ramp-Up	₹12, ₹20, ₹24, ₹26, ₹26, ₹26 crore	-₹9.0 crore	8.10%	4.7 years	Approve only with safeguards

The base case shows a positive NPV, but only narrowly. That is the CFO's warning light. A project that barely clears the hurdle rate under normal assumptions can destroy value if demand is delayed, costs rise, or execution slips.

Kael's board note would not say, "The project is viable." It would say: "The project is viable only if the commercial ramp-up is achieved within the first twelve months and capex overrun remains below 5%. Approval should therefore be conditional, not unconditional."

Recommended Approval Conditions

1. No release of full capital without stage-gate review.
2. Commercial orders or customer pipeline to be validated before second tranche.
3. Cost overrun beyond 5% to return to the Capex Committee.
4. Post-completion audit to be conducted after 12 and 24 months.
5. Business sponsor's incentives to be linked partly to actual project returns.

CHAPTER 10

Compliance and Ethics Equation

Integrity as an internal control.

146 · Compliance Landscape Mapping — Statutory + Regulatory

Kael's first step into the compliance maze was not to read laws but to map them. He called it the **Regulatory Topography** — a single-page visual showing every applicable act, filing, reporting frequency, regulator, owner, and jurisdiction across twelve countries.

The output stunned everyone: hundreds of filings, periodic reports, and multiple authorities, all previously scattered across legal, HR, tax, procurement, finance, and operations. Until then, compliance lived in silos, each function guarding its own piece without seeing the whole landscape.

Kael did not aim to control it all personally; he aimed to see it all clearly. Once the full map appeared, ownership began to emerge naturally. Kael understood that *compliance rarely failed because the law was unknown; it failed because the organisation had never seen the full scope of its obligations.*

CFO Practice Note:

• Build a compliance universe covering statutory, fiscal, labour, environmental, data, contractual, and regulatory obligations.

• Tag every obligation to function, frequency, jurisdiction, responsible owner, reviewer, and escalation point.
• Visualise the landscape in one page; a clear map teaches faster than a hundred-page manual.

---

147 · Designing a Unified Compliance Calendar

Kael replaced countless reminders and spreadsheets with a **Unified Compliance Calendar** accessible to finance, legal, HR, tax, operations, and business heads. It merged statutory, regulatory, tax, contractual, board, and reporting commitments into one timeline, colour-coded by jurisdiction, severity, and filing owner.

The new rule was simple: "If it is not on the calendar, it does not exist." Missed filings triggered automated alerts to the CFO office, not to punish, but to protect. Within two months, overdue filings dropped to zero, and external auditors marked the control maturity as high.

The calendar changed compliance from memory into rhythm. Kael understood that *governance became reliable only when responsibility had a visible cadence.*

CFO Practice Note:
• Centralise all compliance obligations into a shared digital calendar with owner, reviewer, due date, and evidence link.
• Automate reminders, escalation flows, and overdue alerts.
• Review calendar completeness every quarter with internal audit and function heads.

---

148 · SOX / Internal Controls Documentation Refresher

The **Sarbanes-Oxley** framework was not new to Kael, but its spirit had diluted into templates. He initiated a **Control Refresher Program** — a back-to-basics exercise to test whether controls were designed for discipline or convenience.

Teams discovered expired access rights, redundant reconciliations, contradictory approvals, and control narratives that existed only because they had always existed. Kael's message was sharp: "We document for discipline, not decoration." He personally reviewed the top control narratives and removed those that no longer protected anything real.

The Audit Committee later described it as the most meaningful internal-controls update in years. Kael understood that *the strongest control was not the longest checklist, but the clearest intent.*

CFO Practice Note:
• Reassess control narratives annually for relevance, ownership, evidence quality, and risk coverage.
• Eliminate redundant, symbolic, or outdated checks that create effort without control value.
• Conduct walkthroughs with process owners to test design against actual practice.

---

149 · Statutory Audit vs. Internal Audit Boundary Clarity

Kael noticed overlapping audit requests frustrating business units. Both internal and statutory audit teams were often checking the same items, asking similar questions, and exhausting the same people.

He convened both audit leads and drew an **Audit Boundary Charter**: statutory audit ensured accuracy of reported results; internal audit tested the integrity of processes, controls, behaviour, and risk response. From then on, duplication reduced, information flow improved, audit fatigue fell, and issues surfaced earlier.

The auditors themselves later remarked that the company had moved from audit-heavy to audit-ready. Kael understood that *controls worked best when accountability had a clear address.*

CFO Practice Note:
• Define statutory and internal audit scopes annually with clear boundaries and shared understanding.
• Maintain an **Audit Boundary Matrix** to avoid duplication, fatigue, and unclear ownership.
• Share key findings across functions in quarterly governance forums.

---

150 · Control Self-Assessment Checklists

Kael introduced **Control Self-Assessments** — quarterly internal declarations by each finance head affirming compliance with core processes. It was not a formality; it was ownership on record.

He signed the first declaration himself, stating that the CFO must be the first controller, not merely the final reviewer. By the second quarter, every regional controller submitted CSAs proactively, identifying issues before auditors did.

The tone changed from catching errors to preventing blind spots. Kael understood that *self-certification built more than compliance; it trained conscience to speak before audit arrived.*

CFO Practice Note:

• Roll out quarterly self-assessment templates to all finance units and control-sensitive functions.
• Track issue resolution rate, ageing, repeat exceptions, and evidence quality.
• Publish a consolidated CSA dashboard to the Audit Committee with themes, not blame.

---

151 · Fraud-Triangle Awareness Training for Finance Teams

Kael did not start fraud prevention with software. He started with psychology.

He held the first **Fraud Triangle Workshop** personally, explaining how pressure, opportunity, and rationalisation converge silently long before detection. Instead of a generic lecture, he used anonymised internal examples — expense manipulation, pre-dated approvals, over-optimistic revenue booking, and vendor exceptions — to show that fraud often begins as moral fatigue, not criminal identity.

By the second session, employees began voluntarily reporting grey zones for clarification. It was not fear that spread; it was mindfulness. Kael understood that *fraud often began where fatigue met justification and no one paused long enough to question it.*

CFO Practice Note:

• Conduct annual fraud-triangle and ethics-fatigue sessions for finance and control-sensitive teams.
• Use anonymised internal cases instead of generic training videos.
• Track behavioural improvement through fewer exceptions, faster escalations, and better documentation.

---

152 · Whistle-Blower Process Testing and Closure Rate Tracking

Kael refused to treat whistle-blower channels as HR formalities. He commissioned a **Whistle Integrity Audit** to test hotline accessibility, anonymity, routing, investigation ownership, and closure timelines.

The results exposed the truth: too many concerns were acknowledged but unresolved. He set a resolution SLA and published an anonymised **Case**

Closure Tracker in quarterly governance reports. For the first time, employees saw the system respond faster than rumours spread.

The channel became credible because it moved. Kael understood that *people stopped speaking up when their words disappeared into silence.*

CFO Practice Note:

• Periodically test the whistle-blower process end to end, including anonymity, escalation, investigation, and closure.
• Track closure cycle time, case ageing, repeat themes, and retaliation indicators as compliance KPIs.
• Share aggregate themes publicly where appropriate to rebuild trust without exposing individuals.

---

153 · Regulatory Reporting Timelines and Ownership Matrix

Missed filings had once been routine, explained away with phrases like "someone from legal will handle it." Kael eliminated that ambiguity through a **Regulatory Ownership Matrix** mapping each filing, deadline, preparer, reviewer, approver, evidence file, and escalation owner.

No submission went out without a digital timestamp and accountable sign-off. The result was zero missed filings across two consecutive quarters, and regulators began referring to the company as a benchmark filer.

Governance moved from paperwork to punctuality. Kael understood that *compliance was not merely about filing; it was punctuality with purpose.*

CFO Practice Note:

• Maintain a dynamic registry of all regulatory filings with deadlines, owners, reviewers, and evidence location.
• Tag primary, secondary, and oversight owners for every material submission.
• Review compliance punctuality in monthly leadership meetings.

---

154 · Leveraging AI for Exception Reporting and Pattern Alerts

Kael saw potential where others saw noise. He worked with IT to deploy AI-based anomaly detection on financial transactions, cross-checking vendor IDs, payment timings, duplicate invoices, split payments, and threshold breaches.

Within two months, the system flagged repeated small transactions below approval limits — a classic micro-leak pattern. The quick fix saved money, but more importantly, it restored internal confidence that technology was an ally of control, not an auditor waiting to punish.

Kael understood that *AI would not replace ethics; it would amplify the signals ethics could no longer afford to miss.*

CFO Practice Note:

• Use AI and machine-learning tools for continuous control monitoring in high-volume transaction areas.
• Focus first on repetitive approval breaches, duplicate vendors, split payments, and unusual timing patterns.
• Treat AI alerts as learning feedback, not disciplinary ammunition.

---

155 · Cyber-Governance and Data-Privacy Compliance

Finance systems held the company's most sensitive data, yet Kael noticed inconsistent access hygiene: multiple administrators, shared passwords, weak segregation of duties, and outdated user rights.

He established a **Finance Cyber-Governance Council** co-led by the CIO. Every privileged access request now required CFO–CIO dual approval. Multifactor authentication became mandatory for treasury, ERP, payment, and reporting modules.

To underline the importance, Kael opened the first Data-Privacy Awareness Week with a simple warning: trust is a balance-sheet asset and must be protected like cash. Kael understood that *modern cybersecurity had become the new internal control.*

CFO Practice Note:

• Establish joint CFO–CIO governance for ERP, treasury, payment, payroll, and reporting systems.
• Implement least-privilege access, multifactor authentication, and periodic user-access reviews.
• Include cyber incidents, privileged-access exceptions, and data-risk trends in quarterly risk reports.

---

156 · Tax-Compliance Review — Direct & Indirect Taxes

Tax compliance had often been treated as a quarterly chore outsourced to consultants. Kael brought it back into leadership view through a **Tax Governance Review** — a quarterly CFO-led meeting covering direct taxes, indirect taxes, filings, litigations, credits, notices, reconciliations, and jurisdiction-level exposure.

He refused to accept "no exposure" as an answer. Each tax head had to show the evidence behind the assertion. Within one quarter, legacy tax balances were reconciled and closed, and external auditors noticed the difference in confidence.

When asked why finance looked stronger, Kael replied that they were finally signing their own truth. He understood that *tax certainty quietly strengthened investor confidence.*

CFO Practice Note:

• Maintain a live tracker for all tax filings, assessments, appeals, credits, notices, and reconciliations.

• Conduct quarterly self-reviews with internal tax teams and external advisors present where needed.

• Align tax documentation standards with statutory audit and board-reporting expectations.

---

157 · Anti-Bribery and Anti-Money-Laundering Controls

In Kael's first internal-audit briefing, he asked a blunt question: "If someone wanted to bribe through our system, how hard would it be?" Silence filled the room.

He introduced **Anti-Bribery and AML Protocols** — mandatory due diligence on third-party vendors, sanctions screening, beneficial-ownership checks, and threshold-based payment approvals. Vendor onboarding now required screening through global lists, while treasury auto-flagged payments to new beneficiaries above preset limits.

When one flag uncovered a false vendor account created by a subcontractor, the message spread quickly: ethics had a phone number. Kael understood that *integrity was protected not only by preventing scandals, but by refusing small shortcuts early.*

CFO Practice Note:

• Enforce vendor due-diligence, beneficial-ownership checks, sanctions screening, and AML procedures.

• Apply the four-eyes principle on high-value, high-risk, and foreign remittances.

• Log all red-flag incidents with investigation outcome, closure evidence, and control correction.

158 · Compliance KPI Dashboard for Board Presentation

Kael knew numbers spoke louder than assurances. He created the first **Compliance KPI Dashboard** — ten metrics, one slide.

It tracked filing punctuality, control breaches, whistle-blower closure rate, audit-finding resolution, repeat exceptions, cyber incidents, access-review completion, and regulatory notices. The Board liked its clarity not because it looked polished, but because it was measurable.

Instead of hearing "all compliant," directors could now see trend arrows and ask intelligent questions. Kael understood that *boards did not need reassurance; they needed radar.*

CFO Practice Note:

• Consolidate material compliance KPIs into one visual summary for board review.

• Include directional trends, owners, ageing, and severity so the dashboard prompts inquiry.

• Circulate dashboards at least 48 hours before Audit Committee meetings.

---

159 · Integration of ESG Disclosures and Non-Financial Metrics

Kael's next frontier was integrating ESG and non-financial compliance into finance routines. He linked carbon metrics, gender ratios, safety indicators, supply-chain ethics data, CSR obligations, and governance disclosures to the monthly performance pack.

When business leaders asked why finance was tracking soft data, Kael answered that investors now often read it before the P&L. The following year, structured disclosure improved the company's sustainability rating and strengthened external confidence.

The change was philosophical: credibility had expanded beyond profit. Kael understood that *the CFO owned credibility, and credibility now included sustainability.*

CFO Practice Note:

• Merge ESG, CSR, and non-financial compliance into the financial-reporting cadence.

• Validate ESG data through internal audit, control owners, and external assurance where required.

• Educate finance teams on sustainability materiality, disclosure quality, and non-financial reporting risk.

---

160 · Creating a Code of Financial Integrity Manual

To hard-wire ethics into systems, Kael authored the **Code of Financial Integrity Manual** — a concise living document endorsed by the CEO.

It was more than a policy; it was a philosophy. It opened with a single sentence: "Integrity is not an act; it is architecture." Every new employee signed it during induction, and senior leaders began quoting from it during reviews. Within six months, the Code became part of the organisation's vocabulary.

Policies became behaviour because they were repeated, taught, and rewarded. Kael understood that *values became culture only when they were written clearly, repeated consistently, and rewarded visibly.*

CFO Practice Note:
• Draft a concise financial-integrity charter signed by the CEO, CFO, and relevant CXOs.
• Reinforce it through onboarding, finance training, leadership reviews, and performance evaluation.
• Refresh the manual annually with lessons from audit, ethics, fraud, and compliance cases.

---

161 · Ethics Simulations in Leadership Development

Kael did not want ethics to remain a policy read; he wanted it to become muscle memory. He designed **Ethics Simulations** for senior leaders — realistic, time-boxed dilemmas played in small rooms: a supplier linked to a senior manager, quarter-end shipment pressure, a travel claim pushed through to "keep morale high," or a side letter requested by a key customer.

The conversations were uncomfortable by design. Participants had to choose, defend, and then watch downstream impacts on a projected control map — audit flags triggered, reputational score falling, whistle channels lighting up. In debriefs, leaders admitted most shortcuts began with emotional convenience, not financial gain.

Kael understood that *culture was built in ten-minute decisions that never appeared on slides.*

CFO Practice Note:
• Run quarterly ethics drills using anonymised internal cases and realistic

leadership pressure.
• Capture decisions, map control impact, and agree countermeasures after each simulation.
• Fold insights into manager onboarding, succession planning, and performance reviews.

162 · CFO's Responsibility in Regulation FD and Public Disclosures

Kael reset disclosure discipline. Before every market-facing interaction, he created a **Disclosure Control Room** where investor relations, legal, and finance aligned on equal access, consistent numbers, and approved language.

If a question drifted toward non-public data, Kael parked it for formal filing. He also instituted a **Disclosure Log** — who said what, when, to whom — so that every analyst briefing could be reconciled to public material. The outcome was not merely lower risk; it was higher credibility.

Analysts began describing the company's calls as tight and transparent. Kael understood that *fair disclosure was how internal truth became external trust.*

CFO Practice Note:
• Pre-clear talking points with investor relations, legal, finance, and disclosure owners.
• Maintain a disclosure log and reconcile post-call comments with public materials.
• Train spokespeople to pause and file when uncertain, rather than improvising around sensitive information.

163 · Periodic Board Certification of Compliance Framework

Rather than relying on year-end representations, Kael moved the Board to a quarterly **Compliance Certification** — a one-page attestation covering filings, controls, open investigations, remediation status, repeat exceptions, and high-risk matters.

It turned governance from annual ritual into ongoing dialogue. Directors began asking sharper questions earlier, and management learned that the easiest certification was the one prepared for all quarter, not written at midnight.

The format was brief, but the discipline behind it was deep. Kael understood that *boards did not need more pages; they needed earlier certainty.*

CFO Practice Note:
• Use a standard one-page certification covering status, exceptions, actions, owners, and evidence.
• Time the certification with Audit Committee reviews and archive all support documents.
• Track repeat exceptions and escalate pattern failures.

---

164 · Designing a Crisis-Disclosure Protocol

A small plant incident exposed confusion: legal drafted, communications waited, finance hesitated. Kael codified a **Crisis-Disclosure Protocol** covering triggers, first responder, holding statement, investor timeline, regulator timeline, approval owner, and publication authority.

They rehearsed it like a fire drill. When a cyber outage hit a quarter later, the company communicated quickly, quantified impact within a defined window, and recovered goodwill faster than peers who stayed silent.

The protocol worked because it was prepared before emotion entered the room. Kael understood that *in crisis, speed protected accuracy when governance had rehearsed the message in advance.*

CFO Practice Note:
• Define disclosure triggers, spokesperson hierarchy, approval flow, and pre-cleared holding language.
• Drill quarterly with investor relations, legal, IT, operations, and communications.
• Maintain a secure crisis binder with statements, contact trees, regulator FAQs, and escalation routes.

---

165 · Coordination with External Auditors for Regulatory Updates

Kael reframed auditor meetings from inspection to anticipation. Each quarter, finance and external auditors ran a **Regulatory Horizon Session** covering accounting updates, tax changes, ESG assurance trends, cyber expectations, disclosure developments, and regulator focus areas.

Each update received an internal owner, system-impact note, process change, and target date. By the time new rules arrived, process notes, controls, and systems were already prepared.

Audit letters began using a new phrase for the division: change-ready. Kael understood that *great finance teams met new rules at the gate, not after they had entered the building.*

CFO Practice Note:
• Calendar quarterly regulatory horizon scans with external auditors and relevant advisors.
• Log each update with owner, system impact, control impact, target date, and board relevance.
• Share a short "what changes for us" memo with leadership.

---

166 · Annual Compliance Report to Board — Format and Frequency

Instead of a thick binder, Kael sent the Board a concise **Annual Compliance Report** supported by a live appendix. It opened with a heat map by jurisdiction and risk, followed by filing punctuality, closure cycles, repeated exceptions, whistle case themes, cyber matters, audit trends, and the forward agenda.

The brevity forced clarity. Directors could see trend lines in minutes and spend their time on judgement, not navigation. The live appendix remained available for anyone who wanted evidence behind the dashboard.

Kael understood that *brevity did not mean fewer facts; it meant faster access to truth.*

CFO Practice Note:
• Start the report with a heat map and close with a forward compliance plan.
• Use trend arrows, owner names, severity levels, and ageing on every major KPI.
• Host a Board Q&A clinic after circulation where directors can probe evidence without crowding the main meeting.

---

167 · AI-Driven Continuous Controls Monitoring

Kael plugged **Continuous Controls Monitoring** analytics into payables, receivables, travel claims, vendor master, user access, and approvals. Algorithms searched for split invoices, midnight approvals, duplicate vendors, privilege creep, round-number claims, and repeated threshold exceptions.

Flags went to process owners daily; unresolved items escalated weekly. Within two months, micro-leaks dropped sharply and the team had objective proof that controls were always on, not sampled occasionally.

Automation reduced the alibis that usually hide between audit cycles. Kael understood that *automation did not replace judgement; it removed excuses from the places judgement could not watch continuously.*

CFO Practice Note:

• Start CCM where transaction volume is high and rules are clear.

• Route alerts to process owners with SLA clocks and escalation rules.

• Measure not only findings, but time-to-close, repeat exceptions, and control redesign.

---

168 · Embedding Ethics into Performance Measurement

Kael added ethics multipliers to leadership scorecards: whistle-closure timeliness, repeat exception rate, access-review hygiene, training completion, control remediation, and culture-survey integrity.

A perfect P&L could no longer carry a poor integrity score. Leaders quickly learned that values were not slogans; they were compensation variables. Behaviour shifted faster than any memo could have achieved.

The change made ethics visible in performance conversations. Kael understood that *what the company rewarded revealed what the company truly believed.*

CFO Practice Note:

• Add appropriate integrity KPIs to leadership incentives without turning ethics into mechanical scoring.

• Publish the rubric clearly so leaders understand what behaviour is expected.

• Celebrate teams that fix root causes, not merely those that close tickets quickly.

---

169 · CFO Decision Tests — Would You Sign It Under Oath?

Kael carried a simple test into difficult calls: if this were under oath, would I sign it?

He used it on grey judgements — provisioning, estimates, side letters, quarter-end shipment timing, revenue cut-off, impairment assumptions, and disclosure language. The question quieted noise and focused the room.

Over time, the phrase became cultural shorthand. People arrived with cleaner proposals because they anticipated the oath test. Kael understood that *the best control was sometimes a sentence strong enough to survive at two in the morning.*

CFO Practice Note:
• Use an explicit oath-test box in approval templates for material judgements.
• Require written rationale for provisions, estimates, revenue assumptions, and disclosure decisions.
• Keep a private register of high-judgement calls for CFO and board review.

---

170 · Building a Compliance-First Finance Culture

Policies can be copied; culture must be lived. Kael closed the loop by aligning rituals, symbols, and systems: weekly cash and control huddles, ethics recognition at town halls, access reviews tied to appraisals, and dashboard visibility for control closure.

Compliance stopped being a department and became a way of working. Turnover fell in controller roles, audit findings declined, and hotline traffic shifted from complaints to clarifications. The culture had begun measuring itself.

Kael understood that *compliance was not the brake on business; it was the steering that kept speed from becoming damage.*

CFO Practice Note:
• Make control rituals visible, time-boxed, and linked to decision-making.
• Recognise everyday integrity, early escalation, and clean remediation — not only large financial wins.
• Keep asking what behaviour each rule produces; culture follows the incentives hidden inside process.

90-Day Dashboard — Compliance Integrity Index

Metric	Baseline (Day 0)	Target (Day 90)	Outcome Owner
Filing On-Time Rate (all jurisdictions)	92%	100%	Tax & Legal Controllers
Whistle Case Median Closure Days	58	≤ 30	Ethics Office
Repeat Control Exceptions (Top 10)	14 per qtr	≤ 3	Process Owners
CCM Alert Time-to-Close (Median)	9 days	≤ 3 days	Operations Finance
Access Review SLA Compliance	61%	≥ 95%	IT + Finance
Board Certification Exceptions	7 open	≤ 1	CFO Office
Crisis-Disclosure Drill Time (to first statement)	2h 40m	≤ 45m	IR + Legal + CIO
ESG/Non-Financial Disclosure Assurance	Partial	Limited assurance complete	Sustainability + IA

By Day 90, compliance moved from paperwork to posture — visible, rehearsed, and measurable. Finance no longer *reported* integrity; it **operated** it.

"Trust is the only asset that compounds without capital."
— **Soumen Ray, CFO L&T Finance** *(leadership forum paraphrase)*

CHAPTER 11

Board & Audit Committee Engagement

Every boardroom question is an invitation to earn trust.

171 · Structuring the CFO–Board Relationship Charter

When Kael took charge, he found Board interactions fragmented — emails routed through assistants, finance decks arriving late, and discussions dominated by post-fact explanations. He restructured this through a **CFO–Board Relationship Charter** — a compact three-page protocol endorsed by the Chair.

It outlined engagement rhythm, monthly calls, quarterly meetings, data-flow ownership, escalation etiquette, and pre-read discipline. Most importantly, it defined how surprises should be handled — through pre-emptive disclosure, not polished hindsight. Within two cycles, the Chair remarked that finance had stopped arriving at meetings and started arriving prepared.

Kael understood that *governance trust began when the CFO treated the Board not as an audience, but as a partner in enterprise judgement.*

CFO Practice Note:
• Document a CFO–Board Charter covering frequency, format, data ownership, escalation standards, and feedback loops.

• Schedule informal Chair check-ins between formal meetings to prevent avoidable surprises.
• Pre-commit to disclosure standards for emerging risks, material deviations, and unresolved concerns.

---

172 · Understanding the Chair and Audit Committee Priorities

Kael learned that each Chair carries a personal compass — some prioritise control hygiene, others investor narrative, regulatory posture, capital discipline, or reputational resilience. He began with a **Board Priority Audit**: confidential one-on-one conversations with the Chair, Audit Committee head, and independent directors.

Patterns emerged quickly — risk appetite, transparency preferences, communication cadence, sensitivity to surprises, and tolerance for uncertainty. By aligning his updates with these mental models, Kael reduced surprise questions and made Board engagement more intentional.

What looked like intuition was structured empathy. Kael understood that *Boards may not change often, but their anxieties do; the CFO must learn the anxiety before presenting the answer.*

CFO Practice Note:
• Conduct one-on-one onboarding dialogues with the Chair, Audit Committee head, and key independent directors.
• Document the top three expectations, concerns, and communication preferences of each director.
• Map Board concerns to agenda items so likely questions are answered before they are asked.

---

173 · Preparing Concise Board Packs and Dashboards

The first Board pack Kael inherited ran 187 slides — most unread. He tore it down to fifteen dashboards covering financial, operational, risk, compliance, capital, culture, and cash indicators, each with one clear narrative and traffic-light status.

He adopted a ruthless rule: if the Board could not discuss it meaningfully in ten minutes, it did not belong in the main pack. His decks became visual, trend-based, and self-explanatory. The Chair later told him, "You made finance legible."

Kael understood that *strong Boards needed insight, not information weight; clarity was the CFO's first act of respect.*

CFO Practice Note:

• Limit Board packs to essential dashboards and move supporting detail to controlled appendices.
• Use trend views, variance bridges, and decision notes instead of static number dumps.
• Circulate packs at least 48 hours in advance with contextual notes from the CFO office.

---

174 · Pre-Emptive Briefings with Chair and CEO

Kael institutionalised a rhythm known internally as the **Thursday Pre-Reads.** Every Thursday before a Board or Audit Committee meeting, he spent thirty minutes each with the Chair and CEO separately, previewing possible concerns, aligning tone on sensitive disclosures, and clarifying decision points.

This simple act turned potential confrontation into collaboration. The CEO once told him privately, "You don't brief me for optics — you prepare me for honesty." Kael knew that pre-briefings were not manipulation; they were governance hygiene.

Kael understood that *a short pre-brief could prevent a long post-meeting crisis when it surfaced truth before tension did.*

CFO Practice Note:

• Hold pre-meeting syncs with the Chair and CEO to align facts, risks, narratives, and likely sensitivities.
• Log all likely hot topics and prepare concise CFO responses with evidence.
• Maintain consistency; never allow leadership to be surprised alongside the Board.

---

175 · Translating Financial Data into Strategic Insight

Kael banned the phrase "as per last quarter" from Board decks. Instead, every slide had to answer three questions: So what? What is changing? What should we do?

Finance updates now began with strategic context — margins explained through customer mix, working capital through pricing shifts, debt ratios through scenario projections, and cash through operating behaviour. Numbers became stories that moved decisions. After two quarters, the CEO asked Kael to open Board meetings with a five-minute macro briefing, a privilege previously reserved for Strategy.

Kael understood that *the CFO who could translate numbers into direction shaped the company's future, not merely its history.*

CFO Practice Note:

• Convert every metric into meaning by linking it to decision, risk, capital, cash, or strategic consequence.
• Use visuals and comparative narratives to show movement, not isolated figures.
• Train finance VPs in executive storytelling so the finance function speaks with one strategic voice.

---

176 · Managing Q&A Under Pressure — Grace Under Scrutiny

Boardrooms test not only numbers, but nerve. Kael learned that tone determines whether truth lands as clarity or defence. When faced with rapid-fire questioning — "Why this variance?", "Why now?", "Why missed?" — he resisted the urge to over-explain. He paused, acknowledged, and answered only what data could prove.

His calm became contagious; the CEO later remarked that Kael's composure had become the company's new control system. In post-meeting reviews, Kael coached his team to never debate urgency when accuracy was still being established.

Kael understood that *composure was the CFO's first form of compliance under scrutiny.*

CFO Practice Note:

• Practise rapid-fire Q&A drills before every Board or Audit Committee meeting.
• Train team members to answer with evidence, limitation notes, and next steps — not emotion.
• Keep a variance war-room sheet covering likely questions, data owners, explanations, and corrective actions.

---

177 · Financial Statement Narratives and Story Discipline

Kael believed a balance sheet could be read like a story — assets as choices, liabilities as consequences, and cash flow as the plot twist. He rewrote the financial statement commentary into a clear sequence: context, cause, consequence, and correction.

The Audit Committee began calling his reports readable. More importantly, directors could now trace decisions to numbers and numbers back to decisions. Prior decks had delivered information; Kael's narratives delivered accountability.

Kael understood that *narrative was not decoration; it was disclosure made understandable enough to govern.*

CFO Practice Note:

• Draft commentary in a storyline sequence: context, cause, consequence, correction.

• Avoid jargon and replace raw percentages with business impact statements.

• Peer-review narratives internally before Board circulation or external publication.

---

178 · Audit Committee Calendar & Risk Heat-Map Updates

Previously, risk reviews happened reactively. Kael created a twelve-month **Audit Committee Calendar** linking each quarter's agenda to defined risk domains — financial controls, cyber, compliance, tax, liquidity, culture, and governance.

He complemented this with a live **Risk Heat Map**, colour-coded by likelihood and impact, updated monthly through internal audit and finance feeds. Now, when an issue appeared red, it was not news; it was already in motion for remediation.

Kael understood that *visibility was not governance by itself, but it was where governance began.*

CFO Practice Note:

• Publish an annual Audit Committee calendar with fixed risk themes and review cycles.

• Maintain a live heat map showing risk owner, action plan, closure date, and movement since last review.

• Use trend views; red zones must show movement, not permanence.

---

179 · Internal vs. External Audit Alignment

Kael convened what he called the **Audit Trialogue** — quarterly coordination among Internal Audit, External Audit, and the CFO office. It replaced duplicate checks with shared insight.

Internal teams focused on control design and operating discipline. External auditors focused on validation and reporting assurance. The CFO office focused on remediation, accountability, and board communication. This division of labour restored mutual respect and reduced audit fatigue. The Audit Committee Chair noted that meetings now sounded like one team speaking three dialects.

Kael understood that alignment was not about everyone agreeing; it was about seeing risk through a shared lens.

CFO Practice Note:

• Host joint audit-planning sessions annually with internal audit, external audit, and finance leadership.
• Share top findings, root causes, and closure evidence across audit teams.
• Track combined audit effort hours; efficiency is also a control outcome.

---

180 · Handling Management Letters and Findings

Most companies treat audit letters as post-mortems; Kael treated them as operating manuals. He created a three-column tracker — finding, root cause, behavioural fix — and circulated it to every functional head.

Closure was not marked until the control survived one full quarter of testing. He personally signed off only after seeing evidence, often asking teams whether the issue would have failed again if no one had checked. That standard turned fear into discipline; letters became learning logs.

Kael understood that *controls aged quickly, and the cure was not apology but iteration.*

CFO Practice Note:

• Convert audit letters into live remediation dashboards with owners and timelines.
• Assign each finding a cross-functional owner, not only a finance owner.
• Review status monthly and publish repeat-finding reduction goals.

---

181 · Designing Executive Summaries for Non-Finance Directors

Kael observed that several directors came from engineering, law, policy, operations, or public leadership backgrounds. They did not need accounting jargon; they needed clarity. He introduced a two-page **Executive Summary** for every Board pack, structured as **Five Things to Know** and **Three Decisions to Make**.

Charts replaced dense tables, and commentary replaced codes. The difference was immediate: meetings moved from clarification to conversation. The Chair joked that Kael had turned finance into subtitles the whole Board could read.

Kael understood that *a good CFO translated complexity into confidence without diluting the truth.*

CFO Practice Note:

• Draft short summaries tailored for non-finance directors.

• Use visual ratios, trend lines, and impact statements instead of raw number blocks.

• Frame each summary around what changed, why it matters, and what decision is needed.

---

182 · Conducting Quarterly Board Deep-Dives

Rather than scatter focus, Kael launched **Quarterly Board Deep-Dives** — sixty-minute thematic sessions led by finance but co-owned by business heads. Topics rotated across working capital, tax exposure, ESG financing, culture risk, cyber readiness, and capital allocation.

This rhythm allowed directors to engage early with strategy, not after results had already hardened. One independent director said, "We finally see finance as a telescope, not a microscope."

Kael understood that *depth created credibility; breadth became useful only after the Board trusted the depth.*

CFO Practice Note:

• Schedule four Board deep-dives annually aligned to strategic and risk priorities.

• Blend quantitative analysis with frontline narratives and management accountability.

• Capture action items and assign ownership within 48 hours.

---

183 · Integrating ESG and Non-Financial Metrics into Packs

Kael made ESG inseparable from performance. Each Board pack now included ESG KPIs: carbon per revenue, gender mix, ethical-sourcing scores, safety incidents, training completion, and supplier compliance.

He reframed them as risk mitigants rather than CSR optics. Directors began asking how ESG trends correlated with margin stability, cost of capital, brand trust, and retention — a sign that non-financial data had achieved financial relevance.

Kael understood that *ESG had become part of the CFO's cost-of-capital conversation, not a decorative disclosure.*

CFO Practice Note:

• Integrate ESG metrics into the same dashboard cadence as financial KPIs.
• Cross-link ESG outcomes to investor sentiment, credit ratings, risk exposure, and operating resilience.
• Seek limited assurance for material ESG disclosures before public release.

---

184 · Crisis Communication with Board — When and How to Inform

During a regional fraud alert, Kael realized most leaders wait too long to inform the Board out of caution, fear, or incomplete facts. He changed policy: bad news travelled to the Board within 24 hours; good news could wait.

He created a **Crisis Communication Grid**, classifying events by materiality and setting escalation bands. The Board appreciated early signals even when details were incomplete; confidence rose because transparency replaced surprise.

Kael understood that *Boards forgave mistakes faster than omissions when management respected their right to know early.*

CFO Practice Note:

• Define escalation timelines by event type, severity, financial impact, legal exposure, and reputational risk.
• Maintain a Board-alert protocol with clear authorisation levels and message owners.
• Debrief after every incident to identify what worked, what lagged, and what must be refined.

---

185 · CFO as Bridge Between Governance and Operations

Kael viewed his role not as a mere interpreter, but as a translator between boardroom expectations and ground realities. He built **line-to-board feedback loops** — quarterly CFO field visits feeding qualitative insights into Audit Committee meetings.

This grounded governance in reality; dashboards now carried human context. The CEO often said, "Kael does not just bring numbers upstairs; he carries intent downstairs."

It was governance with empathy, and that earned lasting trust. Kael understood that *the CFO turned oversight into understanding when he carried truth in both directions.*

CFO Practice Note:

• Dedicate field time each quarter to experience operations firsthand.

• Channel operational learnings into Board reports with context, not anecdote alone.

• Position finance as interpreter of both performance and behaviour.

---

186 · Documenting Board Decisions and Follow-Up Actions

Kael disliked minutes that were merely transcripts. He created **Decision Registers** — living ledgers listing every Board or Audit Committee resolution, owner, deadline, dependency, and status.

Each item was revisited at the next meeting with commentary. The simple change converted discussion into discipline. Within two quarters, the Chair began referring to the Decision Register before asking any question — a subtle signal that the Board trusted follow-through.

Kael understood that *Boards remembered promises longer than they remembered numbers.*

CFO Practice Note:

• Maintain a running Decision Register updated after every Board or committee meeting.

• Tag owners, deadlines, dependencies, risks, and next-review status.

• Circulate updates periodically so promises remain visible between meetings.

---

187 · AI-Driven Board-Pack Automation and Visuals

Board packs consumed hundreds of finance hours. Kael brought in an AI-assisted reporting module within the ERP, auto-pulling dashboards, variance charts, cash indicators, risk summaries, and ESG metrics directly into presentation templates.

The human role shifted from compilation to insight. Errors dropped, turnaround time reduced, and finance finally had time to challenge the story behind the data. When asked how it felt, Kael smiled: "We did not lose control to AI — we gained time for thinking."

Kael understood that *automation freed the CFO's mind for judgement when controls protected the data beneath it.*

CFO Practice Note:

• Integrate ERP and BI tools to auto-populate Board visuals from controlled data sources.

• Lock narrative fields for CFO review so automation does not dilute judgement.

• Validate AI output monthly for data integrity, classification errors, and version control.

---

188 · Ethics in Board Discussions — Guarding Objectivity

Kael noticed that even Boards carry biases — regional pride, loyalty to founders, optimism fatigue, fear of public embarrassment, or reluctance to reopen old decisions. He developed a practice of **ethical anchoring**. Whenever a contentious issue arose, he reminded the room to separate facts from feelings for the next five minutes.

That pause alone changed conversations. It allowed emotion to exhale and reason to return. The Chair later admitted that Kael kept the Board from crossing the line between confidence and conviction.

Kael understood that *integrity in the boardroom often began with the courage to pause before certainty hardened.*

CFO Practice Note:

• Introduce reflection pauses in heated Board debates before recommendations or voting.

• Sequence discussion through facts, assumptions, implications, and decision options.

• Note dissent objectively; disagreement is governance oxygen, not disloyalty.

---

189 · Post-Meeting Reflection Notes for CFO Learning

After every Board or Audit Committee session, Kael spent twenty minutes writing **Reflection Notes** — what worked, what questions repeated, which slide drew silence, which comment shifted tone, and where his own answer could have been sharper.

He used these notes to refine decks, tighten narratives, mentor his team, and prepare for future scrutiny. Over time, they became a self-training library — a mirror to his own evolution. He told his team that every meeting left a footprint, and finance had to trace it before time erased it.

Kael understood that *self-audit was the CFO's quietest form of growth.*

CFO Practice Note:

• Maintain a confidential post-meeting reflection log after Board and committee sessions.
• Identify question patterns, weak slides, blind spots, tone shifts, and unresolved concerns.
• Use insights to mentor upcoming finance leaders and improve future Board preparation.

---

190 · Building a Board Relationship Scorecard

Relationships cannot be seen on spreadsheets, but they can be managed with discipline. Kael built a **Board Relationship Scorecard**, rating each director relationship on trust, transparency, traction, responsiveness, and quality of dialogue.

Scores were based on feedback tone, query depth, turnaround, collaboration frequency, and the nature of questions asked. The scorecard was not vanity; it was calibration. It helped Kael see which relationships needed more data, which needed more dialogue, and which needed more distance.

Kael understood that *influence was earned one conversation at a time, and the CFO had to steward those conversations deliberately.*

CFO Practice Note:

• Review Board interactions quarterly across trust, transparency, traction, and responsiveness.
• Record qualitative signals such as tone, curiosity, turnaround time, and depth of questions.
• Use findings to tailor communication rhythm and evidence style for each director.

90-Day Dashboard — Board Trust Index

Metric	Baseline (Day Zero)	Target (Day Ninety)	Outcome Owner
Board-Pack Volume	187 slides	≤ 20 concise dashboards	CFO Office
Pre-Read Circulation Timeliness	30 hrs before meeting	≥ 48 hrs before	Finance Secretariat
Average Board Q&A Resolution Lag	10 days	≤ 3 days	CFO Office
Decision Register Closure Rate	62%	≥ 95%	Function Heads
Audit-Finding Repeat Rate	12%	≤ 3%	Internal Audit
ESG Metrics Inclusion	0	100% of quarterly packs	Sustainability Lead
Director Satisfaction (Survey)	7.1 / 10	≥ 9.0	CFO + Chair
Crisis Escalation Compliance	Inconsistent	100% within 24 hrs	CFO + Legal + Comms

By Day 90, Kael had transformed Board meetings from defensive rituals into disciplined dialogues.
Finance wasn't *reporting to* the Board anymore — it was *partnering with* it.
The trust was visible not in applause, but in silence — the kind that signals respect.

"A trusted CFO doesn't just earn time on the agenda — he earns time in the Chair's mind."
— **Brian Olsavsky, CFO Amazon Inc.** *(Board Governance Panel, 2023)*

Practical Tool: From Data Dump to Board-Ready Insight

Board packs fail when they confuse volume with clarity.
A CFO should never walk into the boardroom with a document that merely reports numbers. Directors do not need more data. They need judgement, context, risk, and decision options.
Kael Cipher inherited board packs that were technically accurate but strategically weak. They contained dozens of slides, multiple reconciliations, and long operational notes. Yet after reading them, a director could still ask: "So what exactly requires our attention?"
That was the problem.

Before: Weak Board Slide

Title: Q2 Financial Performance Update

- Revenue increased by 8% compared to last quarter.
- EBITDA margin declined from 18.5% to 16.8%.
- Receivables increased due to delayed collections from key customers.
- Inventory increased due to higher procurement in anticipation of future demand.
- Net debt increased because of working capital requirements.
- Management is monitoring the situation and expects improvement in the next quarter.

This slide gives information, but not interpretation. It reports symptoms but does not separate normal movement from board-level concern.

After: Board-Ready CFO Slide

Title: Q2 Performance: Growth Remains Positive, but Cash Discipline Requires Board Attention

Area	Current Position	CFO Interpretation	Board Attention Required
Revenue	Up 8% QoQ	Growth is volume-led, but margin quality is mixed	Monitor customer/product mix
EBITDA Margin	Down from 18.5% to 16.8%	Discounting and input costs reduced operating leverage	Approve pricing discipline review
Receivables	Up by ₹86 crore	DSO moved from 52 to 64 days; two customers driving 70% of delay	Support escalation with strategic customers
Inventory	Up by ₹72 crore	Procurement exceeded confirmed demand; risk of slow-moving stock	Freeze non-critical purchase orders
Net Debt	Up by ₹110 crore	Working capital, not capex, is driving borrowing	Approve 60-day cash recovery plan

CFO Recommendation

Management should implement a 60-day cash recovery plan with three immediate actions:

1. Customer-level collection escalation for top five overdue accounts.
2. Temporary freeze on non-critical inventory purchases.
3. Weekly cash reporting to the CEO and Audit Committee Chair until DSO returns below 55 days.

Decision Required from Board

Approve management's proposed cash discipline plan and authorize the CFO to escalate collection discussions with strategic customers where commercial teams require board-level support.

The difference between the two slides is not design. It is leadership.

The first slide says what happened. The second explains what it means, what may go wrong, and what decision is required.

Kael's rule for board packs was simple:

"Every board slide must earn its place by answering one of three questions: What changed? Why does it matter? What decision is needed?"

CHAPTER 12

BUILDING YOUR FINANCE LEADERSHIP TEAM

A CFO is only as strong as the bench he builds. Move from command to collaboration; build a finance team that lasts.

191 · Mapping Current Org Structure vs. Desired Future State

On Day 1, Kael inherited an org chart frozen in time — titles stacked vertically, decisions clogged at the top, and accountability travelling slowly through hierarchy. He redrew it into a **Future-State Blueprint** that mirrored the business's five value streams instead of its five cost centres.

Each node showed current headcount, capability depth, process ownership, automation coverage, and decision dependency. The first insight was uncomfortable: the company was not short of people; it was short of clarity.

Kael understood that *organisation charts did not fail overnight; they fossilised when structure stopped following the work.*

CFO Practice Note:
• Overlay major finance processes on the current structure to identify duplication, delay points, and dependency chains.
• Design the two-year target structure before hiring new roles or replacing existing ones.
• Align structure to value streams, decision speed, control ownership, and future automation needs.

---

192 · Assessing Competency Gaps Across Finance Verticals

Kael ordered a **Finance Capability Audit**, not an appraisal. Each controller, FP&A lead, tax head, treasury manager, and compliance owner self-scored proficiency across analytics, digital tools, governance, business partnering, and executive storytelling.

Results were visualised as a **Heat Map of Readiness**. Patterns emerged: strong compliance minds, weak forecasting depth; strong closing discipline, weaker board communication. Rather than criticise, Kael converted the findings into a **Skill-Investment Plan**.

Kael understood that *competence was the currency through which finance culture earned future relevance.*

CFO Practice Note:
• Conduct finance skill self-assessments annually across technical, digital, governance, and communication capabilities.
• Cluster findings into three priorities — strengthen, stretch, and sustain.
• Pair technical experts with strategic mentors so capability grows across verticals, not inside silos.

---

193 · Building Role-Clarity Documents and Accountability Matrices

Ambiguity kills speed. Kael launched **Role-Clarity Sheets** — one-page statements for every key finance role specifying decision rights, risk limits, escalation thresholds, recurring deliverables, and stakeholder ownership.

He tied them into a **RACI Matrix** — Responsible, Accountable, Consulted, Informed — for core processes such as closing, collections, payments, treasury, tax, compliance, and board reporting. Within weeks, cross-emails reduced and approval loops shortened. People stopped copying everyone; they started owning outcomes.

Kael understood that *speed was the dividend of clarity.*

CFO Practice Note:

- Draft RACI matrices for recurring finance processes and high-risk decision flows.
- Publish role-clarity documents on the finance portal and review them quarterly.
- Use performance reviews to correct overlaps, ownership gaps, and escalation confusion.

---

194 · Leadership Pipeline and Succession Framework

Kael refused to let succession become an obituary topic. He built a **Finance Talent Pipeline** in three tiers: **Emerging**, **Ready-Soon**, and **Ready-Now**.

Every tier carried exposure goals — cross-functional rotation, project ownership, board-pack contribution, crisis simulation, and external learning. He presented the pipeline to the Audit Committee alongside cash-flow charts, signalling that leadership continuity was a control metric too.

Kael understood that *bench strength was a financial ratio in disguise; weakness in succession eventually became weakness in control.*

CFO Practice Note:

- Maintain succession lists for all critical finance roles, not only the CFO position.
- Define readiness through skills, behaviour, exposure, judgement, and stakeholder maturity.
- Review the pipeline quarterly with the CHRO and CEO.

---

195 · Recruiting for Judgement Over Experience

When a senior controller resigned, Kael shortlisted two candidates — one with longer audit experience, another with broader industry exposure and sharper judgement under ambiguity. He chose the latter.

His logic was clear: systems could teach process, but judgement had to be tested before hiring. Six months later, that hire prevented a mis-posting that could have inflated earnings materially. Kael turned the case into a hiring philosophy lesson for the finance leadership team.

Kael understood that *experience could fill a chair, but judgement created direction when the rules were incomplete.*

CFO Practice Note:
• Test decision reasoning, ethical clarity, and ambiguity handling during interviews — not only credentials.
• Use situational caselets involving revenue pressure, control exceptions, and stakeholder conflict.
• Add a **Judgement Index** to senior finance hiring scorecards.

196 · Balancing Internal Promotion vs. External Hires

Kael believed every vacancy asked a strategic question: grow or buy? He built a **Talent-Mix Matrix** mapping every role by internal succession depth, external benchmark, capability gap, and urgency.

If a role had two ready-soon internal successors, the position was ring-fenced for internal growth. If not, external search began. This balance preserved loyalty without limiting learning. When a global treasury role opened, he promoted an internal manager and hired an outsider as deputy; both thrived.

The signal was clear: performance earned opportunity, not proximity. Kael understood that *great finance teams imported capability without forgetting to export talent upward.*

CFO Practice Note:
• Maintain a live Talent-Mix Matrix showing internal readiness and external market benchmarks.
• Use external hiring to fill capability gaps, not to bypass internal development laziness.
• Celebrate internal promotions publicly and explain external hires transparently.

197 · Capability Matrix for FP&A, Treasury and Compliance

Kael designed a **Finance Capability Matrix** listing core skills across FP&A, Treasury, Compliance, Tax, Controllership, and Business Partnering — from forecasting logic to hedging discipline, regulatory fluency, board storytelling, and risk interpretation.

Each skill had four levels of mastery: **Aware**, **Applied**, **Advanced**, and **Advisor**. Every leader self-rated quarterly, with Kael reviewing movement rather than static scores. The pattern of improvement became a measure of leadership vitality.

Kael understood that *capabilities compounded when CFOs tracked them with the same seriousness as capital.*

CFO Practice Note:
• Maintain one capability map across all finance verticals.
• Rate skills quarterly and track momentum, not perfection.
• Link capability progress to succession readiness, project allocation, and mentoring plans.

---

198 · Establishing Daily and Weekly Rhythms of Review

Kael replaced scattered updates with a **Finance Rhythm Calendar** — daily cash huddles, weekly variance reviews, fortnightly control reviews, monthly strategy syncs, and quarterly board-readiness sessions.

Each forum had fixed participants, agenda, time limit, escalation path, and expected output. What looked rigid soon became liberating: teams knew when to speak, so they stopped interrupting the rest of the week. Noise reduced because rhythm absorbed anxiety.

Kael understood that *rituals were the operating software of culture.*

CFO Practice Note:
• Define review cadence by risk velocity — daily liquidity, weekly performance, monthly governance, quarterly strategy.
• Fix calendars at least one quarter ahead to reduce ad-hoc chaos.
• Close every review with a three-point action note, owner, and deadline.

---

199 · Delegation Without Abdication — Trust and Verify

Delegation was Kael's quiet superpower. He issued **Delegation Charters**: every transferred decision carried the required data set, tolerance band, approval threshold, escalation trigger, and review frequency.

Once delegated, he never second-guessed publicly. Review replaced rework. Controllers joked that Kael's greatest compliment was silence; it meant he trusted the math and the person behind it.

Kael understood that *delegation failed when leaders handed over power but kept the fear.*

CFO Practice Note:
• Document decision rights with thresholds, data requirements, escalation triggers, and fallback paths.

• Audit delegated outcomes quarterly, not daily, unless risk triggers are breached.
• Praise discretion that protects principle, not ego.

200 · Designing KPIs for Functional Heads

Kael unified all finance verticals under a **Balanced KPI Framework**. Every functional head carried three types of metrics: performance outcomes, governance discipline, and people development.

No scorecard was complete without evidence of mentoring at least one successor. The Board soon saw the shift: quarterly reviews began focusing on forward indicators, not only post-mortems. Finance leadership became measurable beyond closing books and meeting deadlines.

Kael understood that *KPIs were contracts of clarity between expectation and behaviour.*

CFO Practice Note:
• Limit functional KPIs to five to seven measurable outcomes.
• Include at least one governance metric and one people-development metric by design.
• Review KPI quality, not only KPI results; ask what each metric teaches the organisation.

201 · Continuous Learning and Cross-Training Programmes

Kael considered stagnation the silent risk in finance. He launched **Finance 360**, a cross-learning initiative where controllers shadowed treasury analysts, FP&A staff learned audit walkthroughs, compliance leads joined budget calls, and tax managers attended business reviews.

Every rotation ended with a teach-back session — learning through explanation, not attendance. Within months, internal mobility improved and team confidence rose because finance people began seeing beyond their own desks.

Kael understood that *learning agility was the hedge against professional obsolescence.*

CFO Practice Note:
• Implement rotational learning every quarter across finance verticals.
• Use micro-learning formats — short, practical, peer-led sessions.

• Reward knowledge sharing with visibility, stretch roles, and leadership exposure.

---

202 · Coaching High-Potential Finance Leaders

Kael saw raw potential everywhere, but knew potential without polishing could burn out. He started **CFO Office Hours** — monthly one-on-one coaching with five emerging finance leaders.

Conversations focused not only on numbers, but on mindset: influence, resilience, brevity, judgement, and confidence under scrutiny. One analyst later wrote, "You did not mentor my career; you mentored my confidence." Kael knew that was the real multiplier.

Kael understood that *leadership scaled only when it was taught before it was needed.*

CFO Practice Note:
• Identify the top finance talent by initiative, curiosity, ownership, and judgement — not only grade.
• Schedule structured mentoring and track behavioural shifts, not merely promotions.
• Pair coaching with visibility through presentations, task forces, and leadership forums.

---

203 · Handling Legacy Teams and Change Resistance

Legacy teams often resist not because they dislike change, but because they fear irrelevance. Kael managed this with **Respectful Transition Plans**, inviting senior controllers to mentor new hires on institutional memory while learning digital workflows themselves.

He never replaced experience; he repurposed it. By giving veterans ownership of training manuals, audit-liaison roles, and process-history documentation, he turned resistance into reassurance. The past stopped blocking the future because it had been given a role inside it.

Kael understood that *the past became an asset only when it was invited into the future with dignity.*

CFO Practice Note:
• Pair digital adopters with experienced mentors so both sides gain relevance.
• Document legacy wisdom, informal controls, process history, and recurring

judgement calls.
• Offer reskilling before reallocation wherever capability can be renewed.

204 · Crafting a Finance Team Charter Aligned to Purpose

To Kael, purpose was not poetic; it was operational. He drafted a **Finance Team Charter** that opened with one line: "We exist to protect trust and accelerate performance."

The charter defined collective behaviours: facts before opinions, questions before decisions, unity before credit, and escalation before surprise. Copies hung in every finance office and appeared in onboarding decks. Slowly, it became the invisible code that guided tone and trust.

Kael understood that *purpose was not painted on walls; it was printed on daily choices.*

CFO Practice Note:
• Co-create the charter with finance team participation, not only CFO authorship.
• Refresh it annually during offsites and major transformation cycles.
• Integrate charter language into onboarding, appraisals, and leadership conversations.

205 · Remote and Hybrid Team Governance

As work turned hybrid, Kael saw control gaps widening. He created a **Virtual Governance Protocol** defining digital attendance norms, data-access boundaries, meeting documentation, review rituals, and decision logging.

Dashboards updated live during review calls; decisions were logged instantly on shared boards. Hybrid no longer meant diluted accountability; it meant distributed ownership. Performance consistency rose even as office presence became more flexible.

Kael understood that *trust travelled at the speed of visibility.*

CFO Practice Note:
• Define data-access controls, approval rules, and documentation standards for remote finance roles.
• Standardise digital rituals such as daily huddles, audit-ready notes, and decision logs.
• Use collaboration logs as control evidence where remote work affects governance.

206 · Measuring Team Engagement and Retention Drivers

Kael did not rely on HR surveys alone. He built a **Finance Engagement Index** combining pulse-survey sentiment, turnover analytics, workload balance, closing-cycle fatigue, error rates, and manager feedback.

He tracked flight-risk heat zones — teams with rising attrition, declining survey energy, or repeated overtime spikes. Instead of slogans, he offered schedules: recharge days after closings, Friday no-meeting blocks, and workload rebalancing after peak cycles.

Kael understood that *retention was a finance KPI disguised as HR data.*

CFO Practice Note:

• Integrate engagement analytics with productivity, error rates, closing pressure, and overtime trends.
• Act on fatigue signals early through schedule redesign, workload balancing, and manager intervention.
• Treat recovery as ROI, not recreation.

---

207 · Designing Succession Folders for Critical Roles

Kael institutionalised continuity through **Succession Folders** — one-page blueprints for every critical finance role. Each folder contained KPI maps, process notes, control logs, stakeholder lists, recurring decisions, system access requirements, and handover protocols.
When a senior controller took sudden medical leave, her replacement restored process flow within 48 hours using that folder. The incident quietly proved the value of documentation.
Kael understood that *succession was continuity with a documented heartbeat.*

CFO Practice Note:

• Identify all positions with material decision authority, control ownership, payment access, or regulatory responsibility.
• Create digital succession folders and review them semi-annually.
• Store them securely in the CFO vault with controlled access for audit, HR, and emergency continuity.

---

208 · AI-Based Skill-Gap Analysis Tools

To future-proof capability, Kael implemented an AI-driven **Skill-Gap Scanner**. It compared individual competencies with role requirements and generated learning prescriptions from the corporate LMS.

FP&A teams discovered their modelling skills were ahead, but narrative communication lagged. Treasury had strong execution discipline but weaker scenario storytelling. The algorithm flagged capability gaps before stakeholders felt them.

Kael understood that *AI could coach patterns, but human judgement still had to read potential.*

CFO Practice Note:

- Use AI to analyse skills by recency, relevance, role requirement, and future business need.
- Keep human review on interpretation; algorithms see patterns, not ambition or maturity.
- Connect skill gaps to succession readiness, rotation planning, and mentoring assignments.

---

209 · Creating a Finance Leadership Handbook

Kael compiled every policy, protocol, and philosophy into a **Finance Leadership Handbook** — part manual, part manifesto. It opened with a dedication: "For those who balance trust before balance sheets."

Each chapter included caselets, decision tests, role expectations, escalation rules, board-pack principles, and Kael's own emails as learning moments. The handbook became mandatory reading for every finance manager worldwide.

It did not merely document process; it scaled judgement. Kael understood that *codifying wisdom was the first step toward making leadership transferable.*

CFO Practice Note:

- Publish a living handbook that is digital, searchable, and version-controlled.
- Include decision principles and examples, not only procedures.
- Review the handbook annually during leadership offsites and after major governance events.

---

210 · Annual Talent Review and Development Agenda

Each January, Kael chaired a **Finance Talent Review Council** with the CHRO and CEO. The agenda mirrored financial planning: people budgets, learning ROI, leadership bench health, succession risks, capability gaps, and critical-role coverage.

Every promotion carried a learning commitment; every development plan carried an impact metric. The Board noticed that the company's people forecast finally felt as rigorous as its cash-flow forecast.

Kael understood that *talent was capital with a heartbeat, and it deserved forecasting discipline.*

CFO Practice Note:

• Hold annual talent reviews before budget finalisation, not after compensation decisions are frozen.

• Quantify learning investments as a percentage of finance operating cost and leadership-risk reduction.

• Present bench strength, succession depth, and capability gaps as governance metrics to the Board.

Appendix A — The 90-Day CFO Dashboards

"Execution becomes evidence when measured through dashboards."
— **Global CFO Leadership Forum (2023)**

These 90-Day Dashboards are designed as measurable control panels for first-time CFOs.
Each grid outlines 30–60–90-day milestones with qualitative and quantitative targets, helping CFOs transform credibility into visible performance.

How to Use This Appendix

Each dashboard is meant to be updated weekly across the first quarter of the CFO's tenure.
At the **30-, 60-, and 90-day reviews**, progress should be presented to the CEO and Audit Committee as evidence of control maturity, leadership cadence, and ethical culture alignment.

These dashboards collectively build the **CFO Credibility Index** — a measurable bridge between **trust and transformation**.

"Control systems stabilise companies; dashboard cultures scale them."
— **HBR CFO Playbook, 2023**

---

1. Cash-Flow Credibility Index *(From Chapter 8 – Cash-Flow Redesign & Receivables Discipline)*

Objective: Restore rhythm, predictability, and trust in liquidity management.

Metric	30 Days	60 Days	90 Days	Outcome / Target
Forecast Accuracy	Establish baseline (±10%)	Reduce variance to ±6%	Achieve ±3%	Forecast precision certified by internal audit
Receivables Aging	Map top 20 delayed accounts	Launch early-payment incentives	Reduce >60-day receivables by 50%	Receivables <30 days = 70%+
Weekly Cash Governance	Create weekly review rhythm	Integrate with ERP dashboard	Automate exception alerts	Zero-surprise liquidity reports
Vendor Terms Discipline	Identify high-dependence vendors	Negotiate term alignment	Institutionalise rolling payment calendar	Vendor trust score ≥ 90%

2. Capital Discipline Index *(From Chapter 9 – Capex Pause and Rationalization)*

Objective: Reprioritize investments and protect returns on capital.

Metric	30 Days	60 Days	90 Days	Outcome / Target
Capex Evaluation Matrix	Build master inventory of all projects	Apply hurdle rate + WACC filters	Publish priority Capex list	Capex ROI > 15% (weighted)
Post-Completion Audits	Identify 5 major projects for review	Complete 60% audits	100% post-audit closure	ROI variance <10% vs. plan
Capex Governance Charter	Draft charter with CFO sign-off	Obtain Board approval	Integrate into ERP workflow	Governance cycle time <7 days
Asset Reallocation	Identify idle assets	Begin divestiture / leasing program	Complete first asset sale	5% capital release vs. budget

3. Compliance Integrity Index *(From Chapter 10 – Compliance and Ethics Equation)*

Objective: Embed integrity as an internal control and governance practice.

Metric	30 Days	60 Days	90 Days	Outcome / Target
Compliance Calendar	Consolidate statutory obligations	Roll out unified calendar	Zero overdue filings	100% adherence verified
Control Self-Assessments	Create checklists for key controls	Launch pilot testing	Full division-wide rollout	>95% completion
Whistle-Blower Closure	Review pending cases	Reduce closure cycle to <30 days	Zero backlog	Transparency index >90%
Continuous Control Monitoring (CCM)	Deploy AI-based alerts	Integrate with audit workflow	Activate exception analytics	Real-time compliance alerts active

4. Board Trust Index *(From Chapter 11 – Board & Audit Committee Engagement)*

Objective: Earn Board confidence through transparency, brevity, and foresight.

Metric	30 Days	60 Days	90 Days	Outcome / Target
Board-Pack Design	Audit existing pack for clarity	Redesign into concise dashboards	Roll out globally	Slide count ↓ 40%; comprehension ↑
Audit Finding Closure	Track open items	Reduce open cases by 50%	Zero critical items pending	Closure cycle <45 days
Governance Dashboard	Create prototype dashboard	Share preview with Chair & CEO	Implement fully	Board approval rating ≥ 4.5 / 5
Ethics Heat Map	Compile region-wise data	Present trend to Audit Committee	Integrate into quarterly reports	Culture-temperature >80% positive

5. Finance Leadership Index *(From Chapter 12 – Building Your Finance Leadership Team)*

Objective: Build a finance organisation that thinks independently and operates interdependently.

Metric	30 Days	60 Days	90 Days	Outcome / Target
Org Blueprint	Map current structure	Publish desired-state design	Begin migration	100% role clarity achieved
RACI and Role Sheets	Draft for all verticals	Finalise and socialise	Embed into ERP	Approval cycle ↓ 30%
Mentoring & Coaching	Identify top 10% talent	Launch CFO Office Hours	Review first coaching cycle	90% feedback positive
Attrition & Engagement	Establish baseline data	Implement rotation & recharge days	Reduce voluntary attrition by 20%	Engagement index >85%

PART III

THE FIRST 180 DAYS: BUILDING THE MACHINE

Theme: Institutionalise Systems | Modernize Finance | Align with Strategy
Deliverable: Finance Transformation Blueprint — Reporting to Strategic Enablement

Introduction

By the six-month mark, Kael had crossed the invisible line between *stabilizing performance* and *engineering permanence.*
The first 90 days were about credibility — proving that numbers could be trusted.
The next 90 days are about **capability — building a machine that can think, learn, and act without constant supervision.**
This phase is the CFO's true test: converting a function into an **institution**. Controls must evolve into systems; routines into rhythms; and data into intelligence.
Kael now moves from verifying accuracy to **architecting autonomy** — embedding the discipline of finance into the very circuits of the enterprise.
"A CFO's legacy begins when the company stops asking for reports and starts receiving insight."
— **Amy Hood, CFO Microsoft Corp.**

Purpose of the First 180 Days

- **Institutionalise Systems:** Shift from person-driven execution to process-driven reliability.
- **Modernize Finance:** Integrate ERP, automation, analytics, and real-time dashboards.
- **Align with Strategy:** Ensure every financial metric tells the story of the business plan.
- **Elevate Governance:** Build audit trails, predictive control loops, and ethical automation.

By Day 180, the CFO's office must operate as an **engine of strategic intelligence** — where reporting, risk, capital, and culture converge into a single, self-learning ecosystem.

"If the first 90 days earn you trust, the next 90 must build what endures."
— **Global CFO Leadership Forum (2023)**

Structural Journey

Phase	Focus Area	Expected Outcome
Days 1–90	Build financial credibility and operational rhythm	Liquidity stable · Controls trusted · Team aligned
Days 91–180	Institutionalise digital systems and cross-functional governance	Automated reporting · Analytics-driven decisions · Finance integrated with strategy

Each chapter in this part ends with a **180-Day Strategy Map** — a 90–150–180-day grid translating transformation themes into measurable milestones. Together they form the **Finance Transformation Blueprint**, the CFO's first tangible proof that modern finance can be both intelligent and ethical.

"Systems, not speeches, sustain excellence."
— **Soumen Ray, CFO L&T Finance Holdings**

CHAPTER 13

DESIGNING FINANCE SYSTEMS & DIGITAL WORKFLOWS: ERP Discipline, Automation and MIS Cadence

From data entry to decision intelligence. Build visibility before velocity; introduce shared services, RPA, and analytics.

211 · Defining the Finance Digital Blueprint

By the 180-day mark, Kael understood that technology was not an IT agenda; it was a finance design problem. He began with a **Finance Digital Blueprint**, a single visual architecture mapping every flow of data, decision, document, approval, and report.

The blueprint separated transactional work from analytical intelligence, defining which parts could be automated, centralised, standardised, or deliberately left judgement-driven. It served as the constitution for every subsequent system initiative, anchoring digitisation to business value rather than vendor ambition.

Kael understood that *digital finance began with intent, not infrastructure.*

CFO Practice Note:

• Create a one-page finance system landscape showing data inputs, flows,

owners, controls, and outputs.
• Align every automation project to one of three goals — speed, accuracy, or insight.
• Review the blueprint annually to ensure systems follow strategy, not the other way around.

---

212 · ERP Architecture Audit — What Exists vs. What's Needed

Kael resisted the instinct to upgrade for optics. He conducted a neutral **ERP Architecture Audit**, cataloguing modules in use, modules unused, process overlaps, manual patches, reporting latency, and integration gaps.

What emerged was fragmentation: regional systems talking through spreadsheets, manual reconciliations disguised as local flexibility, and reporting delays accepted as normal. Kael framed the issue not as technology cost, but as control risk. A global ERP core with local configuration became the target state.

Kael understood that *every ERP decision was a governance decision wearing a technology label.*

CFO Practice Note:
• Benchmark current ERP utilisation by modules activated, modules used, and modules bypassed.
• Identify manual patches and calculate their control, time, and reconciliation cost.
• Define a three-tier plan — stabilise, standardise, then scale.

---

213 · Data Governance and Master-Data Management

Kael saw data inconsistency as the silent destroyer of credibility. He launched a **Finance Data Governance Council** with shared ownership between Finance Operations, IT, HR, Sales, and Procurement.

Master-data dictionaries were rebuilt from the ground up — customers, vendors, chart of accounts, tax codes, cost centres, employee codes, product hierarchies, and approval roles — each assigned a data steward. The principle was simple: no analysis was better than wrong analysis.

Kael understood that *when the data foundation shook, even perfect logic collapsed.*

CFO Practice Note:
• Create a single master-data owner for every critical domain.

• Track data-quality KPIs such as completeness, accuracy, duplication, timeliness, and ownership.
• Embed data-stewardship metrics in performance reviews for relevant owners.

---

214 · Automation Priorities across AP, AR and GL

Kael identified automation not as an end, but as a sequence of trust-building steps. He started where control pain was highest — Accounts Payable, Accounts Receivable, and General Ledger reconciliations.

Through process mining, he measured cycle time, error frequency, manual touchpoints, rework cost, and exception volume before deploying RPA bots. Manual voucher entries reduced, close cycles shortened, and the CEO finally saw automation as a finance credibility project, not a technology experiment.

Kael understood that *automation should remove friction, not replace thinking.*

CFO Practice Note:
• Prioritise automation by volume, risk, rework cost, and control impact.
• Run a pre-automation baseline study and measure post-deployment ROI quarterly.
• Involve controllers early so automation has ownership, not only implementation.

---

215 · Workflow Standardisation for Approvals and Reconciliations

Standardisation was Kael's quiet revolution. He introduced a **Global Approval Matrix**, digitised in ERP workflow, so every disbursement, journal, vendor change, and exception followed consistent logic.

Reconciliations moved to a unified checklist with maker-checker sign-offs visible on dashboards. What had once been seventeen email threads became one traceable transaction chain. Approval stopped depending on personality and started following policy.

Kael understood that *process clarity was culture in motion.*

CFO Practice Note:
• Define approval thresholds in both monetary and risk terms.
• Automate escalation alerts for delayed reconciliations, approvals, and exceptions.
• Publish monthly exception reports to reinforce accountability.

---

216 · System Integration with HR, Sales and Operations

Kael believed finance's digital transformation could never live in isolation. He initiated a cross-system integration audit linking HR for cost of talent, Sales for receivables and incentives, and Operations for inventory, production, logistics, and capacity.

The goal was one version of truth across all functions, so forecasts, hiring, procurement, and working-capital planning spoke the same financial language. Integration exposed gaps that were not merely technical: delayed inputs, siloed ownership, competing KPIs, and inconsistent definitions.

Kael understood that *if data could not travel across functions, strategy could not travel either.*

CFO Practice Note:
• Build API-level connections between ERP, CRM, HRIS, procurement, and operations systems.
• Define reconciliation checkpoints at every major integration node.
• Measure data-latency impact on forecast quality and financial close cycles.

---

217 · Building Real-Time Dashboards for Key Metrics

When weekly reviews still relied on Excel attachments, Kael knew visibility was an illusion. He mandated **real-time dashboards** powered directly from transactional systems, allowing leadership to view cash, collections, spend, margins, and working-capital movement by region in minutes.

Visuals replaced verbal updates. CFO insights became live rather than lagged. Finance earned a new reputation: the first to show, not merely the last to explain.

Kael understood that *every live number reduced debate and moved attention closer to decision.*

CFO Practice Note:
• Identify five headline KPIs for dashboard launch — liquidity, DSO, DPO, operating cash flow, and forecast accuracy.
• Enable drill-down by entity, geography, currency, customer, vendor, and business line.
• Review dashboard usage analytics; adoption is proof of relevance.

---

218 · MIS Calendar — Frequency and Ownership

Reporting chaos was Kael's early inheritance. Different units submitted MIS reports at uneven intervals — some weekly, some monthly, some quarterly, and some whenever convenient.

He enforced a discipline of cadence through a single **MIS Calendar** defining frequency, owner, approver, data source, review forum, and escalation path for every report. The act was administrative in form, but transformational in impact. Finance stopped chasing data; business heads began anticipating it.

Kael understood that *rhythm was the unsung KPI of high-trust organisations.*

CFO Practice Note:
• Publish an MIS Calendar visible to all CXOs and report owners.
• Automate reminders, submission logs, version control, and escalation alerts.
• Conduct quarterly reviews of report usefulness and stop producing reports no one reads.

---

219 · Documenting Report Definitions for Consistency

Kael discovered that the same "gross margin" meant three different numbers across regions. He commissioned a **Finance Reporting Glossary** — a controlled vocabulary defining every metric, formula, data source, owner, and approved usage.

Each report carried a footnote or link back to this dictionary, ensuring comparability. Over time, the glossary became the backbone of reporting governance and one of the few documents the Audit Committee quoted verbatim.

Kael understood that *definition drift could become more dangerous than a data error because it allowed everyone to believe they were right.*

CFO Practice Note:
• Maintain a live repository of report definitions, formulas, sources, and ownership.
• Lock version control through document-management systems.
• Align metrics with Board-approved KPIs before automating dashboards.

---

220 · AI and Predictive Analytics for Forecast Accuracy

Forecasting accuracy was Kael's favourite obsession. He introduced AI-driven predictive models combining historical trends, seasonality, customer payment behaviour, commodity prices, FX volatility, and regional demand signals.

Machine learning became finance's new co-pilot, offering probability bands rather than false precision. Kael made one rule: forecasts must learn faster than the market moves. Analysts were trained not to worship the model, but to challenge its confidence levels.

Kael understood that *the best CFOs did not pretend to know the future; they simulated it before it arrived.*

CFO Practice Note:

• Use rolling forecasts integrated with AI inputs at least every 30 days.
• Measure prediction accuracy through variance against actuals.
• Train analysts to interpret confidence intervals, not only point estimates.

---

221 · Robotic Process Automation in Routine Finance

Kael approached automation like a surgeon, not a shopper. He began with routine, rule-based processes — vendor invoice matching, tax validation, GL postings, reimbursements, account coding, and duplicate checks.

RPA bots quietly took over repetitive strain, reducing manual effort and shortening process cycles. Instead of eliminating roles, Kael re-channelled people into analytics, exception management, controls, and business partnering. Automation became a showcase of doing more without exhausting people more.

Kael understood that *automation was not about fewer people; it was about freeing people for higher-value problems.*

CFO Practice Note:

• Begin with three to five high-volume, low-judgement use cases.
• Map exception paths before deploying bots.
• Measure automation ROI through error-rate reduction, cycle-time savings, and redeployed capacity.

---

222 · Cybersecurity and Data-Integrity Controls

Digitisation meant Kael had to guard not just cash, but code. He elevated cybersecurity from an IT memo to a Board-monitored finance risk.

Every payment gateway, reporting tool, ERP workflow, RPA node, and dashboard interface was tested for role-based access, segregation of duties, and audit-trail integrity. Kael personally approved the first **Finance Cyber Charter**, mandating dual authorisation for system edits and ethical firewalls between users and administrators.

Kael understood that *in digital finance, security had become the new segregation of duties.*

CFO Practice Note:
• Conduct quarterly vulnerability assessments on all finance applications.
• Introduce multi-factor authentication, privilege-expiry cycles, and periodic access reviews.
• Report cybersecurity metrics in the quarterly Audit Committee pack.

---

223 · Cloud vs. On-Prem Deployment Decision

Vendors sold cloud as magic; Kael treated it as mathematics. He compared total cost of ownership, latency, data-sovereignty laws, disaster recovery, regulatory comfort, control thresholds, and vendor-lock risk.

Certain modules — travel, reimbursements, workflow tools, analytics — moved to cloud for agility, while core-ledger data remained on-prem or in controlled environments where regulation demanded comfort. The hybrid model balanced speed, sovereignty, and security.

Kael understood that *technology strategy had to respect jurisdiction before ambition.*

CFO Practice Note:
• Perform a five-year cost-benefit analysis for each deployment model.
• Evaluate local data-protection, tax, regulatory, and audit requirements before cloud migration.
• Define exit clauses and portability requirements for vendor-lock scenarios.

---

224 · Vendor Evaluation and Implementation Governance

ERP vendors and consultants arrived with glossy decks; Kael countered with governance. He set up a **Digital Finance Steering Committee**, chaired by himself and co-sponsored by the CIO.

Every proposal faced three filters: business outcome, control compliance, and payback period. Implementation partners were rated on transparency, auditability, delivery discipline, change support, and evidence of similar deployments. The committee minutes became the most-requested internal reading — proof that discipline scales faster than software.

Kael understood that *the vendor's true deliverable was not code; it was accountable value.*

CFO Practice Note:
• Evaluate vendors on domain experience, SLA discipline, auditability, security, and implementation realism.
• Insist on milestone-linked payments and documented acceptance criteria.
• Include user-adoption metrics in project-closure criteria.

225 · Change-Management Plan for System Rollout

Kael knew technology failed where people were unprepared. He invested early in a **Finance Change-Management Office** — training, FAQs, pilot champions, adoption dashboards, issue clinics, and digital buddy networks.

When the new workflow went live, adoption rates rose quickly because users were not meeting the system for the first time on launch day. His mantra was simple: teach before you toggle. Change became less of a complaint and more of a shared migration.

Kael understood that *transformation succeeded when adoption became identity, not instruction.*

CFO Practice Note:
• Run pre-rollout demos by function, geography, and process owner.
• Identify early adopters as local evangelists and first-line support.
• Track user-adoption scores monthly for at least six months after go-live.

226 · Post-Implementation Audit and User Adoption Score

Kael refused to declare victory on go-live day. He instituted a **Post-Implementation Audit** after 90 days of usage, measuring user adoption, error recurrence, data latency, exception rate, and process adherence.

Every process owner was rated on a **System Adherence Index**, correlating actual usage with the designed workflow. Where adoption lagged, he held dialogue before discipline, turning audit findings into mentorship moments. Finance became the only function where system feedback loops also drove human growth.

Kael understood that *automation without adoption was only a mirage of progress.*

CFO Practice Note:

• Conduct post-implementation audit within three months of go-live with an independent reviewer.

• Use adoption heat maps by process, role, and geography.

• Report corrective actions to the Digital Finance Steering Committee.

---

227 · Data-Visualisation Best Practices for Leadership Reports

Kael discovered that presentation quality often shaped perception quality. He created a **Finance Visualisation Standard** specifying colour codes, chart templates, variance bridges, commentary hierarchy, traffic-light rules, and one-line insight structure.

Reports now spoke the language of decision-makers: concise, comparable, and credible. Board packs shrank, but comprehension improved. Numbers no longer shouted; they spoke with clarity.

Kael understood that *great visuals did not simplify truth; they amplified it without distortion.*

CFO Practice Note:

• Train analysts in visual hierarchy — context before colour, trend before decoration.

• Standardise templates across dashboards and recurring leadership reports.

• Include one clear "so what" statement per chart.

---

228 · Continuous-Improvement Loops in Digital Finance

Transformation without iteration is decoration. Kael built a **Continuous-Improvement Loop**, where quarterly feedback from controllers, users, internal auditors, process owners, and IT support teams was logged into a digital tracker.

System enhancements were prioritised using effort–impact matrices. He called it **Finance Kaizen**. Within two cycles, error recurrence fell and manual work reduced because improvement stopped being an annual project and became a habit.

Kael understood that *sustainable finance transformation was maintenance with purpose.*

CFO Practice Note:
• Maintain a live CIL dashboard with owner, issue, impact, priority, and closure status.
• Close the loop by documenting fix, validating result, and communicating the update.
• Tie CIL metrics to both IT and finance KPIs.

---

229 · AI-Augmented Audit-Trail and Compliance Checks

To Kael, AI was not a shiny accessory; it was a sentinel. He deployed machine-learning models to review audit trails, flag anomalies, and pre-empt control violations.

The system learned behavioural baselines: who approved faster than normal, who edited entries after cut-off, which vendors triggered frequent reversals, and which access rights expanded quietly. Auditors began asking for access to Kael's dashboard because the machine had become the first line of audit defence.

Kael understood that *AI did not replace oversight; it multiplied the reach of oversight when humans could no longer watch everything continuously.*

CFO Practice Note:
• Deploy AI models on approval logs, payment histories, vendor changes, journals, and access activity.
• Integrate alerts with ERP and GRC systems for real-time visibility.
• Review false positives monthly to fine-tune thresholds and preserve credibility.

---

230 · Creating a Digital Finance Health Index

Six months into transformation, Kael unveiled the **Digital Finance Health Index** — a composite score combining automation adoption, data accuracy, dashboard timeliness, system adherence, user satisfaction, and insight usage.

Every function's score was published on the enterprise intranet. What started as an internal tool became a competitive benchmark across regions. The CFO's role evolved from custodian of numbers to architect of digital discipline — a transformation measurable in both bytes and trust.

Kael understood that *digital maturity was not measured by technology count, but by decision confidence.*

CFO Practice Note:

• Build the DFHI around process automation, data quality, user adoption, system adherence, and insight timeliness.
• Refresh scores quarterly and share transparently across finance leadership.
• Celebrate top-performing units publicly to reinforce digital finance culture.

180-Day Strategy Map — Digital Finance Transformation

Phase	Key Milestones	Measurable Outcomes
Days 90–120	Launch Finance Digital Blueprint, complete ERP audit, and establish governance committee.	Digital baseline mapped · System risk log created
Days 120–150	Deploy automation pilots in AP/AR/GL, standardize workflows, and finalize MIS Calendar.	40% cycle-time reduction · Real-time dashboards live
Days 150–180	Complete post-implementation audit, roll out AI-based audit trail, and publish DFHI.	90% user adoption · Predictive-accuracy variance <5%

By Day 180, Kael had built the **engine room of reliability** — where systems, data, and people operated in synchronized cadence.
The organisation no longer *closed books*; it *opened insight.*

CHAPTER 14

Partnering Beyond Numbers

Influencing operations, HR, and sales with data.

231 · Role of Finance as Strategic Business Partner

By the seventh month, Kael had earned his seat at the executive table not because he asked for it, but because every decision now demanded his lens. He redefined finance from a reporting centre to a reflection centre — where business heads could see cause and effect, not just variance and ratio.

His mantra became simple: *"Finance is not a department; it is a perspective."* Kael began each business review with three slides — revenue quality, capital velocity, and risk exposure — turning financial language into management instinct. The CEO later remarked that meetings no longer began with what went wrong, but with what was worth scaling.

Kael understood that *true finance partnership began when finance stopped policing decisions and started improving the questions behind them.*

CFO Practice Note:

• Anchor every business discussion to value drivers — margin, cash, risk, growth, and capital discipline.
• Translate financial outcomes into business levers, not accounting language.
• Build credibility through problem-solving, not policing.

232 · Building Joint Review Rhythms with Function Heads

Kael institutionalised **Joint Performance Reviews** — monthly 90-minute sessions where finance sat alongside sales, HR, supply chain, marketing, and operations. He treated these meetings as laboratories of alignment: realigning incentives, clarifying cost ownership, and linking forecasts to action.

The rhythm changed behaviour. Cross-functional trust began replacing departmental defence. Finance was no longer the post-mortem doctor arriving after results; it became the co-pilot helping functions adjust direction before performance drifted.

Kael understood that *business rhythm was leadership's invisible structure; without it, alignment became accidental.*

CFO Practice Note:
• Co-create JPR agendas with business heads so finance enters as a partner, not an inspector.
• Assign one finance liaison per major function with clear review responsibility.
• End every JPR with three decisions and one cross-functional action item.

---

233 · Translating Financial Language into Business Impact

Kael noticed how easily numbers got lost in translation. He reframed financial statements into business stories: revenue became customer stickiness, EBIT became pricing courage, cash flow became execution credibility, and working capital became operating discipline.

Suddenly, strategy reviews carried heartbeat and consequence. Business leaders were no longer merely hearing finance; they were seeing how financial outcomes connected to their own decisions. Finance became the function that could make clarity feel motivating.

Kael understood that *the CFO's job was not to make everyone fluent in finance, but to make finance fluent in the language of the business.*

CFO Practice Note:
• Build a glossary of business analogies for recurring finance terms.
• Train analysts in storytelling, visualisation, and business-context explanation.
• Replace variance slides with impact-to-action narratives.

---

234 · Cost-to-Serve Analysis by Segment and Channel

Kael introduced **Cost-to-Serve Analytics** to uncover silent profitability leakages hidden under growth. Each product, geography, customer segment, and channel was mapped for its full delivery cost — logistics, credit, support, returns, service time, discounts, and collection effort.

The results shocked management. Some high-volume channels were quietly destroying value. With data in hand, sales strategy shifted from volume-first to value-first. Kael called it commercial courage built on cost truth.

Kael understood that *the company could not fix what it feared to measure, and could not measure what it kept hidden under average margins.*

CFO Practice Note:

• Attribute indirect costs using driver-based logic such as shipment count, transaction volume, service time, and return frequency.
• Pair every sales report with cost-to-serve visibility by segment and channel.
• Review loss-making channels quarterly and redefine pricing, terms, or service levels.

---

235 · Margin Bridge Analytics — Price, Volume, Mix

Kael replaced single-line profit explanations with a **Margin Bridge** — a dynamic waterfall chart decomposing performance into price, volume, mix, cost, currency, and productivity effects.

This visual changed leadership discussions quickly. Instead of debating opinions, the team debated levers. Sales saw their wins, supply chain saw its friction, and finance gained the authority of objectivity. Margin was no longer a result at the end of the month; it became a map of choices made across the business.

Kael understood that *margin transparency became influence because it showed not only what changed, but who could act next.*

CFO Practice Note:

• Build automated margin bridges in BI tools by business line, product, geography, and customer segment.
• Disaggregate profit drivers monthly into price, volume, mix, cost, currency, and productivity.
• Use bridge discussions to trigger tactical actions, not merely analysis.

---

236 · Demand Planning and Supply-Chain Alignment

Kael's next integration frontier was demand planning. He joined the monthly S&OP meeting not as a spectator, but as a calibrator of assumptions.

By aligning sales forecasts with procurement, production, inventory, and cash-flow data, finance became the arbiter of realism. Every production surge now carried a liquidity tag; every delay carried a working-capital cost. Forecast debates shifted from emotion to evidence.

Kael understood that *when finance sat inside S&OP, forecasts stopped being guesses and started becoming commitments.*

CFO Practice Note:
• Integrate finance into monthly S&OP cycles as a standing participant.
• Model the end-to-end cash impact of demand shifts, production changes, and inventory builds.
• Track forecast accuracy jointly across sales, supply chain, and finance.

---

237 · Linking Sales Targets to Cash-Collection Plans

Revenue meant nothing to Kael unless it converted into cash. He introduced **Cash-Aligned Sales Targets**, linking commission eligibility and regional performance reviews to actual collection within agreed terms.

This simple recalibration improved DSO and changed the relationship between sales and finance. Sales leaders began asking about credit quality before chasing volume. Finance and sales stopped being adversaries and became allies in liquidity.

Kael understood that *revenue without cash discipline was optimism sold on credit.*

CFO Practice Note:
• Embed collection milestones and payment discipline into sales-incentive design.
• Review top-customer receivables jointly with sales leaders every month.
• Publish monthly DSO and cash-velocity scores by sales region.

---

238 · Partnering with HR on Payroll Efficiency and Headcount Planning

Kael treated payroll not as an expense, but as an investment portfolio of human capacity. Working with HR, he launched a **Finance–HR Efficiency Program** to map people cost to productivity, absenteeism, attrition, role duplication, and revenue per employee.

Automation of payroll validation reduced errors and freed HR to focus on engagement. For the first time, manpower planning spoke the same language as margin planning. Headcount was no longer defended emotionally; it was linked to capacity, growth, risk, and productivity.

Kael understood that *talent allocation had become another form of capital allocation.*

CFO Practice Note:

• Co-own a workforce-planning model tied to revenue per FTE, productivity, attrition, and role criticality.
• Implement automated payroll audits and exception reporting.
• Present HR cost variance and headcount productivity in financial dashboards quarterly.

239 · Designing Shared Dashboards for Cross-Function Visibility

Kael believed transparency dissolved politics. He commissioned **Shared Enterprise Dashboards** — unified BI screens showing sales, supply chain, HR, operations, and finance metrics side by side.

The dashboard ended the argument over whose data was more accurate. Teams now discussed trends, causes, and actions rather than ownership of numbers. Cross-functional trust became a measurable output of shared visibility.

Kael understood that *when everyone saw the same number, alignment stopped depending on persuasion and started becoming habit.*

CFO Practice Note:

• Use one enterprise BI tool or governed data layer for all major functions.
• Enforce identical data definitions, refresh cycles, and ownership rules.
• Measure dashboard usage to confirm decision adoption, not just technical deployment.

240 · Evaluating Operational KPIs and Cost Drivers

Kael introduced **Operational KPI Audits** — quarterly reviews where finance dissected which metrics truly drove cost, margin, cash, quality, and customer outcomes.

Plant OEE, procurement cycle time, customer returns, energy cost per unit, logistics cost per shipment, and service turnaround were linked directly to margin bridges. Performance metrics shifted from vanity into value. Operations began using finance dashboards as their own improvement compass.

Kael understood that *every KPI needed a profit logic behind it, or it risked becoming decoration.*

CFO Practice Note:
• Identify the top five operational cost drivers affecting margin and cash movement.
• Quantify the correlation between operational KPIs and financial outcomes.
• Review driver-impact matrices each quarter with operations heads.

---

241 · Facilitating Budget Ownership Across Departments

Kael realized budgets often failed not because of numbers, but because of distance — finance owned them, while everyone else merely used them. He reversed the model: every department now co-signed its budget with a clear accountability statement.

Monthly reviews shifted from justification to ownership. Business heads began defending their own forecasts, trade-offs, and assumptions. Finance stopped allocating and started enabling responsibility.

Kael understood that *ownership was the currency of execution; without it, budgets became rented promises.*

CFO Practice Note:
• Co-author budgets with department heads and clearly document cost drivers, assumptions, and owners.
• Embed budget KPIs into each function's scorecard.
• Recognise accurate forecasters and disciplined owners, not only aggressive target-setters.

---

242 · ROI Analysis on Marketing and Digital Campaigns

When Kael joined campaign reviews, creative decks suddenly acquired numbers. He instituted a **Marketing ROI Framework** connecting every rupee of spend to leads, conversions, retention, customer lifetime value, payback period, and brand impact where measurable.

The shift was cultural. Discussions moved from aesthetics alone to analytics with imagination intact. Marketing leaders began saying that finance helped them prove impact, not limit ambition.

Kael understood that *a CFO who understood marketing metrics could become the CMO's strongest ally, not the campaign's natural enemy.*

CFO Practice Note:

• Link campaign spend to measurable outcomes such as leads, conversion, retention, repeat sales, and lifetime value.
• Track payback period and cash impact for major initiatives.
• Include marketing ROI in quarterly business reviews.

243 · Using Finance Insights for Pricing and Discount Strategy

Kael's team built a **Pricing Profitability Model** that simulated margin impact for every proposed discount. Sales leaders began previewing financial effects before finalising deals.

What started as analysis soon became behaviour. No major discount went live without finance validation. Revenue quality rose because the company stopped confusing volume with value.

Kael understood that *price moved profit faster than most cost programmes, which made discount discipline a CFO responsibility.*

CFO Practice Note:

• Automate price–margin simulations in BI tools for key products, customers, and deal types.
• Track discount elasticity and contribution impact from every major price concession.
• Review lost margin due to discounts monthly with sales leadership.

244 · Collaborating on Inventory and Logistics Optimization

In Kael's view, inventory was not stock; it was trapped cash. He collaborated with supply-chain heads to redesign reorder points, safety-stock logic, freight contracts, warehousing terms, and logistics routing.

Finance introduced carrying-cost dashboards, converting tonnes, pallets, and transit days into currency exposure. Working-capital turnover improved because operations could finally see the cash cost of planning habits.

Kael understood that *inventory was one of the most honest reflections of planning discipline.*

CFO Practice Note:

- Integrate finance metrics into warehouse, procurement, and logistics dashboards.
- Quantify carrying cost per SKU, region, warehouse, and product family.
- Establish joint finance–supply-chain ownership for inventory KPIs.

---

245 · Cost Reduction Without Culture Damage

When asked for cost cuts, Kael responded, "We will remove waste, not worth." He led a **Zero-Based Mindset** exercise where every expense had to justify its relevance from zero, but always through respect for people and purpose.

Unproductive travel, unused subscriptions, duplicate vendors, idle licences, and low-value routines went first. Learning budgets, welfare support, safety spends, and capability investments were protected. The result was structural savings without cultural injury.

Kael understood that *sustainable cost culture was empathy expressed through efficiency.*

CFO Practice Note:

- Run quarterly spend-rationalisation workshops with department heads.
- Protect investments in innovation, safety, learning, and critical capability.
- Communicate savings as value unlocked, not benefits withdrawn.

---

246 · Building Finance Liaisons Within Other Functions

Kael created a new class of ambassadors — **Finance Liaisons** embedded within sales, HR, operations, supply chain, and marketing.

These individuals were not auditors; they were translators of performance. They attended huddles, decoded business trends early, and brought insights back to the CFO office. The result was striking: business teams began calling finance before decisions, not after mistakes.

Integration replaced interpretation. Kael understood that *when finance walked the floor, trust climbed the charts.*

CFO Practice Note:

- Assign one finance liaison per major function and rotate the role every 12–18 months.

• Define joint KPIs such as forecast accuracy, initiative ROI, and decision turnaround.
• Train liaisons in both business storytelling and financial analytics.

247 · Training Non-Finance Leaders in Financial Literacy

Kael knew influence depended on understanding, not authority. He launched **Finance for Non-Finance Leaders** — quarterly workshops simplifying P&L logic, cash cycles, working capital, pricing, capex, and cost of capital.
Within six months, business heads began discussing ROIC and cash conversion in everyday meetings. Empowerment replaced dependency; financial thinking became cultural currency.
Kael understood that *a financially literate organisation was one of the CFO's strongest internal controls.*

CFO Practice Note:

• Curate simple case studies drawn from the company's own data.
• Use visual dashboards and business scenarios instead of technical ratio lectures.
• Assess impact through decision quality, forecast discipline, and ownership, not quiz scores.

248 · AI Tools for Cross-Functional Data Correlation

Kael deployed AI not to replace analysts, but to reveal unseen connections. Machine-learning models cross-linked HR attrition spikes with regional profitability, logistics delays with receivable ageing, customer service complaints with renewal rates, and marketing spend with cash conversion.
The correlations exposed hidden cost levers no dashboard had previously shown. Finance's analytical edge now powered strategic decisions across functions, not just finance reports.
Kael understood that *AI's greatest gift to finance was not hindsight or foresight alone, but the ability to connect signals humans had kept apart.*

CFO Practice Note:
• Use AI models to identify three to five high-correlation business patterns each quarter.
• Validate insights with functional owners before turning correlations into action.
• Build a central **Insight Register** for recurring data themes and leadership decisions.

249 · Continuous Feedback Loop Between CFO and Business Heads

To institutionalise alignment, Kael introduced **CFO–Business Feedback Dialogues** — short, structured sessions after every quarter-end. Each functional head rated finance on clarity, speed, usefulness of insights, responsiveness, and business relevance.

Scores were discussed openly inside the CFO leadership team. Finance's responsiveness became a leadership KPI. The CFO's credibility was no longer anecdotal; it became quantified trust.

Kael understood that *transparent CFOs did not merely manage perception; they measured whether finance was actually useful.*

CFO Practice Note:

• Create a quarterly feedback form covering timeliness, transparency, collaboration, usefulness, and decision impact.

• Discuss results at CFO leadership meetings and convert criticism into action.

• Track improvement trends year over year.

---

250 · Framing Finance as Enabler, Not Controller

Kael's closing message to his team was simple: "We do not own compliance; we enable confidence." He repositioned finance's role through an internal campaign — storytelling videos, success dashboards, business-partner wins, and recognition for cross-functional decisions improved by finance insight.

The mindset shift was profound. People stopped seeing finance as the department of no and started seeing it as the function of how. Control remained essential, but enablement became the leadership posture.

Kael understood that *control was table stakes; enablement was leadership.*

CFO Practice Note:

• Share finance success stories enterprise-wide, especially where finance helped another function perform better.

• Recognise business teams that achieve goals through finance insight, not despite finance discipline.

• Embed the enabler mindset into finance performance reviews, mentoring, and team rituals.

180-Day Strategy Map — Business Partnership Maturity Index

Phase	Key Milestones	Measurable Outcomes
Days 90–120	Launch Finance Liaisons, conduct joint reviews, and integrate cost-to-serve dashboards.	Unified reporting cadence · Improved forecast accuracy
Days 120–150	Roll out finance-literacy programmes, embed cash-linked sales metrics, initiate feedback loops.	10% DSO reduction · Cross-functional trust index baseline
Days 150–180	Deploy AI-correlation models, publish partnership scorecards, and formalize CFO–function charters.	Predictive insight adoption >80% · Finance cited as enabler in CEO reviews

By Day 180, Kael had **transformed finance from a gatekeeper into a growth partner**.
The board began introducing him not as Chief Financial Officer but as Chief Facilitation Officer — proof that credibility, once earned, can be scaled through collaboration.

CHAPTER 15

Raising Capital and Investor Readiness

From repair to reputation. Frame your funding story; engage bankers and investors through clarity.

251 · Capital Structure Diagnostic — Debt vs. Equity Mix

By his eighth month, Kael had rebuilt operational control; now he had to shape the capital narrative. He began with a **Capital Structure Diagnostic** — a precise review of debt, equity, internal accruals, leverage ratios, repayment capacity, and funding flexibility aligned to the company's risk appetite.

He evaluated peer leverage, sector volatility, interest-rate sensitivity, liquidity shocks, and future growth funding. The insight was sobering: the company's cost of debt was lower than perceived risk, but its equity story remained under-communicated to the market.

Kael's conclusion was bold: optimising capital was not only about raising funds; it was about raising credibility. Kael understood that *capital structure reflected corporate character — how much risk the company could carry without pretending to be stronger than it was.*

CFO Practice Note:

• Benchmark industry leverage against growth volatility, cash stability, covenant headroom, and peer capital structures.

• Maintain a rolling three-year capital-structure simulation covering debt, equity, internal accruals, and stress scenarios.
• Present funding capacity, leverage movement, and credit headroom in every Board capital review.

---

252 · Evaluating Cost of Capital — WACC and Leverage Tolerance

Kael revisited the company's **Weighted Average Cost of Capital** not as a finance metric, but as the threshold of ambition. He ran multiple stress cases, varying debt composition, equity dilution, tax-shield benefit, interest-rate movement, and rating sensitivity.

The analysis revealed that the organisation could carry limited additional leverage without impairing its credit profile, provided cash conversion and interest coverage remained disciplined. He used this headroom to fund automation and growth without unnecessary equity dilution, proving that prudence and performance could co-exist.

Kael understood that *WACC defined how brave the company could be before courage became recklessness.*

CFO Practice Note:
• Re-evaluate WACC semi-annually using updated risk-free rates, beta, borrowing cost, tax assumptions, and market risk premium.
• Define leverage tolerance through interest-coverage, DSCR, covenant, and cash-flow stress tests.
• Communicate WACC impact clearly in capital-allocation and investment approval discussions.

---

253 · Building the Investor Information Memorandum

Kael prepared the company's first **Investor Information Memorandum** — a disciplined synthesis of strategy, performance, governance, risk, capital structure, growth runway, and execution proof.

Every figure was traceable to audited or management-approved sources; every claim had evidence behind it. The IIM became a mirror of discipline, not decoration. When shared with institutional investors, it shifted perception: the company was not undervalued because the market was blind; it was under-communicated because management had not told the story with enough structure.

Kael understood that *an investor document was not a brochure; it was the company's credibility placed in sequence.*

CFO Practice Note:
• Structure the IIM around vision, strategy, execution, governance, risk, financial performance, and capital need.
• Align all numbers to audited statements, management accounts, board-approved plans, and traceable assumptions.
• Refresh the IIM every six months; market confidence erodes when capital stories become stale.

---

254 · Preparing Financial Models and Sensitivity Cases

Kael built a three-statement integrated model with dynamic assumptions on growth, margin, working capital, debt, tax, capex, and currency exposure. He treated modelling as the Board's rehearsal room — the place to test ambition before announcing it.

Every investor scenario — base, bull, and bear — was validated against liquidity buffers, covenant compliance, interest coverage, and debt-servicing capacity. When bankers asked how resilient the projections were, Kael replied that they had already been interrogated before leaving the company.

Kael understood that *forecasts alone rarely persuaded sophisticated investors; scenarios did, because scenarios revealed preparation.*

CFO Practice Note:
• Maintain linked P&L, balance sheet, and cash-flow statements with consistent drivers and audit trails.
• Conduct quarterly assumption reviews with business heads, treasury, tax, and FP&A.
• Include downside protection ratios such as DSCR, interest coverage, covenant headroom, and liquidity buffer in every model pack.

---

255 · Rating-Agency Interaction Strategy

When Kael first met the rating agency, he did not carry spreadsheets alone; he carried stories of systems. He walked analysts through digital finance controls, real-time dashboards, liquidity cadence, compliance rhythm, risk heat maps, and Board reporting discipline.

The analysts' questions shifted from "Can you repay?" to "How did you reform?" Within one review cycle, the firm's outlook improved because transparency had made risk more understandable. Kael proved that credibility was not built only by tenure; it was built by evidence.

Kael understood that *rating confidence was earned when governance became fluent enough for outsiders to trust the numbers behind the story.*

CFO Practice Note:

• Prepare a rating-agency briefing deck covering business model, liquidity, leverage, governance, controls, risk, and capital strategy.
• Respond to rating queries with data, decision evidence, policy discipline, and board-approved assumptions.
• Maintain a formal agency-interaction calendar aligned with audit reviews, board packs, and debt maturity planning.

---

256 · Understanding Various Funding Instruments — Bonds, ECBs, CPs, NCDs

Kael believed that a CFO who did not understand the architecture of capital eventually became its prisoner. When liquidity tightened, he did not call the banker first; he opened his own **Funding Instrument Matrix**.

Every option — bonds, external commercial borrowings, commercial papers, non-convertible debentures, working-capital loans, and private placements — was scored on cost, control, tenor, covenant load, currency risk, regulatory requirement, speed, and market appetite.

He taught his team that money was never free; it was merely differently priced trust. Kael understood that *capital markets rewarded CFOs who knew how every rupee travelled, what obligation it carried, and what story it told.*

CFO Practice Note:

• Maintain a funding matrix comparing cost, tenor, covenants, security, currency risk, regulatory approvals, and execution speed.
• Match funding instruments to purpose — short-term liquidity, long-term capex, refinancing, growth, or balance-sheet repair.
• Review funding options before crisis; the best capital is negotiated when the company still has choices.

---

1 · Academic Core — *What each instrument really means is given on the next page*

Instrument	Nature	Typical Tenor	Cost Profile	Best Used For	Key Risks / Watchpoints
Corporate Bonds	Long-term debt raised from capital markets	3 – 10 yrs	Medium (6–9%)	Stable cash-flow businesses needing predictable interest expense	Market appetite, disclosure burden, refinancing exposure
NCDs (Non-Convertible Debentures)	Secured or unsecured fixed-income instruments issued to institutions	1 – 5 yrs	Slightly higher than bonds	Medium-term projects; refinancing existing debt	Covenant complexity, early-redemption penalties
Commercial Papers (CPs)	Unsecured money-market instruments	3 – 12 months	Low (linked to T-Bills + spread)	Working-capital cycles	Rollover risk, rating dependency
ECBs (External Commercial Borrowings)	Foreign-currency loans from offshore lenders	3 – 7 yrs	Low nominal cost (LIBOR / SOFR + margin)	Capex / import financing / global subsidiary funding	FX risk, hedging cost, compliance (ECB Master Direction)

Academic Reference: RBI Master Direction on ECB (2023), SEBI (NCD Listing Regulations 2019), and ICMA Bond Market Practices.

2 · CFO's Strategic Screen — Choosing the Right Source for the Right Need

Kael created a **Funding-Source Decision Compass**, now used across all group entities:

Need / Scenario	Preferred Instrument	Rationale
Short-term liquidity (< 6 months)	CP or Invoice Discounting	Quick, low-cost funding; maintains credit-line headroom
Expansion / Growth capex	Bonds or NCDs	Predictable service cost; suitable for investor visibility
FX-linked imports / foreign subsidiaries	ECB	Currency-matched funding; global lender diversification
Project finance / Infrastructure	Term Loan or Infra Bonds	Long tenor; asset-liability matching
Temporary bridge before equity raise	Mezzanine Debt / Bridge Loan	Convertible option for flexibility; maintains momentum
Leveraged M&A / Buyout	Structured Debt / PE Bridge	Customized tranches tied to cash-flow stages
Balance-sheet deleveraging	Bond refinance or Rights Issue	Reduces cost of capital while retaining control

Kael insisted the funding choice must pass three filters:

1. **Tenor Match:** Debt shouldn't outlive the asset.
2. **Currency Match:** Borrow in the currency of cash flows.
3. **Signal Effect:** Funding form must reinforce the company's narrative (stability vs growth vs innovation).

---

3 · Operational Checklist Before Commitment

- Conduct **WACC-vs-Instrument Cost** benchmarking every quarter.
- Run **FX and interest-rate stress simulations** for ECBs and variable-rate bonds.

- Map **covenant interdependencies** — one breach can trigger cross-default.
- Standardize **treasury approval workflows** for new issuances.
- Ensure **RBI / SEBI / FEMA compliance** documentation is digitized and ready before execution.

---

4 · Kael's Lesson — Finance as a Portfolio of Choices

When the board once asked why he chose an ECB over a domestic NCD, Kael's reply was surgical:
"Because the interest rate gap is smaller than the reputational premium of showing global lender confidence."
That single explanation elevated the discussion from borrowing to signaling. Finance had evolved from *seeking money* to *curating capital.*

CFO Practice Note

- Maintain a **live Funding Dashboard** — cost, maturity ladder, currency mix.
- Diversify at least three sources of funding per year to build optionality.
- Revisit instrument choices quarterly under stress and growth scenarios.
- Conduct annual workshops on debt-instrument mechanics for finance teams.

---

257 · Relationship-Building with Banks and Institutional Lenders

Kael viewed lenders not as sources of capital, but as partners in continuity. He restructured the company's banking panel, diversifying exposure across global banks, domestic institutions, and specialist lenders.

Quarterly reviews with each relationship bank became two-way dialogues — not pitch meetings, but trust meetings. Kael shared performance updates, covenant comfort, funding needs, risk signals, and upcoming decisions before stress arrived. When a crisis hit a regional subsidiary, response times dropped from days to hours.

Liquidity was now a product of reputation capital. Kael understood that *banking relationships were built between disclosures, not during drawdowns.*

CFO Practice Note:

• Conduct at least two structured relationship reviews per year with each major lender.
• Share quarterly management commentary proactively, including liquidity, risk, and covenant signals.
• Maintain a lender satisfaction index covering response time, support quality, pricing discipline, and perception.

---

258 · Preparing Covenant-Light Negotiation Strategies

Kael's goal in refinancing was not only lower rates; it was flexibility. He worked with legal counsel to draft **Covenant-Light Negotiation Strategies** that still signalled prudence.

He used data from digital dashboards — real-time liquidity, DSO, compliance health, covenant history, cash-flow discipline, and board reporting cadence — to argue for relaxed maintenance clauses. The conversation shifted from "Can you comply?" to "You already demonstrate discipline."

The outcome was not merely pricing improvement; it was operational breathing room. Kael understood that *the best negotiation leverage was a history of discipline made visible before the lender asked for comfort.*

CFO Practice Note:

• Enter covenant negotiations with metrics, trend evidence, and control history — not emotion.
• Highlight internal dashboards, liquidity discipline, and governance systems to justify covenant flexibility.

• Align legal, treasury, FP&A, and finance teams early to avoid documentation delays.

---

259 · Evaluating Hybrid Instruments and Convertible Debt

Kael explored **hybrid capital instruments** — convertible debentures, warrants, perpetual bonds, and structured securities — as middle paths between dilution and debt load.

He modelled conversion scenarios under different market valuations, ensuring no unexpected control loss, covenant stress, EPS distortion, or rating discomfort. The CFO's message to the Board was clear: flexibility could be cheaper than immediate equity if the structure respected control, timing, and disclosure.

When structured correctly, hybrid funding gave the firm a growth cushion without altering its balance of power. Kael understood that *hybrid capital was the creative compromise between control and confidence.*

CFO Practice Note:

• Simulate dilution, conversion triggers, interest cost, coverage ratios, and control impact before issuance.

• Review accounting treatment, tax impact, rating implications, and disclosure requirements.

• Disclose hybrid exposure transparently in annual reports and investor communications.

---

260 · Bridge Financing and Mezzanine Structures

When a strategic expansion required fast liquidity, Kael engineered a **Bridge Financing** structure backed by receivable securitisation and short-term commercial paper. He complemented it with a mezzanine tranche from a local NBFC, layered for flexibility and early repayment.

The transaction closed quickly not because of financial wizardry, but because of operational readiness. Every document, covenant, security note, forecast, valuation update, and lender checklist had been pre-vetted and digitised.

Finance had become the company's fastest responder. Kael understood that *speed in funding was earned long before the transaction entered the room.*

CFO Practice Note:

• Maintain ready-to-deploy bridge-finance templates, lender checklists, and security documentation.

• Keep valuation updates, receivable schedules, and forecast models current for

fast execution.
• Track blended cost of capital for every financing layer, including mezzanine and short-term instruments.

261 · Private Equity and Venture Capital Readiness Checklist

Kael understood that investor readiness was not a pitch; it was an audit of preparedness. Before approaching funds, he built a **Private Capital Readiness Checklist** covering governance hygiene, shareholder structure, exit scenarios, ESOP clarity, use-of-proceeds logic, compliance history, and audit trail quality.

He ensured board minutes, statutory filings, management accounts, legal documents, cap tables, and internal controls could withstand forensic scrutiny. When investors arrived, there were no surprises — only conviction supported by evidence.

Kael did not chase funding; funding began taking him seriously. Kael understood that *private capital did not back ambition alone; it backed discipline that could survive diligence.*

CFO Practice Note:
• Create a readiness checklist covering legal, financial, governance, tax, HR, cap table, and strategic hygiene.
• Align shareholder agreements, ESOP plans, and dilution models before term discussions begin.
• Document capital-use priorities clearly before approaching investors.

262 · Crafting Equity Storylines for Investors

Kael reframed capital raising as storytelling with numbers. He built a coherent **Equity Storyline** — why the business existed, what pain it solved, how its growth flywheel worked, and how revenue translated into resilience.

Each investor conversation started with vision and ended with value-creation logic. The storyline was not theatre; it was structured reality. Every claim had a metric, every metric had a source, and every source had a decision behind it.

Kael understood that *investors invested in stories only when those stories could survive scrutiny.*

CFO Practice Note:
• Anchor the equity storyline on purpose, proof, profitability, resilience, and capital discipline.

• Use consistent language across investor decks, filings, media notes, and management commentary.
• Test the narrative internally before investor meetings so leadership speaks with one voice.

---

263 · Managing Due Diligence Data Rooms

Kael treated the data room as the investor's first impression of governance DNA. He created a structured **Due Diligence Data Room** with folders for financials, legal, tax, HR, intellectual property, operations, contracts, litigation, compliance, and board records.

Every upload had a version tag, validation date, owner, and access trail. Nothing was left ambiguous. When diligence began, investors remarked that the process felt like working with a listed company.

Kael understood that *the strongest defence in diligence was preparation before persuasion became necessary.*

CFO Practice Note:
• Use secure, version-controlled data-room platforms with audit trails and access logs.
• Designate a diligence SPOC for document flow, query tracking, and version control.
• Refresh key files quarterly, even when no transaction is active.

---

264 · Investor Communication Protocols and Disclosure Norms

Kael institutionalised investor communication into cadence, not chaos. He set quarterly briefings, investor FAQs, approved spokesperson rules, disclosure templates, and communication protocols aligned with applicable regulations and market expectations.

No informal leaks, no selective briefings, no improvised numbers. Only structured transparency. Over time, the market rewarded consistency more than charisma because investors knew what to expect and where to verify it.

Kael understood that *disclosure was not merely compliance; it was culture expressed to the capital market.*

CFO Practice Note:
• Define investor communication protocols covering timing, approval matrix, spokespersons, tone, and permitted content.

• Train leadership on fair-disclosure principles, SEBI / Regulation FD sensitivity, and insider-information boundaries.
• Archive all investor communications for audit traceability and future consistency checks.

---

265 · Term-Sheet Negotiation Principles

For Kael, the term sheet was never only a legal document; it was a mirror of alignment. He approached it as the first real test of partnership chemistry between capital and conviction.

Every clause was a question in disguise: how much control were they giving, how much freedom were they preserving, how much time were they buying, and what signal would the terms send to future investors? He entered each negotiation with three preparations — a valuation narrative, a risk map, and a signal plan.

He understood that capital raised wrongly could become costlier than capital never raised at all. Kael believed that *a term sheet was not about who won the negotiation; it was about whether both sides still wanted to build together after signing.*

CFO Practice Note:
• Prepare a valuation narrative, risk map, dilution model, and control-impact summary before term-sheet discussions.
• Review clauses on liquidation preference, anti-dilution, governance rights, exits, vetoes, and information rights carefully.
• Treat every term as both economics and signal; today's clause may shape tomorrow's investor confidence.

The Strategic Lens: Finance as the Translator of Trust

Kael reframed the negotiation: investors talked in clauses, founders in ambition, lawyers in risk.
Finance had to **translate ambition into acceptable risk**, turning aspiration into arithmetic.
He created a "Red Flag Matrix" to categorize clauses into:

- **Negotiable (yellow):** valuation timing, option pools.
- **Non-negotiable (red):** liquidation preference, board control.
- **Deferred (blue):** exit timelines, IPO rights.

His approach made discussions clinical, not confrontational — data replaced emotion.

The Technical Core: CFO's Must-Know Clauses

Every CFO must master the architecture of a term sheet — not for legal drafting, but for *value defense.*

1. **Valuation Mechanics:** Understand pre- and post-money adjustments, equity linkages, and ESOP dilution impact.
2. **Liquidation Preference:** Guard against "participating preference" that allows investors double-dip rights.
3. **Anti-Dilution Provisions:** Choose *weighted-average* over *full-ratchet* — it protects both control and credibility.
4. **Conversion Rights:** Model forced conversion or redemption clauses under best and worst scenarios.
5. **Board & Voting Rights:** Maintain CFO oversight on information and audit rights; ensure parity between equity and governance.
6. **Drag-Along / Tag-Along Rights:** Synchronize exit timing to avoid minority blocking.
7. **Exit & IRR Clauses:** Model investor IRR targets against cash flows — avoid clauses that mortgage future growth.
8. **Representations & Warranties:** Confirm disclosure capacity before signing — these can convert into liabilities.

Kael's golden rule: **read every clause twice — once as a CFO, once as a future CEO.**

Please refer ***Funding Source Decision Grid*** *— Choosing the Right Capital Path on the next page.*

CFO Application Tip: Map every funding proposal against these **three filters:**

1. *Flexibility,*
2. *Control,*
3. *and Reputation Impact.*

The cheapest money isn't always the right money; credibility compounds faster than capital.

Funding Source Decision Grid			
Business Context	**Preferred Funding Source(s)**	**CFO Decision Lens**	**Strategic Considerations**
Early-Stage / Start-Up	Venture Capital · Angel Funding · Strategic Seed Partners	Focus on governance hygiene, scalability narrative, and founder dilution thresholds.	Choose partners with ecosystem value; structure liquidation preferences clearly.
Growth / Expansion	Term Loans · Private Equity · Mezzanine Finance · Convertibles	Balance cost of capital vs. control. Model EBITDA impact and debt-service ratios.	Align funding tenure with asset life; build early exit flexibility.
M&A / Strategic Acquisition	Syndicated Loans · Bridge Finance · Structured Debt · PE Co-Invest	Prioritize speed and certainty of funds. Integrate deal timeline with financing close.	Maintain covenant flexibility for post-merger integration.
Pre-IPO / Late Stage	Institutional Investors · Sovereign Funds · Convertible Notes · Pre-IPO Rounds	Strengthen disclosure discipline and forecasting accuracy.	Optimize valuation optics; build investor confidence through audit readiness.
Restructuring / Turnaround	Distressed Debt Funds · Special Situation Investors · Asset-Backed Lending	Preserve liquidity and control; avoid predatory dilution.	Focus on governance restoration and operational stabilization.

Choosing the Right Source of Funding: The CFO's Compass

Kael created a **Funding Decision Matrix** that every new CFO in the company could use:

Stage / Need	Preferred Source	Why / When to Use	Key Risks / Watchpoints
Working Capital Gaps	Short-term loans / CPs / Invoice Discounting	Quick liquidity with manageable tenor	Renewal risk, rate volatility
Growth Expansion	Term Loans / NCDs / ECBs	Predictable amortization and cost	Covenant discipline, FX exposure
Strategic Projects / New Markets	Private Equity / Venture Capital	Long-term capital + expertise	Dilution, control rights
Infrastructure / Capex-Heavy Investments	Project Finance / Infrastructure Bonds	Asset-backed, longer horizon	Pledge conditions, DSRA requirements
IPO Preparation or Pre-Listing	Convertible Debt / Mezzanine Capital	Flexibility with equity upside	Complex valuation triggers
Distress / Turnaround	Structured Debt / Special Situation Funds	Time-buying liquidity	Governance interference, pricing penalty

He taught his team: *"The right source of funds depends not on cost, but on consequence."*

Negotiation Framework: The CFO's 3-Lens Test

Before signing, Kael passed every term through three screens:

1. **Strategic Lens:** Does it preserve control and long-term independence?
2. **Financial Lens:** Does it align with WACC, DSCR, and projected free cash flow?
3. **Reputational Lens:** How will this clause be perceived by analysts, regulators, and future investors?

If a clause failed two lenses, it was struck off the table.

CFO Practice Note

- Maintain a **Term-Sheet Comparison Dashboard** for all potential investors — highlight control vs. capital trade-offs.
- Conduct **sensitivity modeling** for dilution, IRR, and liquidation impact across scenarios.
- Document **non-financial obligations** — reporting frequency, ESG disclosures, information rights.
- Use the **CFO–Legal dual sign-off rule** — both must independently certify comprehension of every clause.
- Post-closure, hold a **Board learning session** on term-sheet implications to institutionalise knowledge.

By mastering this language of investors, Kael didn't just raise capital — he **raised confidence**.
The board no longer saw fundraising as a transaction; they saw it as a governance milestone.
Finance became the *custodian of consequence*, balancing ambition with arithmetic — one clause at a time.

---

266 · Convertible Note and Warrant Mechanisms

Kael explored **convertible notes** and **warrants** as flexible bridge instruments for early investors. He designed structures with clear conversion triggers, valuation caps, discount thresholds, maturity timelines, and investor-protection clauses.

By simulating dilution under multiple conversion scenarios, he ensured the company's future equity rounds remained predictable. Flexibility was useful only when it did not create hidden control risk or future valuation confusion.

Kael understood that *convertibles worked only when clarity was stronger than complexity.*

CFO Practice Note:

• Define conversion triggers, valuation caps, discount thresholds, and maturity dates before issuance.

• Simulate dilution under multiple future valuation and conversion scenarios.

• Disclose warrant valuation impact and potential equity overhang transparently.

---

267 · Pricing Discussions — Valuation and Dilution Logic

When investors quoted numbers, Kael focused on logic. He reframed valuation not as aspiration, but as consequence — of performance, potential, cash-flow visibility, governance quality, and market perception.

By demonstrating revenue durability, exit comparables, cost of equity, and dilution impact, he justified fair pricing without emotional negotiation. His message was simple: valuation was earned, not granted.

Kael understood that *the company should price what it could prove and negotiate only what it could sustain.*

CFO Practice Note:

• Anchor valuation around cash-flow multiples, peer comparables, growth quality, and risk profile.

• Quantify dilution per round and explain ownership continuity to founders, board, and investors.

• Maintain a sensitivity table linking valuation to revenue growth, margin, cash conversion, and market assumptions.

---

268 · IPO Readiness Assessment Framework

Kael treated IPO readiness as a governance audit before a market event. He initiated a twelve-month **IPO Readiness Assessment Framework** across finance, legal, HR, investor relations, compliance, internal controls, tax, and reporting cadence.

Internal controls were benchmarked to listed-company standards; quarterly closes became as tight as public reporting. By the time the Board approved the IPO path, the organisation had already begun behaving like a public company.

Kael understood that *a company should not go public to become disciplined; it should go public because discipline was already visible.*

CFO Practice Note:

• Conduct a gap analysis against listing, disclosure, governance, control, and reporting requirements.
• Build a mock-IPO financial model including underwriter fees, listing costs, dilution, and post-listing compliance load.
• Begin investor-style quarterly reporting at least one year before the planned IPO window.

---

269 · Understanding Underwriter and Regulatory Processes

Kael recognised that the underwriter relationship defined the credibility of the issue. He spent months aligning draft red-herring prospectus disclosures, audited financial, legal confirmations, SEBI filings, risk factors, and pricing-band logic with syndicate banks.

His calm command over timelines and transparency-built regulator confidence. The IPO review moved through approvals with minimal queries because finance had removed reconciliation gaps before outsiders could find them.

Kael understood that *regulatory trust was not earned through speed; it was earned through accuracy repeated without drama.*

CFO Practice Note:

• Map prospectus disclosures to audited financials, board records, legal confirmations, and management data with zero reconciliation gaps.
• Maintain a single-source data room for underwriters, legal counsel, auditors, and internal owners.
• Keep a daily regulatory-interaction log during filing and approval phases.

---

270 · Alternative Funding — REITs, InvITs and Green Bonds

Kael diversified funding channels beyond conventional debt and equity. He evaluated real-asset monetisation through **REITs** and **InvITs**, and sustainability-linked issuance through **green bonds**.

Each instrument was tested for strategic fit, regulatory suitability, asset eligibility, investor appetite, rating impact, and disclosure burden. The diversified approach reduced dependence on traditional markets while strengthening reputation capital.

Kael understood that *innovation in finance was not invention; it was alignment between capital source, asset purpose, and long-term trust.*

CFO Practice Note:

- Evaluate asset pools suitable for REIT or InvIT monetisation based on stability, yield, legality, and investor appetite.
- Align green-bond frameworks with credible ESG standards, eligible projects, and assurance requirements.
- Disclose post-issuance impact metrics clearly and consistently.

---

271 · Managing Investor Expectations Post-Funding

Once capital was raised, Kael's task shifted from persuasion to performance. He set quarterly expectation-alignment calls comparing promises against delivery, including revenue milestones, cash use, governance commitments, and strategic progress.

Any deviation was explained with context, not excuses. This proactive candour built a reputation that outlasted market cycles. Investors stopped guessing because management had created a rhythm of honest updates.

Kael understood that *credibility compounded faster than capital when delivery and disclosure moved together.*

CFO Practice Note:

- Publish variance analysis against investor promises within a disciplined post-close timeline.
- Use forward guidance bands instead of fragile single-point forecasts.
- Track investor-trust indicators such as query tone, repeat concerns, and confidence in management explanations.

---

272 · Shareholder Relations and Investor Call Preparation

Kael approached every investor call like a Board presentation. He rehearsed Q&A grids, anticipated activist questions, tested sensitive topics, and briefed leadership on consistent narratives.

By controlling tone, timing, and transparency, he ensured that even difficult calls strengthened confidence. Shareholder relations became not public relations, but performance communication.

Kael understood that *the investor call a CFO feared most often revealed the maturity of the finance function.*

CFO Practice Note:

• Maintain an investor-question tracker across earnings cycles and funding discussions.
• Circulate call briefs to the CEO, investor relations, legal, and finance leadership at least 48 hours before the call.
• Record, archive, and analyse sentiment trends after each call.

---

273 · Periodic Investor Reporting Templates

Kael standardised investor updates into modular **Investor Reporting Templates** covering financials, operations, ESG, governance, capital allocation, risk, and strategic milestones.

This consistency made comparison intuitive and confidence measurable. Reports moved from reactive disclosures to proactive engagement tools. Investors no longer read only the numbers; they began reading reliability.

Kael understood that *consistency became the language of trust when every update helped investors compare progress without confusion.*

CFO Practice Note:

• Design quarterly and annual templates aligned with applicable reporting, disclosure, and governance expectations.
• Automate data linkages from ERP and reporting dashboards wherever controls allow.
• Include qualitative commentary for context, not just metric tables.

---

274 · Creating CFO Investor Dashboards

Kael visualised transparency. He built **CFO Investor Dashboards** integrating liquidity metrics, capital allocation, ROIC, debt movement, working-capital trends, ESG indicators, and value-creation summaries.

Real-time insight replaced static reporting, giving the Board and investors a clearer pulse of enterprise value. Numbers turned into narrative, and precision became persuasion.

Kael understood that *data without design became noise; dashboards turned it into conviction when the story was honest.*

CFO Practice Note:

• Integrate investor dashboards with finance ERP, BI tools, and investor-relations systems.

• Display capital-efficiency ratios such as ROIC, CFROI, EVA, leverage, and cash conversion visibly.

• Refresh internal visual layers weekly and publish investor-ready summaries at defined intervals.

---

275 · Communicating Value Creation vs. Profit Creation

Kael often reminded teams that profit was arithmetic; value was architecture. He differentiated quarterly earnings from structural wealth creation by emphasising ROIC, brand equity, resilience multiples, customer quality, governance strength, and cash durability.

By shifting focus from margin obsession to market relevance, he changed investor dialogue from short-term gain to sustainable growth. Profit still mattered, but it was no longer allowed to pretend it was the whole story.

Kael understood that *profit explained the past, while value showed whether the future deserved investor belief.*

CFO Practice Note:

• Present both profit and value-creation scorecards in investor and Board decks.

• Link major growth initiatives to long-term shareholder returns, resilience, and capital efficiency.

• Use capital-efficiency metrics in CEO and leadership evaluations.

---

276 · Annual Capital Market Engagement Plan

Kael closed the funding cycle with discipline through an **Annual Capital Market Engagement Plan**. He scheduled investor conferences, lender reviews, non-deal roadshows, ESG briefings, analyst meetings, and governance updates across geographies.

This rhythm institutionalised visibility and prevented reactive storytelling. Markets rewarded predictability; investors valued access because access reduced uncertainty.

Kael understood that *engagement was the dividend of transparency when communication became planned rather than improvised.*

CFO Practice Note:

- Publish an annual investor-engagement calendar aligned with results releases, board cycles, and funding milestones.
- Balance domestic and global investor interactions across equity, debt, ESG, and institutional audiences.
- Review perception studies annually to recalibrate messaging, disclosure quality, and investor priorities.

CHAPTER 16

Mergers, Acquisitions & Strategic Investments

Growth through intelligence, not impulse. Evaluate deals through culture, integration, and cash discipline.

277 · M&A Strategy Map — Buy, Merge, or Ally

Kael viewed inorganic growth as a chessboard, not a casino. He created an **M&A Strategy Map** comparing acquisition, merger, alliance, and build options against capability gaps, market timing, capital availability, and execution readiness.

Each route was filtered through synergy realism, cultural compatibility, return on integration, and board appetite. The outcome was a disciplined playbook: no deal conversation began without strategic intent, and no target was pursued merely because it looked available.

Kael understood that *acquisitions succeeded only when strategy made the choice before ambition entered the room.*

CFO Practice Note:

- Maintain an M&A strategy map linking corporate goals to inorganic growth levers.
- Quantify capability gaps before scouting targets.
- Build early Board alignment on buy, merge, ally, or build scenarios.

278 · Evaluating Acquisition Targets — Qualitative Filters

Beyond numbers, Kael screened targets for culture, leadership integrity, governance maturity, employee morale, brand reputation, customer retention history, and compliance behaviour.

He designed a **Qualitative Target Filter** that forced the deal team to evaluate whether the target could truly integrate into the enterprise. Financial synergies mattered only after ethical and cultural compatibility had been understood. Deals passed not only through valuation multiples, but through values.

Kael understood that *soft factors often decided whether hard math survived after closing.*

CFO Practice Note:

• Conduct independent cultural diligence before financial modelling.
• Review leadership succession, governance maturity, compliance history, and customer retention patterns.
• Use ESG and reputation scoring as part of pre-bid screening.

---

279 · Financial Valuation Methods — DCF, Comps, Precedent Deals

Kael insisted that valuation be both art and accountability. He triangulated value using **Discounted Cash Flow**, comparable company multiples, and precedent transactions, stress-testing each model through sensitivity bands.

He never adjusted assumptions to fit a desired price. He adjusted ambition to fit reality. Numbers became negotiation armour, not decorative support for a deal already emotionally approved.

Kael understood that *valuation was not prediction; it was disciplined imagination tested against evidence.*

CFO Practice Note:

• Use at least two independent valuation methods for every acquisition target.
• Document key drivers such as growth, margin, terminal value, discount rate, synergy, and tax impact.
• Apply currency, tax, liquidity, and risk-premium adjustments consistently.

---

280 · Synergy Estimation — Cost, Revenue, Cultural

Kael framed synergies as execution hypotheses, not guaranteed savings. He separated achievable savings from hopeful assumptions by quantifying cost, revenue, operational, and cultural synergies distinctly.

Each synergy line item had an owner, timeline, validation test, required investment, and integration dependency. When the Board reviewed the deal, assumptions already carried accountability. Synergy stopped being a word in the deck and became a delivery contract.

Kael understood that *synergy was not found inside a transaction; it was built after the transaction through disciplined ownership.*

CFO Practice Note:

- Break synergies into cost, revenue, operational, and cultural categories.
- Assign measurable KPIs, owners, timelines, and post-integration scorecards.
- Revisit synergy realisation quarterly for at least two years after deal closure.

---

281 · Accounting for Mergers — Purchase, Cost, Equity, Consolidation Methods

Kael ensured accounting clarity matched strategic ambition. He mapped transaction structures to accounting treatments — purchase method, equity method, cost method, and consolidation impact — aligning them with applicable accounting standards and group policy.

Early consultation with auditors prevented surprises in goodwill, fair-value adjustments, non-controlling interest, and consolidation entries. The balance sheet told the story exactly as the transaction intended, without accounting shock after the celebration.

Kael understood that *accounting was the language investors read after the strategy speech ended.*

CFO Practice Note:

- Determine accounting treatment at term-sheet stage, not after closure.
- Model goodwill, fair-value adjustments, consolidation impact, and impairment sensitivity under each structure.
- Align disclosure format with group consolidation policies and auditor expectations.

---

282 · Pre-Deal Due Diligence — Financial, Tax and Legal

Kael treated due diligence as the firewall between curiosity and commitment. He established parallel workstreams — financial, tax, legal, operational, HR, technology, ESG, and compliance — each with defined risk flags and validation procedures.

Findings were not boxed as generic issues. They were classified as deal-breakers, deal-modifiers, or deal-confirmers. The diligence report became not a binder, but a decision accelerator.

Kael understood that *diligence was the CFO's truth serum; it revealed what ambition preferred to hide.*

CFO Practice Note:

• Build a cross-functional diligence team with clear owners for each domain.

• Quantify risk findings in monetary, legal, operational, or timing terms instead of adjectives.

• Maintain a red–amber–green matrix for pre-closure Board visibility.

---

283 · Integration Planning and Day 1 Readiness

Kael's mantra was simple: integration starts before acquisition. He formed an **Integration Management Office** during deal evaluation itself, identifying Day 1 deliverables across HR, IT, finance, tax, legal, operations, customers, vendors, and culture.

This clarity turned chaos into choreography. Employees and customers felt continuity, not confusion. The success of the deal was visible on the first morning after closing because the organisation knew who had to do what before the ink dried.

Kael understood that *the first 100 days decided whether a merger remained mathematics or became enterprise value.*

CFO Practice Note:

• Draft an integration blueprint parallel to transaction due diligence.

• Appoint Day 1 functional leaders with authority, timelines, and decision rights.

• Simulate first-week operations through mock readiness drills.

---

284 · Cultural and Talent Integration Playbook

Kael viewed culture as the invisible P&L. He built a **Talent Integration Playbook** aligning compensation bands, leadership norms, recognition systems, critical-talent retention, communication rhythm, and employee anxiety management across both entities.

Open town halls replaced closed memos. Leadership listening sessions reduced rumours. By merging emotions before systems, Kael created the one synergy spreadsheets could never fully measure: trust.

Kael understood that *culture was the integration currency no balance sheet recorded, but every failed merger eventually paid for.*

CFO Practice Note:

• Conduct joint cultural workshops during integration planning and execution.

• Map top talent from both sides and design retention incentives before uncertainty spreads.

• Align leadership behaviours before enforcing policy alignment.

---

285 · Legal and Regulatory Compliance — SEBI, CCI, FTC

Kael's deal discipline extended to regulators. He synchronised legal counsel, compliance officers, transaction advisors, and finance owners into a **Regulatory Response Task Force**.

Every filing — whether domestic or cross-border — carried a compliance matrix highlighting ownership, timeline, dependency, supporting data, and approval status. The meticulousness turned regulatory scrutiny into procedural trust, because every question had a prepared trail.

Kael understood that *regulatory comfort was one of the quietest signals of governance strength.*

CFO Practice Note:

• Prepare a consolidated compliance tracker covering domestic and cross-border authorities.

• Align antitrust and competition disclosures with data-driven market-share analytics.

• Hold pre-notification or preparatory meetings with regulators where appropriate to manage timelines.

---

286 · Contingent Payments and Earn-Out Clauses

Kael learned that not every deal ended at closing; some continued inside clauses. He structured **Earn-Out Mechanisms** that balanced seller motivation with buyer protection, pegged to auditable performance metrics rather than vague goodwill.

Each contingent payment was modelled for timing, tax, accounting, cash-flow, and dispute impact. The art was in designing clauses that encouraged delivery without creating future litigation.

Kael understood that *earn-outs were trust written in numbers, and trust needed definitions before it could survive pressure.*

CFO Practice Note:

• Base earn-out triggers on auditable metrics such as EBITDA, revenue, retention, or milestone delivery.
• Cap payout exposure and document dispute-resolution mechanisms clearly.
• Account for contingent liabilities transparently in post-acquisition reporting.

287 · Push-Down Accounting and Goodwill Testing

Kael approached post-acquisition accounting like surgery — precision before presentation. He implemented **Push-Down Accounting** where appropriate to reflect fair values of acquired assets and liabilities at subsidiary level, aligning statutory books with group reporting discipline.

Goodwill was treated not as pride, but as a performance test. It was reviewed annually, challenged through cash-flow assumptions, and never allowed to sit indefinitely as proof of past enthusiasm. This discipline kept financial integrity intact long after deal headlines faded.

Kael understood that *goodwill was confidence with a review date, not a trophy to be carried forever.*

CFO Practice Note:

• Apply push-down accounting only when control is clearly established and standards permit.
• Test goodwill annually for impairment using cash-flow assumptions, discount rates, and sensitivity analysis.
• Disclose valuation methodology and key sensitivity assumptions clearly.

288 · Leveraged Buyouts — Structure and Caution

Kael viewed leverage as a lever, not a weapon. In evaluating **Leveraged Buyouts**, he balanced financing ambition with solvency discipline, modelling cash flows, covenant resilience, interest coverage, refinancing risk, and debt-service ratios under stress.

He rejected glamour models that could not survive a meaningful rate shock or cash-flow delay. For him, every LBO carried the same lesson: control debt, or debt would control strategy.

Kael understood that *leverage amplified leadership when disciplined, and exposed it when ambition outran cash.*

CFO Practice Note:
• Maintain conservative DSCR and interest-coverage thresholds under base and stress cases.
• Structure repayment schedules to match realistic asset cash generation.
• Ensure Board awareness of refinancing triggers, covenant risk, and downside liquidity exposure.

---

289 · Spin-Offs, Carve-Outs and Demergers

Kael treated divestitures as acts of focus, not failure. He orchestrated **Spin-Offs**, **Carve-Outs**, and **Demergers** to unlock hidden value by separating capital-light growth units from legacy-heavy cores.

Each separation plan included tax structuring, legal continuity, shared services, employee transition, customer communication, and cultural stability. What exited the parent balance sheet often re-entered the market as renewed opportunity.

Kael understood that *divestment was not retreat; it was redeployment when the portfolio needed sharper purpose.*

CFO Practice Note:
• Conduct pre-demerger valuation and standalone readiness review for each entity.
• Secure regulatory clearances, tax neutrality, and legal approvals in advance.
• Define shared-service agreements for HR, IT, finance, legal, and procurement before separation.

---

290 · Strategic Joint Ventures — Control and Risk Sharing

Kael saw joint ventures as the art of shared control. He negotiated governance rights, profit-sharing ratios, reporting standards, funding obligations, reserved matters, exit clauses, and dispute mechanisms with mathematical clarity.

By building neutral arbitration terms and transparent reporting standards, he made partnership predictable. For Kael, trust was structured, not assumed. The strength of the JV lay not in enthusiasm at signing, but in clarity when disagreement arrived.

Kael understood that *joint ventures failed less from conflict of interest than from absence of clarity before conflict appeared.*

CFO Practice Note:

• Define control thresholds, veto rights, reserved matters, and exit terms explicitly in JV agreements.
• Align accounting treatment, reporting cadence, and consolidation approach before operations begin.
• Conduct annual partner-alignment reviews covering performance, culture, capital commitment, and governance.

---

291 · Post-Merger Performance Scorecard

Kael believed a deal was not complete until the integration P&L proved it. He designed a **Post-Merger Performance Scorecard** tracking synergy realisation, retention rate, customer continuity, cultural health, system integration, cost overrun, and ROI timelines.

Each metric had Board-level visibility. Accountability continued beyond applause. The scorecard transformed post-merger reviews from ritual into renewal, showing which promises had become value and which remained theatre.

Kael understood that *integration metrics were the real purchase price because they revealed what the company truly paid after closing.*

CFO Practice Note:

• Build a 12–24 month integration scorecard with financial and non-financial KPIs.
• Review synergy progress quarterly with business-unit leaders and integration owners.
• Communicate post-merger value delivery in investor and Board updates.

---

292 · ESG and Sustainability Diligence in Modern M&A

Kael recognised that future-ready deals were measured not only in cash, but in conscience. He integrated **ESG Diligence** into every transaction, evaluating carbon footprint, labour practices, community impact, governance history, compliance exposure, safety culture, and supply-chain ethics.

Targets with weak sustainability profiles were marked as long-term liabilities, regardless of short-term profitability. In Kael's M&A model, ethics had enterprise value because future risk could not be hidden inside current EBITDA.

Kael understood that *sustainability diligence was not activism; it was risk management with a longer memory.*

CFO Practice Note:
• Include ESG criteria in target-scoring templates and investment committee papers.
• Quantify carbon, compliance, labour, safety, and reputation exposure during due diligence.
• Align post-acquisition disclosures with relevant sustainability and governance standards.

---

293 · AI in Deal Screening and Valuation Analytics

Kael embraced artificial intelligence as his quiet analyst. He deployed AI-driven models to scan industries, flag undervalued targets, benchmark transaction multiples, identify synergy patterns, and update comparable transactions in real time.

Pattern recognition replaced gut feel as the starting point, though not the final decision. By automating deal scouting, Kael multiplied insight while preserving human judgement for context, culture, and strategic fit.

Kael understood that *AI did not replace judgement in M&A; it refined the field where judgement had to work.*

CFO Practice Note:
• Use AI tools to screen acquisition targets based on synergy fit, valuation gaps, and performance outliers.
• Integrate market-data APIs to update valuation comparables dynamically.
• Maintain human validation checkpoints for qualitative context, culture, and strategic intent.

---

294 · Deal War-Room Governance Model

Kael built a **Deal War-Room** — both physical and digital — to centralise information flow, decision rights, version control, diligence findings, risk tracking, and integration readiness.

Every major acquisition moved through this command centre, with real-time dashboards for legal, finance, tax, HR, IT, compliance, and integration workstreams. It replaced confusion with cadence, creating a living audit trail of accountability. In Kael's world, discipline was not post-facto; it was process.

Kael understood that *the war-room was where deal chaos learned structure before it could damage value.*

CFO Practice Note:

• Establish a dedicated deal-governance room with version-controlled documentation.

• Define decision escalation protocols, risk ownership tiers, and approval rights.

• Integrate collaboration tools for cross-functional visibility and audit trail.

---

295 · Integration PMO Setup

Kael formalised integration oversight through an **Integration PMO**, chaired by finance but powered by cross-functional leads from HR, IT, legal, operations, tax, procurement, and communications.

The PMO tracked synergy milestones, budget variance, system migration, retention risk, cost overruns, cultural checkpoints, and Day 1 commitments on structured dashboards. Weekly stand-ups converted strategy into momentum. This PMO became the heartbeat of every successful merger.

Kael understood that *PMOs converted merger intent into enterprise muscle only when accountability moved every week.*

CFO Practice Note:

• Define PMO governance structure with clear accountability and functional ownership.

• Use standard templates for synergy, risk, budget, culture, and integration tracking.

• Conduct fortnightly reviews to monitor progress and recalibrate plans.

---

296 · Lessons-Learned Log for Future Acquisitions

For Kael, every deal ended with documentation, not decoration. He institutionalised a **Lessons-Learned Log** capturing missteps, negotiation insights, valuation errors, diligence gaps, cultural surprises, integration challenges, synergy shortfalls, and governance improvements.

This living archive turned experience into a playbook, ensuring the next acquisition began smarter than the last. Reflection became not a postscript, but the hallmark of mastery.

Kael understood that *organisations that recorded memory outperformed those that kept repeating expensive lessons.*

CFO Practice Note:

- Maintain a lessons-learned register after every transaction closure.
- Review insights during the next M&A pipeline and diligence planning cycle.
- Share findings with the Board, deal teams, and integration teams annually.

Practical Tool: CFO Deal Memo and Day 1 Integration Checklist

An acquisition is not successful when the deal is announced. It is successful when the promised value survives integration. Before recommending any transaction, the CFO should prepare a deal memo that separates strategic attraction from financial reality.

Illustrative CFO Deal Memo
Transaction Name: Acquisition of Orion Systems Pvt. Ltd.
Buyer: NextAura Global
Target: Orion Systems Pvt. Ltd.
Transaction Type: 100% equity acquisition
Proposed Consideration: ₹420 crore
Strategic Rationale: Expansion into automation software, access to enterprise customers, margin-accretive digital capabilities.

Review Area	CFO Assessment
Revenue Quality	68% recurring revenue; top 5 customers contribute 41% revenue. Concentration risk requires retention plan.
EBITDA Quality	Reported EBITDA margin 24%; normalized EBITDA estimated at 20% after removing one-time items.
Working Capital	Receivables higher than industry norm; ₹38 crore overdue beyond 90 days.
Valuation	Proposed valuation at 11x normalized EBITDA. Acceptable only if synergy capture exceeds ₹35 crore over three years.
Debt / Liabilities	No major external debt; pending employee claims and tax exposure require escrow.
Technology Risk	Platform scalable but requires cybersecurity review before integration.
Cultural Risk	Founder-led culture; second-line leadership depth limited.
Synergy Potential	Cost synergy ₹18 crore; revenue synergy ₹24 crore over three years.

CFO Recommendation	Proceed to final negotiation subject to price adjustment, escrow protection, customer retention plan, and Day 1 integration controls.

Day 1 Integration Checklist

Area	Day 1 Action
Cash Control	Freeze unauthorized bank changes; map all bank accounts and signatories.
Financial Reporting	Align reporting calendar, chart of accounts, and monthly close timeline.
Delegation of Authority	Issue interim approval matrix for purchase, payment, capex, hiring, and contracts.
Customer Continuity	Communicate ownership transition to top customers without disturbing service confidence.
Vendor Continuity	Confirm critical vendor obligations and payment terms.
Employee Communication	Announce leadership structure, payroll continuity, and benefits stability.
Legal / Compliance	Secure statutory records, contracts, licenses, litigation files, and tax submissions.
IT and Cybersecurity	Review admin access, ERP rights, data backup, and cybersecurity vulnerabilities.
Synergy Tracking	Create synergy dashboard with owners, timelines, and financial impact.
Culture	Identify informal leaders and integration risks within the first 30 days.

Kael believed every acquisition had two prices: the price paid to the seller and the price paid later for poor integration.

The first is visible in the term sheet. The second hides in culture, systems, customers, and people.

A CFO protects value by entering the deal with open eyes and entering Day 1 with operating control.

CHAPTER 17

Risk Management & Scenario Planning

The CFO's superpower is imagination with math. Create the enterprise risk map and run The Liquidity Cliff simulation.

297 · Defining Enterprise Risk Categories — Strategic, Operational, Financial, Compliance

Kael began by mapping risk not as fear, but as foresight. He categorised enterprise risk into **Strategic**, **Operational**, **Financial**, and **Compliance** dimensions — each with clear ownership, measurement logic, escalation cadence, and Board visibility.

The framework transformed ambiguity into accountability. Risks now spoke the same language across business units, functions, and geographies. The Board no longer saw risk as scattered chaos; it saw risk as a structured discipline that could be discussed, owned, and acted upon.

Kael understood that *risk was not a department; it was a mindset that had to travel through every decision.*

CFO Practice Note:

• Define standard enterprise-risk categories across business units and functions.

• Assign risk owners with measurable KPIs, escalation levels, and reporting cadence.
• Review the risk taxonomy annually to reflect new markets, technologies, regulations, and business realities.

---

298 · Creating the Enterprise Risk Register

Kael institutionalised risk management through an **Enterprise Risk Register**, linking each risk to likelihood, impact, velocity, owner, mitigation plan, residual exposure, and review frequency.

It became the single source of truth for Board reviews, internal audits, management discussions, and risk-committee meetings. Every risk carried a name, not just a number — ensuring accountability had a face.

The ERR soon became a mirror of leadership discipline. Kael understood that *when risk had no registry, it rarely had a remedy.*

CFO Practice Note:
• Maintain a live, version-controlled Enterprise Risk Register accessible to authorised risk custodians.
• Include rating scales for likelihood, severity, velocity, control strength, and residual exposure.
• Review and update the register quarterly with executive and Board oversight.

---

299 · Risk Ownership and Escalation Protocols

Kael designed a **Risk Ownership Matrix** defining who identified, who mitigated, who reported, and who escalated each risk. He introduced a three-tier escalation rule — business owner to CFO office, CFO office to Risk Committee, Risk Committee to Board where materiality demanded it.

No longer could risks vanish in silence or wait for quarterly narration. Escalation became an institutional habit, not a personal favour. The process did not eliminate uncertainty; it reduced the possibility of surprise.

Kael understood that *escalation was not panic; it was professionalism before risk became damage.*

CFO Practice Note:
• Establish tiered escalation rules tied to financial exposure, operational disruption, compliance severity, and reputational impact.
• Document response timelines and decision owners for each risk level.

• Conduct quarterly drills to test whether escalation works under pressure.

---

300 · Identifying Black-Swan and Grey-Rhino Scenarios

Kael encouraged the leadership team to imagine the unimaginable. He differentiated **Black Swans** — rare, unpredictable shocks — from **Grey Rhinos** — visible but ignored threats moving steadily toward the enterprise.

Using scenario-modelling workshops, he stress-tested liquidity, supply chain, cybersecurity, customer concentration, regulatory exposure, funding access, and reputation shocks. Preparing for improbables became a competitive advantage because leadership stopped treating surprise as an excuse.

Kael understood that *the only thing worse than failing to predict a crisis was failing to prepare for the risks already visible.*

CFO Practice Note:
• Conduct annual scenario simulations for low-probability, high-impact risks and visible high-impact threats.
• Build cross-functional crisis playbooks for each major risk category.
• Quantify financial resilience under each scenario through cash, EBITDA, covenant, and continuity impact.

---

301 · Risk-Heat Map Methodology

Kael visualised enterprise risk through a **Risk Heat Map**, plotting severity against probability and overlaying control strength, risk velocity, and mitigation status.

The red zones triggered Board and Risk Committee review; amber zones required management action plans; green zones remained monitored by business heads. This visual clarity turned subjective conversations into strategic ones. Risk appetite was no longer rhetoric — it was mapped in colour.

Kael understood that *visualisation converted anxiety into action when risk could be seen, compared, and owned.*

CFO Practice Note:
• Build a risk matrix calibrated to the company's approved risk appetite.
• Update the heat map quarterly using risk-owner inputs, internal audit findings, and real-time analytics where available.
• Use the map as the opening slide in risk-committee discussions so attention starts with priority.

302 · Business Continuity and Disaster Recovery Planning

Kael knew resilience was built in peace, not in panic. He institutionalised **Business Continuity Planning** and **Disaster Recovery** frameworks that mapped every critical process to fallback owners, recovery time objectives, recovery point objectives, alternate systems, and communication protocols.

From IT systems to treasury operations, payroll, collections, vendor payments, and statutory filings, each process had a predefined alternate path. When a regional outage struck, operations resumed within hours because the organisation was rehearsed before disruption arrived.

Kael understood that *business continuity was not insurance; it was intelligence designed before crisis.*

CFO Practice Note:

• Identify mission-critical processes and define recovery time objectives and recovery point objectives.

• Conduct semi-annual BCP and DR simulation drills across finance, IT, treasury, HR, and operations.

• Integrate continuity testing into enterprise risk reviews and Audit Committee reporting.

---

303 · Insurance Portfolio Review and Adequacy Testing

Kael treated insurance as the last line of defence in financial architecture. He performed annual **Insurance Adequacy Testing**, correlating policy coverage with asset growth, inflation, business expansion, cyber exposure, key-person dependency, liability risk, and new market operations.

Coverage gaps were not left as broker notes; they were converted into revised endorsements, updated limits, and claim-readiness protocols. Premiums were no longer seen as administrative cost, but as risk-transfer discipline.

Kael understood that *insurance transferred risk only when the risk had first been properly understood.*

CFO Practice Note:

• Map insurance coverage against the top enterprise risks annually.

• Benchmark deductibles, exclusions, limits, and premiums with industry peers and risk advisors.

• Ensure claims protocols, evidence folders, and documentation trails are audit-ready.

---

304 · Annual Risk Management Report for the Board

Kael reframed the **Annual Risk Management Report** from a compliance summary into a strategic conversation. Each section linked financial exposure, mitigation status, residual risk, readiness index, early-warning signals, and year-over-year movement.

The Board began reading the report not for reassurance, but for foresight. Risk governance moved from paperwork to predictive insight because management could now show not only what might go wrong, but how prepared the organisation was to respond.

Kael understood that *Boards did not need comfort; they needed clarity strong enough to challenge complacency.*

CFO Practice Note:

• Structure the report around risk trends, mitigations, residual exposure, and early-warning signals.

• Quantify the top residual risks by impact on EBITDA, cash flow, compliance, continuity, or reputation.

• Present the executive summary through visual dashboards for faster Board comprehension.

---

305 · Financial Hedging Policies — FX, Commodities, Interest Rate

Kael transformed treasury's defence into a science. He designed a comprehensive **Financial Hedging Policy** defining exposure types, approved instruments, hedge ratios, thresholds, approval limits, counterparty norms, documentation standards, and mark-to-market reporting for FX, commodities, and interest-rate risks.

By embedding hedge-effectiveness reviews and mark-to-market dashboards, he ensured no surprises in P&L, cash flow, investor calls, or covenant discussions. Hedging became not reaction, but rhythm.

Kael understood that *a CFO's reputation was often written in how quietly volatility was managed before it became visible.*

CFO Practice Note:

• Formalise hedging policy with Board-approved limits by exposure type, instrument, counterparty, and tenor.

• Use independent valuation tools to validate hedge effectiveness and mark-to-market impact.

• Disclose unrealized gains, losses, and material hedge positions transparently in quarterly reports.

Practical Tool: Simple Foreign Exchange Hedge Policy Extract

Foreign exchange risk becomes dangerous when it is treated as treasury instinct rather than board-approved discipline.

A CFO does not hedge to predict currencies. A CFO hedges to protect business margins, cash flows, and planning reliability. The purpose of a hedge policy is therefore not to maximize gains from currency movement. It is to prevent currency movement from damaging operating truth.

Illustrative Foreign Exchange Hedge Policy Extract

1. Policy Objective

The objective of this policy is to manage foreign exchange exposure arising from imports, exports, foreign currency borrowings, inter-company transactions, and committed commercial exposures. The company will hedge to protect operating margins and cash-flow predictability. The company will not undertake speculative currency positions.

2. Covered Exposures

The policy applies to:

- Confirmed import payables.
- Confirmed export receivables.
- Foreign currency loans and interest payments.
- Approved forecast exposures where probability is high and documentation is available.
- Inter-company receivables and payables denominated in foreign currency.

3. Hedge Ratio

Exposure Type	Hedge Coverage
Firm committed exposure within 0–3 months	70%–100%
Firm committed exposure within 3–6 months	50%–80%
Highly probable forecast exposure within 6–12 months	25%–50%
Unconfirmed or speculative exposure	0%

4. Permitted Instruments

The company may use simple, transparent instruments such as forward contracts, options, and swaps where commercially justified. Complex derivative structures may be used only with prior approval from the CFO and the Treasury Risk Committee.

5. Prohibited Activities

The following are not permitted:

Currency trading for profit.

Leveraged derivative structures without board approval.

Hedge contracts without underlying exposure.

Rolling losses forward to hide treasury performance.

Oral or undocumented hedge commitments.

6. Approval Authority

Transaction Size	Approval Required
Within treasury operating limit	Treasurer + Controller
Above treasury operating limit	CFO
Complex derivative / strategic hedge	CFO + Audit Committee / Board-approved authority

7. Reporting

Treasury will submit a monthly forex exposure report covering gross exposure, hedged exposure, open exposure, mark-to-market position, hedge maturity profile, and realized/unrealized gains or losses.

Kael's treasury principle was clear:

"A hedge is insurance against uncertainty. The moment it becomes a bet, the CFO has already lost control."

306 · Counterparty Risk Evaluation Models

Kael recognised that a contract was only as strong as the counterparty behind it. He built **Counterparty Risk Evaluation Models** for suppliers, customers, lenders, insurers, distributors, and financial partners, rating them on financial health, reputation, dependency, concentration, payment behaviour, and operational reliability.

When a key vendor collapsed mid-year, contingency sourcing activated instantly because finance had already mapped exposure. Preparedness protected performance, and procurement finally saw risk evaluation as continuity planning, not paperwork.

Kael understood that *the best contracts began with the right counterparties, not merely the right clauses.*

CFO Practice Note:

• Conduct periodic financial health checks for major suppliers, customers, lenders, and strategic partners.

• Diversify exposures where dependency, concentration, or reputational risk is high.

• Maintain a counterparty-risk register linked to procurement, treasury, legal, and credit systems.

---

307 · Cyber-Risk and Data-Protection Frameworks

Kael regarded cybersecurity not as an IT issue, but as a Board-level fiduciary risk. He implemented a layered **Cyber-Risk and Data-Protection Framework** covering access controls, encryption, privileged-user reviews, data classification, backup integrity, and incident-response readiness.

Quarterly ethical-hacking audits exposed vulnerabilities before attackers could exploit them. Finance systems, payment gateways, ERP workflows, and reporting dashboards were treated as critical assets because a cyber breach could become a liquidity event, disclosure issue, or trust failure.

Kael understood that *cyber defence was not only a firewall; it was a culture of disciplined access, awareness, and response.*

CFO Practice Note:

• Conduct annual third-party cyber audits, penetration tests, and finance-system vulnerability reviews.

• Mandate multi-factor authentication, least-privilege access, data classification, and periodic user reviews.
• Align data protection with applicable privacy laws, ISO 27001 principles, and local regulatory requirements.

308 · ESG-Linked Risk Disclosure Standards

Kael integrated environmental, social, and governance dimensions into the **Enterprise Risk Register**. He linked carbon exposure, supply-chain ethics, labour practices, safety performance, governance compliance, and community impact to measurable risk factors.

Disclosures followed recognised frameworks not merely to satisfy investors, but to create accountability inside the business. ESG stopped being an annual-report paragraph and became part of risk language, capital conversations, and Board oversight.

Kael understood that *ESG reporting had moved beyond optics; it had become an obligation of trust.*

CFO Practice Note:
• Embed ESG metrics into quarterly risk dashboards and Board risk discussions.
• Align disclosures with relevant frameworks such as TCFD, GRI, SASB, or applicable local standards.
• Coordinate sustainability assurance with internal audit, external advisors, and functional data owners.

309 · Crisis Simulation and Tabletop Exercises

Kael did not wait for crises; he rehearsed them. He ran **Tabletop Exercises** replicating cyberattacks, liquidity crunches, supply-chain disruptions, regulatory raids, customer defaults, and reputational incidents.

Executives learned to respond under time pressure, separating facts from assumptions and decisions from panic. Every simulation strengthened reflexes that balance sheets alone could not create. The exercise revealed who took ownership, who waited for instruction, and which data arrived too late.

Kael understood that *preparedness was the highest form of confidence because it made panic less necessary.*

CFO Practice Note:
• Conduct semi-annual crisis simulations covering the top enterprise risks.
• Document learning outcomes and update crisis playbooks after every drill.
• Involve external experts where needed to test agility, communication clarity, and leadership response.

---

310 · Embedding Risk in Budgeting and Forecasting Cycles

Kael fused strategy and caution into one process. He embedded **Risk-Adjusted Budgeting** into the planning cycle, ensuring forecasts reflected both ambition and vulnerability.

Scenario planning became integral. Each major revenue stream, cost line, capex commitment, funding plan, and margin assumption was stress-tested for volatility. This was not defensive finance; it was enlightened realism. Budgets became stronger because they admitted uncertainty before uncertainty arrived.

Kael understood that *a forecast without risk weight was fiction with formatting.*

CFO Practice Note:
• Integrate risk parameters directly into budgeting, forecasting, and long-range planning models.
• Present base, optimistic, and stress scenarios during budget reviews.
• Use sensitivity analysis, Monte Carlo analysis, or driver-based modelling for material revenue and cost streams.

---

311 · Outsourced Risk and Control Vendor Evaluation

Kael realized that risk travelled through vendors too. He developed an **Outsourced Risk Framework** evaluating external auditors, IT service providers, payroll processors, logistics partners, compliance consultants, and data vendors on control maturity, cyber hygiene, regulatory readiness, and service reliability.

Every contract renewal required control certifications, data-security attestations, service-level performance, and incident history. Third-party reliability became part of the CFO's reputation because outsourced activity still carried internal accountability.

Kael understood that *activity could be outsourced, but accountability could not.*

CFO Practice Note:
• Conduct annual risk audits of all critical outsourced vendors and service providers.
• Include SLA clauses covering data protection, compliance reporting, incident response, and audit rights.
• Maintain vendor-risk ratings within the enterprise control dashboard.

---

312 · AI-Based Predictive Risk Monitoring

Kael embraced artificial intelligence as an early-warning system. He implemented **AI-Based Predictive Risk Monitoring** to scan financial anomalies, supplier delays, payment behaviour, cyber irregularities, control breaches, and compliance signals before they escalated.

Algorithms converted data noise into decision signals, giving the Risk Committee real-time foresight. Kael did not treat AI as judgement. He treated it as radar — useful only when leaders knew how to interpret what it detected.

Kael understood that *predictive risk models were the CFO's radar: quiet, imperfect, but often lifesaving when watched properly.*

CFO Practice Note:
• Deploy AI tools integrated with ERP, treasury, procurement, compliance, and cyber systems for real-time alerts.
• Build machine-learning models for fraud, credit, vendor, cyber, and compliance-risk detection.
• Review false-positive ratios periodically to maintain model credibility.

---

313 · CFO Dashboard for Risk Metrics

Kael built a **Risk Intelligence Dashboard** that summarised enterprise risk on one screen. Key indicators — liquidity headroom, covenant triggers, audit issues, cyber alerts, regulatory deadlines, counterparty exposure, and operational disruptions — refreshed through live data feeds.

Executives learned to view risk visually, not verbally. The dashboard became the heartbeat of enterprise awareness because it showed movement, severity, owner, and action status without waiting for long narratives.

Kael understood that *if leaders could not see their risks, they could not steer the company with confidence.*

CFO Practice Note:
• Link risk dashboards to live data from finance, compliance, treasury, cyber, and operations.
• Display the top risks with traffic-light indicators, trend graphs, owners, and action status.
• Present dashboard highlights in every quarterly Board or Risk Committee meeting.

---

314 · Creating a Culture of Transparency in Incident Reporting

Kael believed risk maturity began when people stopped hiding problems. He built a culture where teams could report control breaches, ethical lapses, operational errors, cyber concerns, and near-misses without fear of automatic punishment.

Every incident triggered root-cause analysis, not a witch hunt. Transparency stopped being heroic and became normal. Over time, people understood that early reporting protected both the organisation and the person raising the concern.

Kael understood that *a company's integrity was tested not by the absence of errors, but by the speed and honesty of acknowledgement.*

CFO Practice Note:
• Maintain safe reporting channels for employees, vendors, and key stakeholders.
• Reward early disclosure and near-miss reporting through recognition, not fear.
• Publish annual transparency metrics in the CFO's governance or risk report.

---

315 · Risk Training Modules for Finance Leaders

Kael converted risk awareness into a leadership curriculum. He introduced **Risk Training Modules** for finance managers covering scenario modelling, audit coordination, cyber protocols, escalation discipline, compliance dilemmas, fraud signals, and Board communication.

Finance leaders began seeing control as empowerment, not policing. By teaching risk, Kael multiplied resilience beyond his own office. The goal was not to create cautious managers, but leaders who could recognise exposure before exposure became expensive.

Kael understood that *a CFO's legacy lived partly in how risk-ready the next generation became.*

CFO Practice Note:
• Develop modular risk workshops for mid-level and senior finance leaders.
• Include practical simulations covering crisis handling, compliance dilemmas, cyber response, and liquidity stress.
• Track learning impact through post-training case assessments and behavioural improvement.

---

316 · Continuous Risk Review Cadence

Kael embedded risk cadence into the company's DNA. Monthly executive reviews, quarterly Board sessions, and annual deep dives created a rhythm of vigilance across liquidity, compliance, cyber, reputation, operations, tax, and governance.

By institutionalising frequency, he made risk management not a project, but a posture. The company no longer waited for turbulence to explain itself; it learned to anticipate, measure, and prepare.

Kael understood that *risk review was not a meeting; it was a muscle strengthened by repetition.*

CFO Practice Note:
• Establish a monthly risk-review calendar aligned with audit, strategy, treasury, and Board cycles.
• Rotate focus areas each quarter across liquidity, compliance, cyber, reputation, operations, and governance.
• Document outcomes and action tracking within the Enterprise Risk Register.

Practical Tool: CFO Risk Appetite Statement

A risk appetite statement converts vague caution into operating discipline.

Without it, every leader defines risk differently. Sales may call a large credit exposure "strategic." Operations may call vendor dependency "practical." Treasury may call short-term borrowing "temporary." The CFO's role is to create a common language before these interpretations become losses.

Kael Cipher proposed the following risk appetite statement for NextAura Global during his first annual risk review.

Ownership and Review

Each risk must have one accountable owner, one measurable indicator, one escalation route, and one review frequency. The CFO will present a consolidated enterprise risk dashboard to the Audit Committee every quarter, with immediate escalation for any risk crossing approved tolerance.

A risk appetite statement is not a decorative governance document. It is a promise about how the organisation will behave before temptation arrives.

Kael summarized it sharply: "Risk appetite is not how much danger we can tolerate. It is how much discipline we are willing to maintain."

Illustrative CFO Risk Appetite Statement

NextAura Global will pursue growth with disciplined risk-taking. The company recognizes that risk is inseparable from enterprise value creation; however, risk must be understood, priced, owned, monitored, and escalated before it threatens liquidity, reputation, compliance, or strategic continuity.

The company has a moderate appetite for strategic and innovation risk where the expected return is measurable and aligned with approved enterprise priorities. It has low appetite for liquidity risk, compliance risk, financial reporting risk, cyber risk, and ethical risk. It has zero tolerance for fraud, deliberate misstatement, bribery, retaliation against whistle-blowers, or concealment of material information from the board.

Risk Appetite Thresholds

Risk Area	Appetite Level	Illustrative Threshold	Escalation Trigger
Liquidity	Low	Minimum 30 days operating cash visibility	Cash buffer below approved limit
Customer Credit	Moderate	Single customer overdue exposure not above approved limit	Top 5 customers drive more than 50% overdue receivables
Forex Exposure	Low to Moderate	Net unhedged exposure within board-approved band	Exposure exceeds hedge policy limit
Capex Execution	Moderate	Cost overrun tolerance up to 5%	Overrun above 5% or delay beyond 90 days
Compliance	Very Low	100% statutory filing discipline	Any missed material filing or regulatory notice
Cyber Risk	Very Low	No unresolved critical vulnerability	Any high-severity breach or data compromise
Ethics	Zero Tolerance	No deliberate concealment or manipulation	Any suspected fraud or management override
Reputation	Very Low	No avoidable public trust breach	Media, investor, regulator, or customer trust event

Practical Tool: Risk Heat Map Template

A risk register lists what can go wrong. A risk heat map shows what deserves attention first.

For a CFO, the heat map is not a decorative risk-management exercise. It is a prioritisation instrument. It helps the leadership team separate noise from danger, routine issues from board-level exposure, and theoretical concerns from risks that may damage liquidity, compliance, reputation, or enterprise value.

Kael Cipher used the heat map not to frighten management, but to sharpen judgement. Every risk was scored on two dimensions: likelihood and impact.

Likelihood Score

Score	Likelihood Level	Meaning
1	Rare	Unlikely to occur under normal conditions
2	Unlikely	Possible, but not expected in the near term
3	Possible	Could occur if controls weaken or conditions change
4	Likely	Strong probability within the planning period
5	Almost Certain	Already emerging or highly probable

Impact Score

Score	Impact Level	Meaning
1	Insignificant	Limited operational or financial impact
2	Minor	Manageable impact within functional limits
3	Moderate	Requires senior management attention
4	Major	Requires CEO / CFO / board committee attention
5	Severe	Threatens liquidity, compliance, reputation, continuity, or enterprise value

Risk Rating Formula [Risk Rating = Likelihood × Impact]

Rating Range	Risk Level	Action Required
1–5	Low	Monitor through normal process
6–10	Medium	Assign owner and review periodically
11–15	High	Management action plan required
16–25	Critical	Immediate escalation to CEO / Audit Committee / Board

Please refer Illustrative CFO Risk Heat Map on the next page.

Risk Area	Risk Description	Likelihood	Impact	Rating	Risk Level	Owner	Immediate Action
Liquidity	Cash buffer may fall below approved minimum due to delayed collections	4	5	20	Critical	CFO / Treasurer	Weekly cash war-room and bank line review
Cybersecurity	Unauthorized access to financial systems or payment platforms	3	5	15	High	CIO / CFO	Penetration test and payment control review
Compliance	Delay in statutory filing or regulatory submission	2	4	8	Medium	Controller	Compliance calendar and ownership check
Customer Credit	High overdue exposure from top five customers	4	4	16	Critical	Sales Head / CFO	Customer escalation and revised credit terms
FX Exposure	Unhedged foreign currency exposure beyond policy band	3	4	12	High	Treasurer	Hedge review and policy compliance report
Capex Execution	Cost overrun in strategic expansion project	3	4	12	High	Project Sponsor / CFO	Stage-gate review before next tranche
Talent	Dependency on one key finance leader for critical process	3	3	9	Medium	CFO / HR	Succession folder and cross-training
Reputation	Public criticism due to governance or disclosure issue	2	5	10	Medium	CEO / CFO / Legal	Crisis communication protocol

Heat Map Interpretation

Impact ↓ / Likelihood →	1 Rare	2 Unlikely	3 Possible	4 Likely	5 Almost Certain
5 Severe	5	10	15	20	25
4 Major	4	8	12	16	20
3 Moderate	3	6	9	12	15
2 Minor	2	4	6	8	10
1 Insignificant	1	2	3	4	5

CFO Review Questions

Before presenting the heat map to the board, the CFO should ask:

1. Are the top risks truly enterprise risks, or only departmental worries?
2. Is every high and critical risk assigned to a named owner?
3. Is the mitigation action measurable, or merely descriptive?
4. Is there a clear escalation trigger?
5. Has the risk rating changed since the previous review?
6. Are emerging risks being captured before they become losses?
7. Is management underplaying any risk because the truth is uncomfortable?

Kael's rule was simple:

"A risk heat map is useful only when it changes behaviour."

If the map does not influence capital allocation, insurance coverage, control testing, treasury planning, compliance focus, or board discussion, then it is not risk management. It is paperwork.

A CFO must ensure that the heat map becomes a living governance instrument — reviewed, challenged, updated, and acted upon. The purpose is not to predict every storm. The purpose is to make sure the organisation knows which clouds deserve attention before the sky turns dark.

CHAPTER 18

Tax and Transfer Pricing Alignment

Tax strategy is not evasion - Cross-Border Discipline and Treaties — it's intelligent navigation. Build tax transparency across jurisdictions; reduce surprises before they cost trust.

317 · Corporate Tax Structure Review and Rationalisation

Kael began his tax transformation by simplifying the maze. He commissioned a group-wide **Corporate Tax Structure Review**, mapping entities, jurisdictions, inter-company flows, holding patterns, loss-making subsidiaries, tax leakages, and business substance.

Redundant layers were merged, dormant entities were evaluated, and loss-making subsidiaries were restructured for efficiency. The outcome was lower leakage, higher transparency, cleaner audit trails, and fewer surprises at tax review time.

Kael understood that *simplification was often the highest form of compliance because complexity gave risk too many places to hide.*

CFO Practice Note:

• Conduct biennial reviews of group tax structures for redundancy, leakage, substance, and compliance risk.

• Align entity structures with business substance, operational purpose, and transfer pricing rules.
• Maintain updated documentation for tax authority readiness and audit defence.

318 · Direct vs. Indirect Tax Optimisation Map

Kael built a **Tax Optimisation Map** linking direct and indirect taxes to business transactions. By integrating GST, VAT, withholding, customs, and corporate tax planning, he created a unified visibility layer for compliance and efficiency.

Each decision — procurement, pricing, contracting, warehousing, invoicing, inter-company charging, and customer delivery — now carried a tax lens. The finance team stopped treating taxes as a cost after the event and started seeing tax as strategy built into the transaction.

Kael understood that *every percentage of tax saved ethically became capital that could be reinvested intelligently.*

CFO Practice Note:
• Map end-to-end tax impact across supply chains, contracts, pricing models, and operating geographies.
• Integrate tax engines into ERP for automated computation, reconciliation, and reporting.
• Benchmark effective tax rates against peers and explain movement annually.

319 · GST and VAT Compliance Automation

Kael digitalised compliance before regulators demanded it. He rolled out automated **GST / VAT Compliance Engines** integrated with ERP, e-invoicing systems, purchase ledgers, sales ledgers, and statutory return modules.

Discrepancies triggered alerts, not penalties. Input credits, output liabilities, mismatched invoices, vendor filings, and return data could now be reconciled in real time. The audit trail became so clean that compliance turned into competitive advantage.

Kael understood that *automation did not merely file returns; it built credibility before the tax authority asked for proof.*

CFO Practice Note:
• Automate GST / VAT reconciliation with purchase ledgers, sales ledgers, e-invoicing, and statutory returns.

• Conduct monthly data validation for input tax credits, mismatches, blocked credits, and vendor compliance.
• Maintain digital archives aligned with statutory retention and audit requirements.

---

320 · Transfer Pricing Models — TNMM, CUP, CPM, PSM

Kael viewed transfer pricing not as a defensive exercise, but as a governance tool. He designed pricing policies aligned with business substance and transaction reality, applying methods such as **TNMM, CUP, CPM**, and **PSM** depending on the nature of each inter-company transaction.

Inter-company arrangements became transparent, defensible, and documentation-rich. Charges were supported by functional analysis, benchmarking, agreements, and clear value logic. Audits turned from confrontation to confirmation because the company could show why every charge existed.

Kael understood that *transfer pricing was where finance met fairness across borders.*

CFO Practice Note:
• Select pricing methods based on transaction profile, functional analysis, risk allocation, and value contribution.
• Prepare contemporaneous documentation with benchmarking studies and inter-company agreements.
• Update inter-company pricing annually to reflect market shifts, business changes, and regulatory expectations.

---

321 · Advance Pricing Agreements and MAP Strategy

Kael turned potential disputes into pre-emptive agreements. He pursued **Advance Pricing Agreements** and **Mutual Agreement Procedures** where recurring high-value cross-border transactions carried meaningful uncertainty.

This approach reduced litigation risk and brought multi-year predictability to pricing, tax provisioning, cash forecasting, and Board communication. Kael preferred clarity before conflict because ambiguity consumed management attention long after the transaction had passed.

Kael understood that *tax certainty was often cheaper than winning a tax battle after years of dispute.*

CFO Practice Note:
• Identify recurring high-value or high-risk transactions suitable for APA coverage.
• Coordinate with external tax counsel, local advisors, and business owners before authority negotiations.
• Track ongoing MAP cases with financial exposure, expected timeline, and provisioning impact.

---

322 · Tax Due Diligence Checklist for M&A

Kael ensured no acquisition closed without a tax due diligence sweep. He examined historical filings, assessments, contingent liabilities, indirect-tax exposures, withholding compliance, transfer pricing positions, and pending litigation before signing any deal.

By stress-testing deferred taxes, evaluating open notices, and quantifying unrecorded exposures, he prevented post-merger shocks that often erode deal value. For Kael, diligence was not procedural caution; it was defence against regret.

Kael understood that *unseen tax exposures could quietly destroy deal value after the headline celebration ended.*

CFO Practice Note:
• Review at least five years of tax assessments, filings, notices, positions, and litigation cases.
• Reconcile deferred tax positions, credits, provisions, and contingent exposures with statutory books.
• Quantify unrecorded liabilities and include them in valuation, indemnity, or purchase-price adjustments.

---

323 · Cross-Border Remittance and Withholding Controls

Kael tightened control over cross-border fund flows. He established a centralised **Remittance Control Desk** to oversee TDS, withholding tax rates, treaty benefits, documentation, approval trails, and payment purpose before funds left treasury.

Every international transaction carried a compliance checklist. No remittance moved without reason, record, and responsibility. Treasury, tax, and legal now reviewed sensitive payments before execution rather than after audit questions arrived.

Kael understood that *in cross-border finance, precision became protection.*

CFO Practice Note:

• Maintain a country-wise withholding matrix covering treaty rates, domestic law rates, documentation, and approval requirements.

• Automate tax deduction validation inside treasury and payment workflows.

• Retain foreign remittance certificates, tax forms, invoices, and approvals in a controlled digital archive.

---

324 · Treaty Benefit Utilisation and BEPS Vigilance

Kael ensured the company's global tax posture remained transparent, lawful, and defensible. He monitored treaty benefits under DTAAs while staying vigilant against **Base Erosion and Profit Shifting** risks.

Each inter-company payment had to be justified by substance, function, and commercial purpose — not merely routing. His principle was simple: global presence, not tax arbitrage. The organisation could use legitimate treaty benefits, but only where business reality supported the structure.

Kael understood that *the future belonged to transparent tax positions that could survive questions from both regulators and investors.*

CFO Practice Note:

• Periodically review treaty eligibility, residency documentation, beneficial ownership, and substance requirements.

• Implement BEPS-compliant country-by-country reporting systems where applicable.

• Align tax planning with substance-over-form documentation and Board-approved risk appetite.

---

325 · Inter-Company Agreements and Arm's-Length Validation

Kael formalised every inter-company transaction with documented agreements — no verbal understandings, informal allocations, or legacy assumptions. Each contract carried service scope, pricing policy, cost allocation logic, payment terms, tax treatment, and review cadence.

Independent benchmarking validated every charge as arm's length. When auditors arrived, compliance was self-evident because the transaction story, contract, invoice, and pricing logic all spoke the same language.

Kael understood that *transparency was the true transfer price when related parties dealt across borders.*

CFO Practice Note:

• Draft clear inter-company agreements for all cross-border services, royalties, loans, cost allocations, and management charges.
• Conduct annual arm's-length benchmarking using reliable external comparables.
• Align invoice documentation with contractual pricing terms and transfer pricing reports.

---

326 · Deferred Tax Assets / Liabilities Reconciliation

Kael treated deferred taxes as time-travel entries in financial statements. He reconciled **Deferred Tax Assets** and **Deferred Tax Liabilities** quarterly, aligning them with projected profitability, temporary differences, carry-forward losses, and reversal timelines.

By validating recoverability, expiry periods, and future taxable income assumptions, he ensured no deferred benefit remained fiction. Tax notes now spoke the language of foresight rather than accounting mechanics.

Kael understood that *deferred taxes reminded the CFO that timing was one of the quietest forms of risk.*

CFO Practice Note:

• Prepare quarterly reconciliations of DTA and DTL by jurisdiction, entity, and temporary difference.
• Test recoverability of DTA through future profitability assessments and expiry analysis.
• Align disclosures with applicable accounting standards and auditor expectations.

---

327 · Tax Litigation Tracking and Resolution Governance

Kael refused to let tax disputes drift into bureaucracy. He instituted a **Tax Litigation Tracker** consolidating assessments, appeals, tribunal cases, notices, demands, refunds, and settlement opportunities across jurisdictions.

Each case carried quantified exposure, probability assessment, next hearing date, owner, counsel, evidence status, and accounting treatment. Disputes stopped being files and became action items. The Audit Committee could now see tax risk as a portfolio, not as scattered legal noise.

Kael understood that *tax litigation was not a waiting game; it was a governance test with financial consequences.*

CFO Practice Note:

• Maintain a live tracker for all open tax cases with exposure, probability, owner, next step, and timeline.
• Classify matters as probable, possible, or remote in line with accounting standards.
• Escalate high-exposure or precedent-setting cases to the Audit Committee quarterly.

---

328 · AI Tools for Tax-Compliance Analytics

Kael used data intelligence to outpace compliance risk. He implemented **AI-Based Tax Analytics** tools that reconciled returns, flagged anomalies, monitored indirect-tax mismatches, checked vendor compliance, and detected filing deviations before notices arrived.

Predictive algorithms converted tax data from a backward-looking record into an early-warning system. For Kael, automation meant foresight, not shortcuts. The tax team could now ask better questions before regulators did.

Kael understood that *tax compliance powered by AI was not governance on autopilot; it was governance with earlier signals.*

CFO Practice Note:

• Integrate AI tools for transaction-level tax anomaly detection and return reconciliation.
• Build exception dashboards for unclaimed credits, mismatched filings, blocked credits, and unusual tax positions.
• Review analytics summaries before statutory filing deadlines and audit submissions.

---

329 · Tax Audit Preparation — Documentation and Readiness

Kael believed a clean audit began with clean documentation. He created **Tax Audit Readiness Binders** containing reconciliations, statutory registers, tax positions, exemption logic, adjustment notes, remittance records, and evidence for major claims.

His team rehearsed audit queries like pilots rehearsing checklists. By audit week, confidence replaced anxiety because every major position had a file, owner, and explanation.

Kael understood that *readiness was the most credible form of defence because it replaced panic with proof.*

CFO Practice Note:
• Maintain updated reconciliation files for income tax, GST / VAT, withholding taxes, and major adjustments.
• Document logic, approvals, and evidence for significant exemptions, credits, deductions, and positions.
• Conduct internal dry-run audits before regulatory inspections or major assessments.

---

330 · ESG-Linked Tax Transparency Reporting

Kael extended transparency to taxation itself. He published voluntary **Tax Transparency Disclosures** highlighting geographic contribution, effective tax rates, incentives used, tax governance, sustainability-linked benefits, and responsible tax principles.

This openness repositioned the company as a responsible taxpayer, not merely a compliant one. Reputation again became currency because stakeholders could see not only what the company earned, but how responsibly it contributed.

Kael understood that *tax transparency had become one of the ESG frontiers of finance.*

CFO Practice Note:
• Prepare annual tax-transparency statements aligned with recognised responsible-tax reporting standards where applicable.
• Link disclosed tax data to ESG performance indicators, governance posture, and stakeholder trust.
• Engage independent assurance for public tax reports where materiality or investor expectations require it.

---

331 · CFO's Annual Tax Governance Statement

Kael closed each fiscal year with a **Tax Governance Statement** — a declaration of compliance integrity, ethical tax posture, risk exposure, litigation progress, transfer pricing discipline, and major policy changes.

The statement became more than a report. It was a CFO's signature of accountability to shareholders, regulators, employees, and society. It showed that tax was not an afterthought buried in notes, but a leadership position rooted in transparency and responsibility.

Kael understood that *tax governance was not only about what the company paid; it was about how the company chose to think.*

CFO Practice Note:

- Present the annual tax governance statement alongside financial results or Audit Committee reporting.
- Disclose tax policy, risk approach, litigation status, assurance mechanisms, and governance ownership transparently.
- Review alignment with the Board Audit Committee, ESG Committee, and overall enterprise risk appetite annually.

Practical Tool: Transfer Pricing Documentation Checklist

Transfer pricing is not merely a tax file. It is the written evidence that related-party transactions were conducted with commercial fairness, economic substance, and defensible logic.

A CFO should not wait for a tax notice to understand the company's transfer pricing position. The documentation must be ready before questions arrive.

Please check Transfer Pricing Documentation Checklist on the next page

Transfer Pricing Documentation Checklist

Documentation Area	**CFO Review Question**	**Status**
Group Structure	Is the legal and operating structure updated for all jurisdictions?	Pending / Complete
Related-Party List	Are all associated enterprises identified correctly?	Pending / Complete
Transaction Register	Are all inter-company transactions captured — goods, services, royalties, loans, guarantees, cost allocations?	Pending / Complete
Inter-Company Agreements	Are signed agreements available and aligned with actual conduct?	Pending / Complete
Functional Analysis	Is the FAR analysis clear — functions performed, assets used, risks assumed?	Pending / Complete
Method Selection	Is the selected method justified — CUP, TNMM, CPM, PSM, resale price, or other accepted method?	Pending / Complete
Benchmarking Study	Is the comparable company / transaction analysis current and defensible?	Pending / Complete
Pricing Policy	Is the pricing formula documented before the transaction, not after the audit?	Pending / Complete
Invoicing Trail	Do invoices, debit notes, credit notes, and ledgers match the policy?	Pending / Complete
Year-End True-Up	Is there a mechanism to adjust margins before books are finalized?	Pending / Complete

Withholding Tax Review	Are cross-border payments reviewed for withholding tax and treaty implications?	Pending / Complete
BEPS / Substance Review	Does the transaction reflect real commercial substance?	Pending / Complete
Master File / Local File	Are jurisdiction-specific files prepared where applicable?	Pending / Complete
Country-by-Country Reporting	Is CbCR applicability reviewed for the group?	Pending / Complete
Litigation Tracker	Are open tax matters, notices, and exposures monitored?	Pending / Complete
Board / Audit Committee Note	Are material transfer pricing risks reported to governance forums?	Pending / Complete

CFO Review Discipline

A CFO should ask three practical questions:

1. Would the company have entered into this transaction with an unrelated party on similar terms?
2. Does the documentation match the actual conduct of the parties?
3. Can the pricing logic be explained clearly to a tax officer, auditor, or board member?

Kael's view was direct:

"Transfer pricing fails when the paper says one thing, the behaviour says another, and the CFO discovers both too late."

The CFO does not need to personally prepare every benchmarking study. But he must ensure that the company's tax position is timely, documented, commercially rational, and consistent with governance expectations.

APPENDIX B — THE 180-DAY STRATEGIC SCORECARDS

"Transformation is only real when outcomes outlast announcements."
— *Global CFO Leadership Forum (2024)*

These **180-Day Strategic Scorecards** convert the CFO's mid-term vision into measurable transformation outcomes.
Each grid spans **90-150-180 days**, covering the six-month window when systems stabilise, integrations take root, and credibility evolves into capability.

How to Use This Appendix

Each scorecard is designed for **monthly progress tracking** and presentation during **90-, 150-, and 180-day** strategic reviews with the CEO and Board Strategy Committee.
Together, they form the **CFO Transformation Index** — a quantified reflection of scalability, integration, and governance maturity.

"Dashboards show control; scorecards prove change."
— *HBR CFO Playbook (2024)*

1. Digital Finance & Systems Modernisation Index

From **Chapter 13 – Designing Finance Systems & Digital Workflows**
Objective: Transform finance operations from transactional to intelligent through ERP discipline, automation, and data integrity.

Metric	90 Days	150 Days	180 Days	Outcome / Target
Digital Blueprint & ERP Audit	Complete audit of existing ERP and workflows	Finalise architecture upgrades, integration needs	Board-approved Finance Digital Blueprint	ERP scope locked; 100 % process coverage
Automation & Workflow Standardisation	Identify automation candidates in AP/AR/GL	Deploy RPA pilots and e-approval chains	Achieve full workflow standardisation	Manual entries ↓ 70 %
Data Governance & Master Data Integrity	Form data-stewardship team and MDM policy	Cleanse critical data sets; define naming logic	Implement validation scripts across systems	Data-error rate < 1 %
MIS & Analytics Cadence	Publish enterprise MIS calendar	Launch real-time dashboards for cash & margins	Present analytics pack to CXO weekly	MIS latency < 3 days
Cyber & Cloud Controls	Assess current controls and vendor posture	Implement encryption and access reviews	Certify system resilience via audit	100 % ITGC compliance

2. Business Partnership & Performance Index

From **Chapter 14 – Partnering Beyond Numbers**
Objective: Position finance as a strategic partner driving operational performance and decision clarity.

Metric	90 Days	150 Days	180 Days	Outcome / Target
Cross-Functional Review Rhythm	Initiate monthly reviews with Ops, HR, Sales	Expand cadence to all business units	Institutionalise performance forums	100 % BU participation
Cost-to-Serve & Margin Bridge Analytics	Launch baseline margin analysis	Deliver segment/channel dashboards	Embed analytics in budget cycles	Gross-margin variance < 3 %
Finance as Strategic Partner Program	Nominate finance liaisons for key functions	Conduct financial-literacy workshops	Formalise partnership charter & metrics	Stakeholder rating ≥ 4.5 / 5
Operational KPI Integration	Identify 10 shared Ops + Finance metrics	Link KPIs to incentive plans	Automate dashboard visibility	KPI alignment = 100 %
Pricing & Cash-Flow Linkage	Map pricing to collection timelines	Pilot dynamic discounting models	Institutionalise price-to-cash discipline	DSO ↓ 10 days; margin ↑ 1 %

3. Capital Structure & Funding Readiness Index

From **Chapter 15 – Raising Capital and Investor Readiness**
Objective: Balance capital efficiency, investor confidence, and liquidity depth.

Metric	90 Days	150 Days	180 Days	Outcome / Target
Capital Structure Simulation	Build 3-scenario model	Align leverage & equity signalling	Board-approved capital policy	Leverage within ± 10 bps of target WACC
Investor Narrative	Draft IIM + core equity story	Validate through mock investor meets	Publish verified investor brief	Market perception ↑ to "Positive Outlook"
Rating Engagement	Establish data + control cadence	Review with agency analysts	Achieve upgrade / positive re-rating	Outlook ≥ Positive
Post-Funding Governance	Form investor-relations cadence	Deliver Q1 performance vs. promises	Publish first impact report	Variance < 5 % vs. commitments

4. M&A Integration & Synergy Realisation Index

From **Chapter 16 – Mergers, Acquisitions & Strategic Investments**
Objective: Ensure every acquisition delivers measurable and cultural ROI.

Metric	90 Days	150 Days	180 Days	Outcome / Target
Synergy Mapping	Quantify cost & revenue synergies	Assign owners & timelines	Validate realisation through audit	≥ 80 % synergy capture
Integration PMO	Establish governance model	Weekly tracking & issue logs	Mid-integration scorecard review	PMO maturity ≥ Level 4
Cultural Alignment	Conduct joint leadership workshops	Launch common value charter	Survey engagement scores	85 % cross-team trust index
Post-Deal Performance	Build combined P&L dashboard	Link KPIs to executive bonus	Board presentation on integration	ROI > plan ± 5 %

5. Enterprise Risk & Resilience Index

From **Chapter 17 – Risk Management & Scenario Planning**
Objective: Institutionalise predictive risk intelligence and continuity assurance.

Metric	90 Days	150 Days	180 Days	Outcome / Target
Enterprise Risk Register	Build and validate top-20 risks	Integrate heat map + dashboard	Board-approved risk cadence	ERR coverage 100 %
Crisis Simulation	Conduct first tabletop exercise	Capture lessons + update playbooks	Audit response time vs. benchmark	Response < 4 hrs
Cyber & Data Risk	Run penetration tests + training	Patch high-severity issues	Certify ISO 27001 compliance	Zero major incidents
Predictive Monitoring	Deploy AI risk engine	Review alerts + false positives	Present dashboard to Board	≥ 90 % risk detection accuracy

6. Tax & Regulatory Alignment Index

From **Chapter 18 – Tax and Transfer Pricing Alignment**
Objective: Achieve predictable, transparent, and ethical tax governance.

Metric	90 Days	150 Days	180 Days	Outcome / Target
Tax Structure Review	Map group entities & jurisdictions	Implement rationalisation plan	File updated structure with authorities	Leakages ↓ > 10 %
Transfer Pricing Compliance	Update policies & agreements	Complete benchmark study	Submit APA/MAP proposal	Full OECD alignment
Litigation Tracker	Consolidate all cases	Escalate > ₹10 Cr exposures to Board	Close ≥ 25 % pending cases	Exposure ↓ > 15 %
Tax Transparency Report	Draft disclosure framework	Review with Audit Committee	Publish Tax Governance Statement	External assurance obtained

PART IV

THE FIRST 365 DAYS: LEADING AND LEAVING A LEGACY

Theme: From Finance Head to Enterprise Leader
Deliverable: CFO 365-Day Legacy Playbook — Inherited → Stabilised → Built → Institutionalised

"The first 180 days build systems; the next 180 build trust that outlasts you."

By the time Kael reached his twelfth month, finance had already become the organisation's language of truth. Yet the final stretch of a first-year CFO journey isn't about more control — it's about **consolidating credibility into influence.**

Part IV explores how a CFO moves from **functional mastery to enterprise leadership**:
how to work with Boards as a peer, allocate capital with purpose, protect ethics under pressure, and prepare successors who can carry the same torch of integrity.

Here, the dashboards give way to **judgement**, and spreadsheets to **stewardship**. The CFO is no longer just interpreting numbers; they're interpreting intent.

Each chapter closes with a **Year-End Leadership Review**, designed to help the reader document what was inherited, stabilised, built, and ultimately institutionalised.
Together, these reflections form the **CFO Legacy Playbook** — the closing proof that leadership is not about tenure, but about the systems and values that survive it.

CHAPTER 19

Working with the Board and Committees

Governance through clarity and courage.

332 · Framing Tough Messages with Data and Empathy

By the ninth month, Kael realized that numbers were not the hardest part of the CFO role — narratives were. He learned to present unpleasant truths with precision, context, and composure.

When profitability dipped, he led with causes and corrective levers, not excuses. His tone balanced empathy with accountability; he spoke as a custodian of facts, not as a defender of management. Boards trusted him because he could humanise data without softening its truth.

Kael understood that *courage in the boardroom was often expressed through calm clarity, not confrontation.*

CFO Practice Note:

- Lead with validated facts, not adjectives or emotional framing.
- Anticipate emotional reactions and anchor replies to outcomes, not blame.
- Close every tough message with corrective measures, ownership, and a path forward.

333 · Delivering Unfavourable Results Transparently

When quarterly results turned against projections, Kael resisted the instinct to buffer the message. He presented variance analysis line by line, linking every deviation to operational reality.

He disclosed early, spoke plainly, and refused selective optimism. The Board began seeing him not merely as a financial messenger, but as a mirror of truth. Bad news became easier to absorb because it arrived with evidence, context, and action.

Kael understood that *unfavourable results were the highest test of financial integrity because they revealed whether truth could survive pressure.*

CFO Practice Note:

• Present quarterly decks with both variance and causality; avoid cosmetic management adjustments.
• Document lessons learned as part of disclosure discipline, not as a delayed post-mortem.
• Treat transparency as risk insurance because it protects long-term credibility.

---

334 · Quarterly Board Briefing Templates

Kael standardised **Quarterly Board Briefing Templates** — concise, visual, and strategic. Each quarterly pack began with financials, moved into governance metrics, and closed with foresight indicators.

Every page answered one of three questions: where are we, why are we here, and what happens next? The new format replaced sprawling decks with focused dashboards that spoke more powerfully than prose.

Kael understood that *Boards did not need more data; they needed distilled judgement that helped them govern faster.*

CFO Practice Note:

• Design Board decks around three layers: summary, insight, and implication.
• Integrate non-financial indicators such as ethics, ESG, cyber, risk, and talent.
• Enforce brevity; keep the main pack limited unless the Board specifically requests detail.

---

335 · Managing Conflicts Between Management and Oversight

Every CFO eventually stands between operational ambition and fiduciary restraint. Kael learned that resolving tension between management and the

Board was not about taking sides; it was about framing trade-offs in the language of consequence.

He used sensitivity analysis, decision trees, and scenario comparisons to show outcomes under each option. Decisions began to self-correct through logic, not persuasion. Trust replaced friction because both sides could see the same consequence map.

Kael understood that *objectivity was the CFO's diplomacy when ambition and oversight pulled in different directions.*

CFO Practice Note:

• Use decision trees to visualise alternatives, outcomes, risks, and governance consequences.

• Reconfirm minutes and decision rationales after meetings to avoid revisionism.

• Maintain neutrality in tone and firmness in principle.

336 · Structuring Committee Presentations — Audit, Risk, CSR, Remuneration

Kael restructured committee presentation flow from information overload to **Insight Architecture**. Audit Committee packs focused on control effectiveness; Risk Committee decks mapped exposures to mitigations; CSR presentations linked capital with community impact; Remuneration meetings tied pay with ethics and value.

Each presentation was customised to its committee mandate, but unified in logic: evidence before emotion, risk before reassurance, and decision before decoration. Directors began receiving what they needed, not everything finance could produce.

Kael understood that *committees respected CFOs who respected their purpose.*

CFO Practice Note:

• Maintain one-slide executive summaries for each committee with red–amber–green flags.

• Align every agenda with the committee charter; avoid over-reporting beyond mandate.

• Circulate decks at least 72 hours in advance and document follow-ups by owner and date.

337 · Ensuring Board Minutes Reflect Accountability

Kael began reviewing draft Board minutes like audit evidence. Every decision, dissent, dependency, and deliverable had to be captured precisely — not as memory, but as record.

Minutes became institutional truth, resistant to revisionism. He ensured that every unresolved issue carried a clear owner, timeline, and next-review status. The quality of minutes improved the quality of follow-through.

Kael understood that *minutes were not merely a record of meetings; they were the legacy of decisions made under responsibility.*

CFO Practice Note:

• Verify factual accuracy, decision wording, ownership, and resolution timelines before minutes are finalised.

• Use digital annotation or tracking to tag pending items by department and owner.

• Maintain an annual summary of Board actions, closures, and unresolved commitments.

---

338 · Board Education — Explaining Complex Financial Concepts

Kael often found that non-financial directors were intelligent, not financial — and the difference mattered. He simplified derivative exposure, lease liabilities, WACC, impairment, covenants, and hedge accounting into analogies the Board could grasp without diluting technical truth.

When the Board understood, oversight turned into collaboration. He made learning inclusive, never intimidating. Financial education became a governance tool, not a classroom exercise.

Kael understood that *clarity was the ultimate mark of mastery because it allowed complexity to serve judgement.*

CFO Practice Note:

• Create a quarterly **Finance Simplified** note for directors on complex financial topics.

• Use visuals, examples, and business language instead of technical jargon.

• Offer optional deep-dive sessions before major accounting, capital, risk, or policy decisions.

---

339 · Balancing Governance Precision with Business Urgency

In one critical quarter-end, Kael faced pressure to defer expense recognition for optics. He chose governance precision over quarterly perfection.

His message to the CEO was clear: the company served the market through integrity, not improvisation. That decision earned him the Board's respect and the CEO's trust because it protected the future from a convenient present.

Kael understood that *good CFOs closed books fast, but great CFOs closed them clean.*

CFO Practice Note:

• Define immovable accounting boundaries early in the CFO tenure.
• Empower controllers to defend close integrity, cut-off discipline, and recognition standards.
• Use post-close audits to benchmark transparency maturity and identify pressure points.

---

340 · Using Executive Sessions to Convey Integrity, Not Insecurity

Kael learned that closed-door sessions were not for confession; they were for confidence. He used executive sessions to share sensitive insights, ethical risks, unresolved concerns, and future implications candidly.

He never used privacy to settle personal scores or create drama. He used it to protect institutional conscience. Over time, directors understood that when Kael requested an executive session, it was because the truth required a quieter room, not a defensive one.

Kael understood that *integrity was often quiet, but everyone in the room could feel its weight.*

CFO Practice Note:

• Use executive sessions for ethical disclosures, sensitive risks, and forward-looking governance concerns.
• Keep the tone factual, measured, and non-defensive.
• Maintain a confidential log of key Board conversations where governance reference or audit continuity may be required.

CHAPTER 20

Capital Allocation and Strategic Alignment

Link every rupee to purpose.

341 · Defining the Enterprise's Capital Allocation Philosophy

By month ten of his tenure, Kael established the firm's **Capital Allocation Philosophy** not as a spreadsheet exercise, but as a strategic compass for value creation. He convened the executive team and the Board to agree on four priorities: growth, maintenance, compliance, and innovation.

Every investment request thereafter had to map to one of these priorities and explain how it advanced enterprise purpose, resilience, or return. Capital was no longer approved because someone had budget authority; it was approved because it carried conviction.

Kael understood that *capital allocation was not only about how much the company spent; it revealed what the company truly stood for.*

CFO Practice Note:

• Develop a concise capital allocation charter defining priorities, guardrails, thresholds, and decision rights.

• Align the charter with the Board's value-creation agenda and investor expectations.

• Circulate the charter internally so every business unit treats it as the first filter for investment proposals.

---

342 · Translating Strategy into Financial Architecture

Kael refused to treat strategy and finance as adjacent silos. He built a **Financial Architecture** — a live model linking strategic pillars to funding pools, return thresholds, governance paths, and exit criteria.

Each strategic initiative had a mapped capital source, performance owner, and outcome metric. When business heads asked whether something could be funded, Kael redirected the discussion: funding was possible only when the initiative respected the architecture. Strategy stopped being a slogan and became money flow with discipline.

Kael understood that *if strategy was not translated into capital movement, it remained mission language rather than an operating model.*

CFO Practice Note:

• Construct a strategy-to-capital map linking strategic themes to cost centres, funding pools, and expected outcomes.
• Tag each initiative with capital origin, performance owner, governance route, and exit metric.
• Review the map monthly with the CFO office and quarterly with the Board to ensure alignment.

---

343 · Aligning Budgets with Business Vision and Purpose

Kael transformed budgeting from compliance to strategic alignment. The annual budget was structured not only by function, but by vision: where the enterprise was going, what it needed, and how each rupee would help it get there.

He worked with Sales, HR, Operations, Technology, and Supply Chain to embed strategic priorities into financial plans. Each leader had to answer how their numbers changed under different strategic choices. Budget became a narrative, not just a number.

Kael understood that *budgeting was not merely allocation; it was the organisation affirming the story it intended to execute.*

CFO Practice Note:

• Rebuild budget templates around strategic themes, not only cost centres.

• Run at least two what-if budget scenarios per function: baseline and strategy-aligned.
• Start budget review slides with purpose, investment, and outcome before comparing last year with this year.

---

344 · Classifying Capital Use — Growth, Maintenance, Compliance, Innovation

Kael introduced a **Capital Use Taxonomy** and mandated every request be tagged clearly. **Growth** meant new markets or products, **maintenance** meant sustaining existing operations, **compliance** meant regulatory or integrity requirements, and **innovation** meant future-state or disruptive capability investment.

With this classification in place, the Board could compare capital requests across functions without confusion. A maintenance project could no longer disguise itself as growth, and an innovation proposal had to justify uncertainty honestly.

Kael understood that *great capital allocation began by being clear about what the money was truly for.*

CFO Practice Note:
• Build a capital-use taxonomy covering growth, maintenance, compliance, and innovation.
• Tag every project request against the taxonomy and include the tag in submission packs.
• Review capital spend quarterly by category and present category-wise returns to the Board.

---

345 · Evaluating ROI versus ROIC — When Capital Creates versus Consumes Value

Kael refused projects justified by vague optimism. He required **Return on Investment** and **Return on Invested Capital** analysis, comparing proposed returns with hurdle rates and cost of capital.

If ROIC did not exceed the required threshold, the project consumed value even if it looked attractive in revenue terms. By elevating ROIC tracking to the Board's key metric, Kael shifted the conversation from "we grew" to "we created value."

Kael understood that *growth without return was vanity, and capital without return was waste.*

CFO Practice Note:
• Set minimum ROIC thresholds for new investments based on business risk and cost of capital.
• Require every business case to include both ROI and ROIC metrics.
• Report actual ROIC versus forecast every six months and compare it with cost of capital.

346 · Building a Capital Allocation Committee Charter

Kael established a formal **Capital Allocation Committee Charter**, chaired by the CFO and including leaders from Strategy, Finance, Operations, and relevant business units.

The charter defined mandate, membership, investment limits, review cadence, decision rights, escalation protocols, and documentation standards. With the Committee in place, allocation decisions became systematic, transparent, and repeatable instead of personality-led.

Kael understood that *the best Board decisions came from committee discipline, not committee confusion.*

CFO Practice Note:
• Draft a CAC charter covering member roles, mandate, decision rights, thresholds, and escalation path.
• Set approval thresholds for management, CAC, and Board-level capital decisions.
• Meet monthly for reviews and publish decision summaries with conditions, owners, and outcomes.

347 · Decision-Gate Criteria — Risk, Return, Reputation

For Kael, capital decisions were never purely financial. The **Decision-Gate Criteria** integrated three pillars: return through ROI and ROIC thresholds, risk through scenario testing and downside guardrails, and reputation through ESG alignment, regulatory impact, and stakeholder sentiment.

Any project failing one pillar came back for redesign or rejection. This made capital approval sharper because business heads knew the company was not only buying returns; it was buying future consequences.

Kael understood that *allocating capital ment saying no as often as saying yes, because discipline protected the few yeses that mattered.*

CFO Practice Note:

• Define decision-gate filters across risk, return, and reputation.
• Embed these filters directly in investment request templates.
• Maintain a filter-fail register of paused or rejected projects and present quarterly learnings to the CAC.

---

348 · Balancing Shareholder Returns with Reinvestment Discipline

Kael balanced capital-market expectations with long-term reinvestment needs. He developed a policy defining how free cash flow would be split between core reinvestment, dividends, buybacks, debt reduction, and strategic reserves.

The policy gave investors confidence without starving the business of future capacity. Shareholder returns were respected, but not allowed to cannibalise innovation, resilience, or growth. The balance created a more mature capital story.

Kael understood that *short-term returns should never be allowed to weaken long-term opportunity.*

CFO Practice Note:

• Publish a capital allocation policy setting bands for reinvestment, shareholder returns, debt reduction, and reserves.
• Use scenario models to test buybacks, dividends, and reinvestment under low-growth or crisis conditions.
• Communicate the policy clearly to investors and analysts annually.

---

349 · Using Hurdle Rates and Cost of Capital in Funding Priorities

Kael entrenched discipline by linking every major capital request to **Hurdle Rates** derived from the company's **Weighted Average Cost of Capital**. Projects exceeding WACC by a defined premium were prioritised; borderline projects required stronger strategic logic or Board-approved exception.

Finance was no longer asking only whether the company could afford a project. It was asking whether the project would create value above the cost of funding. That shift changed the quality of proposals before they reached the CFO's desk.

Kael understood that *funding without a hurdle was hope dressed as ambition.*

CFO Practice Note:

• Calculate WACC annually and set tiered hurdle rates by project type and risk profile.

• Ensure business cases show incremental IRR above hurdle rate and sensitivity to funding cost.

• Track approved projects' forecast return versus realized return each year.

350 · Allocating Resources Across Short, Medium and Long-Term Horizons

Kael mapped capital pools across three horizons: short term for agile response, medium term for growth initiatives, and long term for innovation and future-state transformation.

He created separate **Horizon Funding Pools**, each with defined criteria, ownership, and oversight. This prevented urgent operating demands from quietly consuming capital meant for future relevance. Patience was no longer a leadership wish; it was funded.

Kael understood that *true capital allocators funded horizons, not only projects.*

CFO Practice Note:

• Tag every major capital item by horizon and funding pool.

• Review allocation percentages each quarter across short, medium, and long-term priorities.

• Present a horizon-wise spend and outcomes dashboard at fiscal year-end.

351 · Linking Capital Projects to Measurable Enterprise KPIs

Kael insisted every capital investment be tied to measurable **Enterprise KPIs.** Whether it was an ERP upgrade, a new production line, or a market-expansion initiative, each funded project needed clear outcomes: cash-flow uplift, margin expansion, market share, risk reduction, or productivity gain.

The discipline made vague ambition difficult to approve. Capital projects could no longer hide behind strategic language without measurable delivery. Every rupee had to point to an outcome the enterprise could track.

Kael understood that *if the outcome could not be measured, the investment was only wishful thinking with a budget code.*

CFO Practice Note:

• Require business cases to include the top three KPIs and milestones for each

funded project.
• Include these KPIs in a monthly capital performance dashboard reviewed by the CFO office.
• Apply post-audit reviews at 12 and 24 months to compare realized versus projected outcomes.

---

352 · Integrating ESG and Sustainability Metrics into Capital Decisions

Kael recognised that modern capital allocation had to include non-financial returns. He expanded the capital decision gate to include carbon reduction, energy efficiency, social impact, safety, governance alignment, and long-term regulatory resilience.

Projects that failed minimum ESG criteria were either redesigned or removed from the funding pipeline. This was not cosmetic sustainability; it was capital discipline that recognised how markets, lenders, regulators, and communities were changing.

Kael understood that *sustainable capital allocation had become a premium asset because trust itself had economic value.*

CFO Practice Note:
• Develop ESG scoring for capital projects, including carbon impact, social footprint, safety, and governance quality.
• Require ESG metrics in every major business case and track realisation during capex review.
• Present an annual Capital Allocation and Sustainability Report to the Board and investors.

---

353 · Periodic Capital-Allocation Review — Freeze, Defer, or Exit Logic

Kael built a capital review cadence, forcing re-evaluation of large programmes at fixed intervals. Projects failing milestones were assessed under a **Freeze, Defer, or Exit Protocol**, releasing funds for better opportunities.

The message was clear: capital was not forever. Commitment did not mean blindness. By creating exit logic before emotional attachment hardened, Kael protected the organisation from funding yesterday's assumptions.

Kael understood that *the best capital allocators did not only commit well; they also knew when to uncommit with discipline.*

CFO Practice Note:

• Implement a capital review protocol covering milestone status, spend variance, and outcome forecast.
• Set criteria for freeze, defer, redesign, or exit based on delay, cost overrun, and value erosion.
• Report flagged projects quarterly to the Capital Allocation Committee.

---

354 · Communicating Allocation Rationale to Board and Investors

Kael knew allocation excellence was invisible unless communicated. He prepared a **Capital Allocation Communication Pack** explaining why funds were deployed where they were, how they tied to strategy, and how returns would be monitored.

The narrative entered Board updates, investor roadshows, and annual reporting. Stakeholders could now see capital decisions as part of a coherent philosophy, not isolated approvals. This reduced misinterpretation and strengthened confidence.

Kael understood that *if the company did not explain its capital decisions, the market would invent its own story.*

CFO Practice Note:

• Develop a capital allocation communication pack for the Board, analysts, and key investors.
• Include investment volumes, horizon split, ROIC versus hurdle, funding source, and ESG impact.
• Distribute quarterly updates and hold an annual capital allocation discussion with investors where appropriate.

---

355 · Publishing an Annual Capital Allocation Statement — A CFO Signature Document

By month eleven, Kael prepared the first **Capital Allocation Statement** — a public-facing document summarising how the company allocated capital during the year, what returns were achieved, what was deferred or exited, and how the next year's capital priorities would be shaped.

It became his signature document as CFO: clear, accountable, and forward-looking. The statement connected capital deployment with performance, discipline, sustainability, and investor trust.

Kael understood that *publishing a capital allocation statement signalled transparency, not merely performance.*

CFO Practice Note:

• Draft the statement with Investor Relations, Strategy, Finance, and Board Governance teams.

• Align it with the annual report, covering deployment, performance, exits, lessons, and forward priorities.

• Use the statement to set next year's allocation targets, horizon split, and thematic capital priorities.

Practical Tool: Annual Capital Allocation Statement

Capital allocation is where strategy becomes visible.

A company may speak of innovation, resilience, sustainability, customer value, or market expansion. But the real truth lies in where capital is committed, protected, delayed, or withdrawn.

The CFO's annual capital allocation statement should therefore become a signature document. It explains how the organisation used capital, why those choices were made, and how those choices connect to enterprise value.

Illustrative Annual Capital Allocation Statement

During the year, NextAura Global allocated capital with the objective of strengthening long-term enterprise value while preserving liquidity, governance discipline, and strategic flexibility.

The company's capital allocation philosophy is guided by five principles:

1. Capital must follow strategy, not internal politics.
2. Growth capital must clear risk-adjusted return thresholds.
3. Maintenance capital must protect safety, reliability, and operating continuity.
4. Innovation capital must be funded through measurable milestones.
5. No capital commitment should weaken liquidity beyond the board-approved risk appetite.

Capital Allocation Summary

Capital Use	Amount	Strategic Purpose	CFO Assessment
Growth Capex	₹260 crore	Capacity expansion and new market entry	Approved through stage-gate controls
Maintenance Capex	₹90 crore	Plant reliability, safety, and compliance	Necessary and non-discretionary
Digital Transformation	₹75 crore	ERP modernization, automation, analytics	Expected to improve control and reporting speed
Debt Reduction	₹120 crore	Lower leverage and interest cost	Strengthens balance sheet resilience
Innovation Projects	₹45 crore	New product and platform development	Funded through milestone-based release
ESG / Sustainability	₹35 crore	Energy efficiency and regulatory readiness	Supports long-term cost and reputation advantage

Capital Discipline Measures

The company applied hurdle-rate discipline to all major growth investments. Projects were evaluated using NPV, IRR, payback, strategic relevance, risk exposure, and liquidity impact. Capital projects exceeding approved tolerance for cost, timing, or return assumptions were referred back to the Capital Allocation Committee.

Freeze / Defer / Exit Logic

The company deferred ₹80 crore of proposed capital expenditure where demand visibility was insufficient or return assumptions were not adequately supported. Two underperforming projects were placed under review, with further funding restricted until revised business cases are approved.

CFO Statement

Capital is not merely a funding resource. It is a declaration of enterprise belief. Every rupee committed by the company must either strengthen growth, protect resilience, improve capability, or preserve trust.

As CFO, my responsibility is to ensure that capital allocation remains disciplined, transparent, and aligned with the company's long-term purpose.

"Capital should not chase enthusiasm. Capital should follow evidence."

This statement should be reviewed annually by the Board and used as a reference point for budgets, capex approvals, investor communication, and leadership accountability.

CHAPTER 21

Ethics and the CFO's Red Lines

The most valuable asset on a balance sheet is still integrity.
Knowing when to dissent, and when to walk away.

356 · Defining the CFO's Ethical Perimeter — What's Non-Negotiable

By month eleven, Kael Cipher redrafted the **CFO Integrity Charter** — a one-page declaration of what the CFO office would never compromise. It covered accounting transparency, regulatory disclosures, vendor ethics, related-party dealings, conflict protocols, and pressure escalation.

He presented it to the CEO and the Board with one line circled in red ink: "Ethics is not a cost centre; it is a continuity centre." The Board adopted it as policy, and every finance manager signed an acknowledgement. It was not performative; it was protective.

Kael understood that *tone at the top became truth at the bottom only when leaders converted values into visible boundaries.*

CFO Practice Note:

- Draft a concise CFO Integrity Charter and publish it internally.
- List five non-negotiables such as no back-dated entries, no side letters, no

unrecorded liabilities, no concealed losses, and no undocumented overrides.
• Get Board ratification and make the charter part of the CFO office induction kit.

---

357 · Identifying Grey-Zone Pressures in Real Boardrooms

Kael learned that true ethical battles rarely came labelled wrong. They appeared as shades of convenience: a delayed write-off, a friendly valuation, an unspoken political favour, a softened disclosure, or a silence everyone hoped would pass.

He began every Board pack with a footnote: "Material judgement areas: to be reviewed independently." That one line protected him more than any clause because it forced judgement into daylight before pressure could reshape it.

Kael understood that *integrity was tested less in obvious crises and more in convenient decisions that looked harmless at first.*

CFO Practice Note:
• Train finance teams to flag material judgement areas in reports, forecasts, valuations, and disclosures.
• Create a **Grey-Zone Log** for decisions requiring CFO, CEO, and Audit Chair review.
• Schedule quarterly ethical-judgement reviews with internal audit.

---

358 · Framework: Fact → Principle → Action → Consequence

During a high-stakes disclosure review, Kael proposed a decision algorithm that soon became Boardroom discipline: **Fact → Principle → Action → Consequence**.

If facts were unclear, the decision was delayed. If principles conflicted, the matter was escalated. If action created material consequence, the rationale was documented. The process shifted ethics from emotion to structure.

Kael understood that *ethics needed systems as much as spreadsheets did, because pressure rarely waits for reflection.*

CFO Practice Note:
• Institutionalise the four-step ethics filter in key decision templates.
• Require Board-minute references for every ethics-based escalation.
• Audit adherence annually through the Compliance and Ethics Committee.

---

359 · Recognising Early Warning Signs of Governance Drift

Kael noticed the early tremors: Board minutes skipping uncomfortable debates, increasing offline approvals, shortened audit reviews, verbal consents, delayed disclosures, and fewer recorded dissents.

He quietly reinstated governance hygiene — pre-reads, dissent capture, conflict logs, decision registers, and Audit Chair check-ins. The organisation did not need a scandal to prove drift; the drift was already visible in behaviour.

Kael understood that *the absence of debate was not efficiency; it was often the beginning of governance decay.*

CFO Practice Note:

- Track attendance, dissent, deferrals, and unresolved matters in Board minutes.
- Maintain a **Governance Drift Checklist** covering unrecorded debates, skipped disclosures, verbal-only consents, and delayed escalations.
- Report findings in quarterly CEO and Audit Chair one-on-one discussions.

---

360 · Handling Pressure from Promoters, Investors, or Politicians

When a major investor suggested adjusting quarterly guidance to protect sentiment, Kael refused. He sent a one-line note: "Transparency costs less than correction."

He earned temporary silence and permanent trust. The moment also clarified his own perimeter: a CFO could listen to pressure, but could not let pressure rewrite truth.

Kael understood that *courage became cash-flow positive in the long run when it protected credibility before correction became necessary.*

CFO Practice Note:

- Document every external pressure communication involving financial reporting, disclosure, valuation, or guidance.
- Escalate ethically questionable demands to the Audit Chair within 24 hours.
- Maintain a private **Pressure Register** reviewed confidentially each quarter.

---

361 · Whistle-Blower Policy Awareness and Safe-Channel Creation

Kael found the whistle-blower line existed but was unused because employees feared identification. He partnered with HR to move it under an independent third-party hotline with protected routing and clear investigation ownership.

Anonymous cases rose sharply, proving that silence had been systemic. Participation did not mean culture had worsened; it meant the system had finally become safe enough to hear what already existed.

Kael understood that *silence was one of the biggest unpaid liabilities on a balance sheet.*

CFO Practice Note:

• Outsource or firewall the whistle-blower channel to protect independence and anonymity.
• Publish anonymised quarterly summaries of investigations, outcomes, and corrective actions.
• Track resolution time as a formal KPI for ethics culture.

---

362 · Managing Conflicts of Interest and Related-Party Transactions

Kael introduced a real-time **Conflict Register** with automated alerts if any vendor, consultant, director, employee, or related party overlapped with internal entities or decision makers.

He enforced one simple rule: if you benefit, you recuse. Related-party transactions were no longer buried in annual disclosures; they were monitored as live governance risks. The system made transparency ordinary rather than dramatic.

Kael understood that *sunlight remained the cleanest control when personal interest entered corporate decision-making.*

CFO Practice Note:

• Digitise related-party transaction tracking within ERP and vendor onboarding workflows.
• Disclose recurring related-party spends in quarterly Board papers.
• Have independent directors and senior leaders sign conflict acknowledgements annually.

---

363 · Disclosure Protocols for Sensitive Board Matters

Kael built a **Disclosure Committee**, chaired jointly by Legal and Finance. Every market-moving disclosure had to pass through four filters: materiality, timing, clarity, and risk.

The protocol prevented leaks, overstatement, panic, and litigation. It also protected leadership from improvising under pressure. Sensitive matters now moved through disciplined judgement before reaching the market, regulators, or investors.

Kael understood that *good disclosure told the truth in proportion, not in panic.*

CFO Practice Note:

• Establish a standing Disclosure Committee with Legal, Finance, Investor Relations, and Compliance representation.
• Define materiality triggers using financial, market, regulatory, and reputational thresholds.
• Audit the disclosure process annually through external counsel or internal audit.

---

364 · Case Reflection: Kael Cipher's Refusal of a Concealed Loss Adjustment

When a regional controller proposed reclassifying a ₹280 million loss as inventory variance, Kael overruled the entry and reported it transparently.

The quarterly results dipped, but the audit letter used a phrase the company had not heard in years: "true and fair." The result hurt the quarter but strengthened the institution. Kael did not treat the incident as heroism; he treated it as the minimum standard of the chair.

Kael understood that *a CFO should lose deals faster than integrity, because integrity was the office's final balance.*

CFO Practice Note:

• Mandate CFO-level approval for all material reclassifications above the approved threshold.
• Introduce a **Loss Transparency Tracker** for recurring anomalies, write-offs, and classification changes.
• Reward disclosure honesty in performance appraisals.

---

365 · Communication Discipline During Ethical Confrontations

Kael maintained composure in ethical standoffs. He never argued through emotion; he presented evidence. Emails were factual, minutes recorded the issue clearly, and tone remained neutral.

He once told his deputy, "Never shout your integrity — write it." That became a finance discipline: dissent had to be documented, routed properly, and preserved without theatrics.

Kael understood that *calm was often the loudest language in a Boardroom when truth needed protection.*

CFO Practice Note:

- Follow every verbal dissent with a written summary to formal minutes or approved governance records.
- Maintain a **Disagreement Journal** with facts, timestamps, participants, and escalation status.
- Escalate in writing through proper channels only; avoid off-record ethical confrontations.

---

366 · Media and Regulatory Disclosure Ethics

Kael handled the press as if the regulator might be reading, because they usually were. Every media briefing carried approved language, defined boundaries, and legal review where sensitivity required it.

His principle was simple: say it only if you can sign it. Selective truth, even when technically defensible, could become instant risk in a market that archived every word.

Kael understood that *in the age of instant communication, selective truth became instant exposure.*

CFO Practice Note:

- Route all media interactions through Corporate Communications, Legal, and authorised spokesperson protocols.
- Maintain an approved commentary library for quarterly results, guidance, risks, and recurring investor questions.
- Document off-record or non-attributable discussions in internal logs where governance sensitivity exists.

---

367 · Building an Internal Culture of Ethical Reporting

Kael tied ethical behaviour to performance metrics. **Integrity Scorecards** became part of manager KPIs, and bonuses could be reduced for control violations regardless of profit delivery.

The message was clear: ethics was measurable. People stopped treating control breaches as administrative inconvenience and began seeing them as leadership failures. Culture changed because incentives changed.

Kael understood that *culture was shaped by what the organisation rewarded when no one was watching.*

CFO Practice Note:

• Introduce integrity KPIs covering whistle-blower response, audit closure, disclosure accuracy, and control discipline.
• Link bonus eligibility to an ethics compliance index.
• Publish an annual internal **Ethics Dashboard** company-wide.

---

368 · Linking Ethics to Performance Appraisals

Kael redesigned appraisal forms so the first question was: "How did you protect the company this year?"

Managers soon realized ethics was not HR paperwork; it was leadership proof. Performance reviews began capturing incident prevention, transparent escalation, disclosure quality, and decision discipline alongside financial outcomes.

Kael understood that *values were not banners; they were boundaries tested through appraisal, reward, and consequence.*

CFO Practice Note:

• Include ethics KPIs such as incident prevention, disclosure quality, control discipline, and escalation behaviour in appraisals.
• Reward transparency equally with financial achievement.
• Ensure HR audits appraisal narratives annually for integrity content.

---

369 · Crafting an Ethical Decision Tree for Daily Judgement Calls

Kael introduced a visual **Ethical Decision Tree** on every finance floor: Is it legal? Is it transparent? Would you defend it publicly? Would you sign it under oath? Would you be comfortable if the Board read it?

The moment all answers were not yes, the file stopped. The tree worked because it simplified hesitation and gave managers permission to pause without appearing weak.

Kael understood that *most ethical failures were not born from confusion; they were born from convenience that no one interrupted.*

CFO Practice Note:

• Design and display a simplified Ethical Decision Tree in all finance departments.

• Train managers through quarterly scenario workshops.

• Monitor decision-halt cases and analyse root causes.

---

370 · Handling Resignations or Walk-Away Decisions with Grace

Kael prepared his resignation letter the same day he signed his CFO appointment — just in case keeping the income ever required losing integrity.

He taught his team that walking away could be the highest professional KPI. A CFO should never dramatise departure, but should know where the final line stands before pressure tries to move it.

Kael understood that *the hardest numbers were sometimes the ones a CFO refused to change.*

CFO Practice Note:

• Maintain a **Resignation Readiness Checklist** covering legal, financial, ethical, and transition implications.

• Communicate departures factually, with timelines and handover discipline.

• Keep personal notes private; let conduct speak after exit.

---

371 · Post-Crisis Recovery — Protecting Reputation and Morale

After an ethics storm, Kael reinstated morale through truth debriefs — open sessions explaining what happened, what changed, and how the company would heal.

He told managers that a crisis was not the fall; the real damage came from cover-up. Employees did not need theatre. They needed honesty, closure, and proof that systems had improved.

Kael understood that *trust rebuilt faster when leadership spoke before being forced to speak.*

CFO Practice Note:

• Run post-crisis town halls within 30 days of incident closure.

• Publish internal lessons-learned memos without blame or unnecessary exposure.

• Track morale recovery through employee sentiment surveys quarterly.

---

372 · Annual Ethics Statement to Board and Employees

In his twelfth month, Kael signed the company's first **Annual Ethics Statement** — a public declaration that integrity benchmarks had been measured, lapses had been disclosed, and corrective actions had been taken.

He closed with a single line: "Ethics is not an agenda item — it is the agenda." The document became more than a statement. It became the CFO office's annual mirror.

Kael understood that *ethics was not one subject among many; it was the discipline that decided whether every other subject deserved trust.*

CFO Practice Note:

• Issue an annual CFO Ethics Statement co-signed by the CEO and Audit Chair.

• Summarise major ethical metrics, cases, resolutions, repeat themes, and improvement actions.

• Include the statement in the annual report and intranet home page.

Practical Tool: The CFO Ethical Decision Tree

Ethics becomes difficult not when the answer is obvious, but when the pressure is respectable.

A CFO may rarely be asked directly to commit fraud. The real pressure usually arrives in polished language: "Can we defer this?" "Can we adjust the assumption?" "Can we wait one quarter?" "Can we avoid unnecessary panic?" "Can we manage the optics?"

That is why a CFO needs an ethical decision tree before the crisis.

THE CFO ETHICAL DECISION TREE

Step 1: Define the Issue
What exactly is being requested, approved, delayed, hidden, accelerated, reclassified, or represented?

Step 2: Separate Fact from Interpretation
What do we know? What are we assuming? What evidence exists? What is missing?

Step 3: Identify the Rule
Which law, accounting standard, company policy, board direction, contract, covenant, or disclosure obligation applies?

Step 4: Identify the Stakeholders
Who may be affected — shareholders, lenders, employees, customers, regulators, auditors, vendors, or the public?

Step 5: Test the Intent
Is the purpose to improve accuracy, or to improve appearance?
Is the decision being made for business substance, or for optics?

Step 6: Apply the Disclosure Test
Would I be comfortable if this decision appeared in the board minutes, audit file, regulator's note, or public report?

Step 7: Apply the Signature Test
Would I sign this personally, under oath, if questioned two years later?

Step 8: Seek Independent Challenge
Has the matter been reviewed by legal, audit, tax, compliance, or an independent finance leader?

Step 9: Escalate if Necessary
If the issue is material, unresolved, or ethically uncomfortable, escalate to the CEO, Audit Committee Chair, Board Chair, or designated governance channel.

Step 10: Document the Decision
Record the facts, alternatives considered, professional advice obtained, final decision, dissent if any, and communication made.

Red-Line Questions

- Is anyone asking finance to hide economic reality?
- Is the proposed treatment technically possible but morally misleading?
- Is management pressure replacing professional judgement?
- Would silence damage stakeholders who trust the company's numbers?
- Is the CFO being asked to protect comfort instead of credibility?

Kael's ethical rule was simple:

"If a decision needs darkness to survive, it does not belong in the accounts."

A CFO is not expected to be fearless. But he is expected to be clear. Ethical leadership begins when clarity becomes more important than convenience.

Bridge Reflection — From Integrity to Influence

By the twelfth month, Kael Cipher's role had evolved far beyond numbers. He had begun as a controller of facts — he now stood as the custodian of **truth**.

Ethics, governance, and courage had not only defined his credibility; they had **redefined his leadership identity**.
Where the first 180 days were about control, the next 180 were about conviction.

In global boardrooms, every first-time CFO eventually faces the same question — not from auditors, but from time itself:

"What will remain when you leave the room?"

Kael learned that balance sheets can be closed, but **cultures remain open**. He realized the ultimate metric of a CFO is not EBITDA or ROIC — it's **trust multiplied across generations of leaders**.

By embedding ethics into systems, he had laid the foundation for succession — a structure that would think, decide, and act with conscience, even in his absence.

The final act was not about **controlling capital**, but about **creating continuity** —

about mentoring the next generation to protect what was built and evolve what was learned.

And thus began his last chapter — not of accounting, but of **accountability through legacy**.

CHAPTER 22

From First-Time CFO to Business Leader

A true CFO builds an independent system — nurturing succession, influence, and legacy.

373 · Transitioning Mindset — From Finance Head to Enterprise Partner

In his thirteenth month, Kael Cipher stopped being introduced only as the CFO. He had become the enterprise's conscience — the leader people looked to when numbers, ambition, and judgement needed to meet.

He had learned that finance leadership was not about reporting to the business, but reporting for it. He joined strategic offsites not merely to present numbers, but to shape narratives, test assumptions, and connect enterprise choices with long-term consequence.

Kael understood that *the ultimate elevation of a CFO was not a title change, but becoming part of the organisation's collective wisdom.*

CFO Practice Note:

- Attend business reviews as a strategy voice, not merely as a finance validator.
- Co-create annual goals with business heads before plans are finalised, not after them.

• Shift communication from numbers to meaning to mission.

---

374 · Creating a Legacy-Ready Finance Organisation

Kael called his final initiative **Project Continuum** — a framework ensuring the finance office would outlast him. He mapped every critical process, risk, relationship, control, approval route, and decision rhythm.

He then institutionalised them through digital SOPs, control matrices, delegation charters, and continuity folders. When asked if he was preparing to leave, he smiled and said he was preparing the company to never pause.

Kael understood that *legacy was not what remained behind him; it was what continued working when he was no longer in the room.*

CFO Practice Note:
• Document all key decisions, protocols, and governance routines in a **Finance Playbook Vault**.
• Automate process continuity across treasury, reporting, compliance, and Board governance.
• Conduct quarterly succession simulations or temporary CFO handovers to test resilience.

---

375 · Documenting CFO Playbooks for Successors

Kael's final act was authoring the **CFO Playbooks Series** — concise guides titled **Liquidity**, **Leadership**, and **Legacy**. Each playbook combined tactical checklists with ethical reflections, decision tests, and crisis-response examples.

They were designed to mentor without his presence. His philosophy was simple: a manual should not merely tell people what to do; it should teach them how to think when the manual is not enough.

Kael understood that *knowledge that could not be transferred was only experience trapped inside one person.*

CFO Practice Note:
• Create three internal playbooks: **Crisis Control**, **Capital Allocation**, and **Culture Continuity**.
• Publish them on the intranet CFO Hub with version control and access discipline.
• Nominate deputy authors to update the playbooks every fiscal year.

---

376 · Mentoring Upcoming Controllers and Future CFOs

Kael turned his office into a leadership lab. Each Friday, two controllers presented a **CFO-for-a-Day** case, defending capital allocation, liquidity choices, control exceptions, or Board questions under scrutiny.

What began as coaching evolved into succession culture. Managers learned to think beyond their ledgers and speak in the language of enterprise consequence. Kael did not want followers; he wanted future custodians of judgement.

Kael understood that *good leaders created competence, but great leaders created successors.*

CFO Practice Note:

- Host monthly **Finance Leadership Fridays** with case-based mentoring and Board-style questioning.
- Track mentee readiness through a **Succession Readiness Index**.
- Align mentorship goals with Board talent-review and leadership pipeline frameworks.

---

377 · Grooming Finance Talent through Stretch Assignments

Kael rotated high-potential managers into unfamiliar territories — treasury into supply chain, audit into analytics, FP&A into operations, and controllers into investor communication.

By discomfort, he built depth. When asked about his retention strategy, he replied that he did not merely retain talent; he expanded it. People stayed longer because the organisation kept making them larger.

Kael understood that *growth began when comfort ended and capability was tested outside its usual room.*

CFO Practice Note:

- Design six-month cross-functional rotations for the top finance talent pool.
- Track leadership agility scores, not only technical KPIs.
- Recognise and promote adaptability, judgement, and learning speed — not tenure alone.

---

378 · Designing a Structured CFO-Succession Roadmap

Kael presented the Board with a three-tier **CFO Succession Roadmap**: emergency cover for zero to three months, transitional leadership for three to six months, and strategic succession for six to eighteen months.

For the first time, the company had clarity on who would lead finance if tomorrow changed everything. Succession stopped being a sensitive HR topic and became an enterprise resilience mechanism.

Kael understood that *continuity was the truest test of leadership because it proved the system could breathe without one person.*

CFO Practice Note:

• Prepare a succession grid with at least two internal backups and one external benchmark option.
• Align HR, CEO, Audit Committee, and Board Nomination Committee on development timelines.
• Simulate CFO absence once a year to test business resilience.

---

379 · Handover Protocols — Data, Decisions, and Discretion

Kael's final week resembled an audit of himself. He handed over data systems, strategic files, open decisions, pending disclosures, key relationships, sensitive negotiations, and unresolved judgement areas.

His last email contained no advice — only access. That was the point. A successor should inherit clarity, not dependence. The strongest departure was not dramatic; it was disciplined.

Kael understood that *true power was leaving no dependency behind.*

CFO Practice Note:

• Maintain a **Handover Manifest** covering open decisions, pending disclosures, unresolved risks, and key relationships.
• Secure the manifest in Board-accessible, permission-controlled cloud storage.
• Conduct a joint handover meeting with the CEO, Audit Chair, CHRO, and successor present.

---

380 · Story Reflection — Gemma Zessar's Final Lesson

At a global CFO forum, Kael recalled a line from Gemma Zessar, the celebrated journalist-turned-executive who had once told him that profit was the past and purpose was the future.

He repeated the thought at his farewell address. "Profit built our foundation," he said, "but purpose will build our story." The room stood in silence — not applause, but understanding.

Kael understood that *profit could explain what the company had achieved, but purpose decided whether the achievement deserved to continue.*

CFO Practice Note:

• Integrate purpose statements into quarterly CFO letters and leadership communication.
• Measure capital deployed toward sustainability, inclusion, innovation, resilience, and long-term capability.
• Report purpose KPIs alongside ROIC and capital-allocation outcomes in Board packs.

---

381 · Writing the Letter to My Successor — Wisdom Transfer

Kael's final act was deeply personal. He wrote a one-page letter, sealed in an envelope titled **To the Next Custodian of Truth**.

Inside, it read: "Guard the trust you inherit. Question loudly. Decide quietly. Leave the system cleaner than you found it." The letter was not a sentimental farewell; it was a transfer of duty from one custodian to the next.

Kael understood that *wisdom transfer was not about preserving personality; it was about preserving principles.*

CFO Practice Note:

• Encourage outgoing finance leaders to draft succession letters for future officeholders.
• Store such letters in Board archives for transparency, continuity, and institutional memory.
• Share selected excerpts during CFO induction as part of the organisation's leadership tradition.

Practical Tool: CFO Competency Reference Map

A CFO's legacy is not measured only by financial results. It is measured by whether the finance function can continue to think clearly after the CFO leaves the room.

For that reason, Kael Cipher built a CFO Competency Reference Map for his successors and senior finance team. It was not designed as an appraisal form alone. It was a mirror — a way to identify capability, succession readiness, leadership gaps, and the next generation of finance leaders.

A first-time CFO should use this map in three ways:

1. To audit personal readiness.
2. To assess the strength of the finance leadership team.
3. To build a succession roadmap for critical roles.

CFO Competency Reference Map

Competency Area	What It Means	Developing	Proficient	Enterprise-Ready
Financial Stewardship	Ability to protect accuracy, liquidity, controls, and financial truth	Understands reporting and compliance requirements	Ensures reliable numbers, clean controls, and timely reporting	Protects enterprise trust under pressure and guides the board with confidence
Strategic Thinking	Ability to connect finance with business direction	Supports budgets and forecasts	Links financial analysis to strategy and performance	Shapes capital allocation, growth choices, and long-term enterprise value
Treasury and Liquidity Judgement	Ability to manage cash, funding, banking, and financial resilience	Tracks cash balances and debt schedules	Builds forecasts, monitors covenants, and manages lenders	Anticipates liquidity risk and protects optionality before crisis arrives
Business Partnering	Ability to influence sales, operations, HR, supply chain, and technology through financial insight	Provides reports to functions	Helps functions understand cost, margin, cash, and ROI	Becomes a trusted enterprise partner who improves decisions before money is spent
Governance and Ethics	Ability to protect integrity, transparency, and responsible conduct	Follows policies and approval rules	Identifies control gaps and escalates issues responsibly	Holds the ethical line even against pressure from powerful stakeholders
Board Communication	Ability to translate financial complexity into board-level clarity	Prepares data and schedules	Explains performance, risks, and corrective actions clearly	Frames decisions, trade-offs, and uncomfortable truths with courage and precision

Risk Management	Ability to identify, measure, own, and reduce enterprise risk	Understands functional risks	Builds risk registers, heat maps, and mitigation plans	Embeds risk thinking into strategy, budgeting, capital allocation, and culture
Systems and Digital Finance	Ability to use ERP, automation, dashboards, data governance, and analytics	Uses systems for reporting	Improves workflows, controls, and MIS discipline	Builds digital finance capability that improves decision speed and control reliability
Capital Allocation	Ability to evaluate where money should be invested, protected, delayed, or withdrawn	Understands capex proposals	Applies NPV, IRR, WACC, payback, and hurdle-rate discipline	Ensures capital follows strategy, evidence, risk, and enterprise purpose
People Leadership	Ability to build, coach, retain, and renew finance talent	Manages tasks and deadlines	Builds role clarity, KPIs, and team capability	Creates successors, leadership depth, and a finance culture that survives transition
Investor and Lender Confidence	Ability to communicate financial strength, risk, and value creation externally	Supports data requests	Handles lender, investor, and due diligence information	Builds credibility with capital providers through transparency, discipline, and foresight
Change Leadership	Ability to lead transformation without damaging trust	Participates in change projects	Manages adoption, communication, and resistance	Turns finance transformation into a cultural and strategic advantage

Illustrative Competency Assessment

Candidate / Role	Financial Stewardship	Strategy	Treasury	Governance	Board Communication	People Leadership	Overall Readiness
Group Controller	5	3	3	5	3	4	Strong technical successor; needs strategy exposure
FP&A Head	4	5	3	3	4	3	High strategic potential; needs control depth
Treasurer	3	3	5	4	3	3	Strong liquidity leader; needs broader enterprise exposure
Tax Head	4	3	2	5	3	3	Strong governance specialist; needs business partnering
Regional Finance Head	4	4	3	4	4	5	Closest enterprise-ready candidate

CFO Competency Scoring Guide

Score	Readiness Level	Meaning
1	Basic Awareness	Understands the concept but needs close guidance
2	Functional Performer	Can execute within defined scope
3	Independent Leader	Can own the area with limited supervision
4	Enterprise Contributor	Can influence cross-functional decisions
5	Successor-Ready	Can operate at CFO / enterprise leadership level

How the CFO Should Use Competency Reference Map

The map should be reviewed at least twice a year with HR and the CEO. It should not become a tick-box appraisal exercise. Its purpose is to reveal whether the finance function has enough judgement depth to survive pressure, growth, succession, crisis, and transformation.

For each critical finance role, the CFO should identify:

1. Current role holder.
2. Possible successor.
3. Readiness level.
4. Key capability gaps.
5. Required exposure over the next 12 months.
6. Emergency backup if the role becomes vacant.
7. Development action — coaching, rotation, external training, board exposure, project ownership, or cross-functional assignment.

Succession Readiness Categories

Category	Meaning	CFO Action
Ready Now	Can step into a larger role immediately	Give board / CEO exposure and retention focus
Ready in 12 Months	Needs limited development and broader visibility	Assign stretch projects and mentoring
Ready in 24 Months	Has potential but needs deeper capability	Build structured development plan
Specialist Only	Strong expert but not enterprise-ready	Retain as domain expert; avoid forced leadership path
High Risk / No Backup	Critical role has no practical successor	Create urgent succession and documentation plan

Kael treated this map as part of his legacy discipline.

He knew that a CFO who builds only numbers creates dependency. A CFO who builds people creates continuity.

The strongest finance function is not the one where everyone waits for the CFO's answer. It is the one where the right people know how to ask the right questions even when the CFO is absent.

Kael's final note on the map read:

"Do not build a finance team that remembers your instructions. Build one that understands your judgement."

That is when finance becomes institutional.
That is when leadership becomes transferable.
That is when the CFO's legacy begins.

---

382 · Defining Your Legacy — Continuity, Credibility, and Culture

As Kael left the Boardroom for the last time, he paused before the company emblem. Twelve months earlier, he had entered carrying numbers. Now, he left behind a system, a team, and a truth.

Legacy, he realized, was not the applause after departure. It was the silence that still carried your principles when you were no longer present to defend them. The strongest CFO legacy was not personality, power, or position; it was continuity, credibility, and culture working without supervision.

Kael understood that *a CFO's legacy was not written in the contracts he signed, but in the controls, leaders, and ethical habits that kept speaking after him.*

CFO Practice Note:

• Document your **Legacy Index** — systems built, leaders grown, controls strengthened, ethics upheld, and risks reduced.

• Conduct a 365-day retrospective report for the Board covering continuity, credibility, culture, and unresolved priorities.

• Archive the report as the foundation for the next CFO handbook and succession playbook.

PART V

THE CFO'S YEAR-END REFLECTION: Reading the Company the Way the Market Does

Theme: Institutionalise Systems | Modernize Finance | Align with Strategy

Deliverable: Finance Transformation Blueprint — Reporting to Strategic Enablement

When Kael Cipher completed his first year at G Z Corporation, he realized something profound: the market does not see a company the way management does.

Boards measure performance in revenue, margins, and control. Markets measure *belief* — the visible proof that those numbers can sustain themselves under stress.

During his year-end review with the Board and the CEO, Kael presented what he called *The Cipher Memorandum* — a confidential 30-lever diagnostic of enterprise perception and resilience.

It wasn't a financial report.

It was an x-ray of belief: what investors, analysts, regulators, employees, and society would conclude if they studied the company as deeply as he had.

He had examined patterns across more than a hundred conglomerates — from America's manufacturing giants and Europe's precision-driven enterprises to Asia's digital ecosystems and India's diversified majors.
He studied what differentiated companies that retained investor confidence through crises: innovation funding, capital discipline, governance transparency, cyber resilience, succession depth, and ESG maturity.
He benchmarked disclosure quality, leverage tolerance, culture stability, and risk narrative management across Fortune 500 filings, investor briefings, and public-market commentaries.

What emerged was not a SWOT matrix but a **continuum of stewardship** — 30 measurable levers that defined how a CFO translates internal performance into external confidence.

"The market doesn't value what we earn; it values what it can believe we'll sustain." — Kael Cipher, Year-End Memorandum to the Board

Each of the following levers begins with that premise.
They are not academic exercises; they are living dashboards for CFOs who must build the story of trust as carefully as they build the story of profit.

Preface to the Matrix

This framework is built after a comparative review of public-domain investor documents — including annual reports, analyst briefings, ESG ratings, and market-facing company analysis. It distills the recurring levers investors use to value resilience, leadership integrity, capital discipline, and long-term trust. All examples are written in original language, independent of proprietary content.

How to Read This SWOT Matrix

This section translates the classic SWOT framework — Strengths, Weaknesses, Opportunities, and Threats — into 30 investor-grade CFO levers. These levers help a CFO understand how capital markets, lenders, boards, analysts, and institutional investors may evaluate the enterprise beyond reported profit.

Strengths represent internal advantages the market rewards — areas where the company already demonstrates resilience, discipline, credibility, or competitive advantage.

Weaknesses represent internal value leaks — areas where the company may be losing efficiency, trust, visibility, or execution strength.

Opportunities represent growth levers the CFO can activate — areas where capital, technology, partnerships, tax strategy, talent, or intangible assets can create future value.

Threats represent external or structural risks that can damage valuation — including cyber incidents, climate shocks, geopolitical instability, succession gaps, reputation events, and audit failures.

The purpose of this matrix is not academic analysis. It is a practical CFO lens for answering one essential question:

How does the market read the company — and what can the CFO do to strengthen that reading?

STRENGTHS — WHAT THE MARKET REWARDS

LEVER 1 — Innovation Pipeline | Strengths

Kael Cipher Reflection

Innovation dies not when budgets shrink, but when finance stops asking what tomorrow must become.

Present Interpretation

A strong innovation pipeline signals future readiness. Investors do not reward innovation merely because a company spends on research, technology, or product development. They reward it when innovation is structured, funded consistently, linked to strategy, and translated into future revenue visibility.

In many companies, innovation becomes episodic. It rises when profits are strong and disappears when margins tighten. Kael saw this as a dangerous signal. A company that cuts innovation without discipline may protect the quarter but weaken the next three years.

At **Helios Industries**, a composite global engineering group, the CFO ring-fenced an internal innovation pool during a downturn. Instead of treating all development spend as discretionary, finance separated speculative ideas from strategic prototypes, customer-backed pilots, and productivity-linked digital initiatives. This allowed the company to continue building future products without losing capital discipline.

Kael called this the finance function's shift from budget control to future stewardship.

Strategic Implication

A visible innovation pipeline strengthens investor confidence because it connects today's capital allocation with tomorrow's relevance. It tells the market that management is not simply defending current earnings but preparing future earnings capacity.

For the CFO, innovation should not be treated as blind spending. It should be governed like strategic capital. The right question is not, "How much are we spending on innovation?" The better question is, "Which innovation investments can create future cash flows, defensible margins, or enterprise resilience?"

CFO Action Plan

1. **Create a protected innovation budget** linked to strategic priorities and reviewed by the Board.
2. **Separate innovation categories** into core improvement, adjacent growth, and future-option bets.
3. **Track innovation yield** through new-product revenue, time-to-market, customer adoption, and margin potential.
4. **Use stage-gate funding** so weak ideas stop early and strong ideas receive disciplined capital.
5. **Build cross-functional ownership** between Finance, Strategy, Technology, Operations, and Business Units.
6. **Report innovation progress** in investor and Board packs through measurable business outcomes.
7. **Review intangible value carefully** through patents, data assets, proprietary tools, and qualifying development costs where accounting standards permit.

Investor Lens

Visibility | Consistency | Future Readiness | Capital Discipline

Investors reward innovation when it is not vague ambition. They look for discipline, repeatability, disclosure quality, and evidence that innovation can improve future revenue, margin, customer relevance, or competitive advantage.

CFO KPI Proposition

Innovation Revenue Ratio

Revenue from products, platforms, or services launched within the defined recent period as a percentage of total revenue.

Innovation Yield Ratio

Commercial value generated from innovation projects compared with approved innovation investment.

Stage-Gate Conversion Rate

Percentage of innovation projects moving from concept to pilot, pilot to launch, and launch to commercial scale.

LEVER 2 — Supply-Chain Resilience | Strengths

Kael Cipher Reflection

When the world stops moving, only supply chains built on visibility, trust, and alternatives keep breathing.

Present Interpretation

Supply-chain resilience has become a valuation factor, not merely an operational concern. A company may report strong sales and margins, but if its inputs depend on fragile suppliers, unstable routes, weak logistics visibility, or concentrated sourcing, investors may treat those earnings as vulnerable.

Kael saw supply chains as extensions of the balance sheet. Every delayed shipment, failed vendor, blocked port, commodity spike, or geopolitical disruption eventually appears in working capital, margin, customer service, or cash-flow volatility.

At **NovaLink Global**, a composite consumer-technology company, the CFO partnered with Procurement to build a **Supplier Resilience Index**. Vendors were not ranked only by cost. They were assessed by financial health, delivery reliability, ESG exposure, geographic concentration, and dependency risk. This shifted supply-chain conversations from purchase price to continuity value.

Strategic Implication

For the CFO, supply-chain resilience protects cash predictability. A resilient supplier base reduces emergency purchases, production stoppages, inventory shocks, and sudden working-capital strain.

The market reads supply-chain discipline as evidence of operational maturity. If the CFO can quantify supplier concentration, logistics exposure, inventory buffers, and alternate sourcing readiness, the company appears more controlled during volatility.

CFO Action Plan

1. **Map the supply chain financially** by vendor concentration, spend dependency, geography, and working-capital exposure.
2. **Create a Supplier Resilience Index** covering financial health, delivery reliability, ESG compliance, and geopolitical exposure.
3. **Reduce single-source dependency** for critical inputs through dual sourcing or qualified alternate suppliers.

4. **Integrate Treasury and Procurement** to manage FX, commodity, and payment-term exposure.
5. **Build disruption scenarios** for logistics delays, vendor failure, commodity spikes, and regulatory interruptions.
6. **Track operational capital at risk** by measuring working capital exposed to vulnerable suppliers or routes.
7. **Report resilience indicators** to the Board alongside cash, inventory, margin, and customer-service metrics.

Investor Lens

Continuity | Working-Capital Control | Vendor Visibility | Crisis Readiness

Investors reward companies that can show continuity under stress. A CFO who quantifies supply-chain risk and explains mitigation clearly projects control before crisis arrives.

CFO KPI Proposition

Supplier Concentration Ratio
Percentage of critical input spend dependent on the top suppliers.

Operational Capital at Risk
Working capital exposed to vulnerable suppliers, routes, or countries.

Supplier Resilience Score
Composite score covering vendor financial health, delivery reliability, compliance quality, and alternate-source availability.

LEVER 3 — Capital Efficiency | Strengths

Kael Cipher Reflection

Capital is the most expensive employee in the organisation — and the CFO is responsible for making it work.

Present Interpretation

Capital efficiency is one of the clearest signals of CFO quality. Investors do not judge a company only by how much capital it raises or spends. They judge how effectively capital is deployed, recycled, protected, and converted into enterprise value.

Kael treated capital as a living resource. If capital sits trapped in idle assets, slow inventory, weak subsidiaries, poor receivables, or vanity projects, it quietly reduces enterprise agility. If capital moves with discipline, it supports growth, resilience, and shareholder trust.

At **Altair Global Systems**, a composite technology conglomerate, revenue growth looked healthy but enterprise value remained flat. Kael's review showed that too much capital was locked in underperforming assets, slow receivables, and low-return expansion projects. Once the company rationalised assets, reviewed working capital, and reallocated funds toward higher-return initiatives, capital productivity became visible to investors.

Strategic Implication

Capital efficiency translates directly into credibility. A CFO who can explain return on invested capital, asset productivity, working-capital intensity, and reinvestment discipline gives the market confidence that growth is not being purchased at any cost.

The strongest companies do not simply grow. They grow with discipline. They show that every unit of capital is either creating value, protecting value, or returning value.

CFO Action Plan

1. **Define the capital philosophy**: capital must grow, protect, transform, or return value.
2. **Track ROIC against cost of capital** and report the spread to the Board.
3. **Identify trapped capital** in receivables, inventory, idle assets, non-core subsidiaries, and underused facilities.
4. **Introduce capital velocity tracking** to measure how quickly invested capital returns as cash or measurable value.
5. **Review dormant assets periodically** for sale, redeployment, restructuring, or closure.
6. **Create a Capital Allocation Committee** for major investment decisions.
7. **Link leadership incentives** to capital productivity, not only revenue or EBITDA growth.

Investor Lens

ROIC | Capital Discipline | Asset Productivity | Shareholder Trust

Investors reward CFOs who can explain not just profit, but the quality of capital behind that profit. Efficient capital deployment signals discipline, maturity, and respect for shareholder funds.

CFO KPI Proposition

ROIC-WACC Spread
Return on invested capital minus weighted average cost of capital.

Capital Velocity Ratio
Speed at which invested capital converts into cash flow or measurable enterprise value.

Idle Capital Ratio
Capital locked in underperforming, unused, or non-core assets as a percentage of total capital employed.

LEVER 4 — Governance Trust | Strengths

Kael Cipher Reflection

When investors cannot see through the books, they start pricing the silence.

Present Interpretation

Governance trust is a financial strength. It reduces uncertainty, strengthens institutional confidence, improves lender comfort, and protects valuation during difficult periods.

Kael believed that good governance is most visible when something goes wrong. Companies that disclose issues early, explain corrective action clearly, and maintain Board independence tend to retain trust even under pressure. Companies that delay, hide, or over-polish uncomfortable facts invite suspicion.

At **Argon Technologies**, a composite global technology company, a subsidiary governance lapse triggered internal concern. Instead of waiting for external pressure, the CFO commissioned an independent review, briefed the Audit Committee, disclosed the issue appropriately, and strengthened the control framework. The market did not reward the error. It rewarded the speed and seriousness of the response.

Strategic Implication

Governance trust acts like ethical liquidity. In normal times, it may appear invisible. In stress, it becomes the reserve that allows investors, lenders, boards, and employees to continue believing management.

For the CFO, governance trust is built through disclosure quality, audit discipline, Board transparency, related-party clarity, whistle-blower responsiveness, and consistent ethical tone.

CFO Action Plan

1. **Create a Governance Response Index** to track time from issue identification to closure or disclosure.
2. **Integrate audit, compliance, risk, and ESG data** into one CFO oversight dashboard.
3. **Improve disclosure depth** beyond minimum statutory language where material judgement is involved.
4. **Run governance simulations** for crisis disclosure, audit escalation, whistle-blower matters, and regulatory response.
5. **Strengthen Audit Committee visibility** on control failures, repeated issues, and remediation quality.
6. **Link leadership evaluation** partly to control discipline and ethical conduct.
7. **Publish an annual integrity statement** covering governance improvements, ethics metrics, and control progress.

Investor Lens

Transparency | Board Confidence | Disclosure Quality | Ethical Tone

Investors reward governance that reduces ambiguity. A CFO who turns governance into measurable discipline lowers the market's fear of hidden risk.

CFO KPI Proposition

Governance Response Cycle Time
Time taken from identification of material governance issue to closure, escalation, or disclosure.

Repeat Observation Ratio
Percentage of audit or compliance observations recurring across review periods.

Disclosure Completeness Score
Internal or independent assessment of whether material risks, judgements, and governance actions are clearly explained.

LEVER 5 — ESG Integration | Strengths

Kael Cipher Reflection

Sustainability is not a slide in the investor deck; it is a test of whether value can endure.

Present Interpretation

ESG integration becomes a strength when it is connected to business economics. If ESG remains a separate reporting exercise, it may satisfy disclosure requirements but rarely changes enterprise value. If ESG is embedded into capital allocation, operating efficiency, risk management, and stakeholder trust, it becomes financially meaningful.

Kael treated ESG as a CFO agenda because environmental exposure, labour practices, governance quality, energy cost, safety standards, and supply-chain ethics all carry financial consequences.

At **Helios Energy Group**, a composite utilities and industrial company, ESG moved from annual reporting to operating dashboards. Carbon intensity, safety performance, supplier ethics, and energy efficiency were linked to capital approvals and leadership scorecards. This changed sustainability from external messaging to internal management discipline.

Strategic Implication

The CFO's role is to translate ESG from intent into measurable enterprise impact. Energy efficiency can reduce operating cost. Better safety can reduce disruption and insurance exposure. Strong governance can lower reputational risk. Responsible supply chains can protect customer and investor confidence.

The strongest ESG story is not moral language. It is credible linkage between sustainability, risk reduction, cost of capital, and long-term resilience.

CFO Action Plan

1. **Map ESG to enterprise value** by identifying cost, risk, revenue, and funding implications.
2. **Embed ESG metrics into capital approval** for major projects.
3. **Digitise ESG data collection** across energy, emissions, safety, diversity, supplier compliance, and governance indicators.
4. **Integrate ESG into Board dashboards** alongside financial, risk, and operating metrics.

5. **Evaluate ESG-linked financing opportunities** where performance targets are credible and measurable.
6. **Obtain assurance over material ESG data** where investor reliance or regulatory requirement is significant.
7. **Publish integrated reporting** that connects ESG performance with financial strategy and risk management.

Investor Lens

Resilience | Sustainability Discipline | Risk Reduction | Funding Advantage

Investors reward ESG when it is measurable, assured, and financially connected. The CFO must make ESG credible by linking it to cash flow, cost, risk, capital access, and governance.

CFO KPI Proposition

ESG Value Linkage Score
Percentage of material ESG initiatives linked to measurable financial, operating, or risk outcomes.

Sustainability-Linked Capital Ratio
Share of funding connected to credible ESG or sustainability-linked instruments.

ESG Data Assurance Coverage
Percentage of material ESG metrics subject to internal audit, external assurance, or formal control review.

LEVER 6 — Data Integrity & Cyber Security | Strengths

Kael Cipher Reflection

Financials do not collapse only because numbers are wrong. They collapse when no one trusts where the numbers came from.

Present Interpretation

Data integrity and cyber security are now core financial strengths. A company can have strong accounting policies, but if the underlying data is fragmented, manually adjusted, poorly controlled, or vulnerable to cyber compromise, investor confidence weakens.

Kael saw data as the hidden foundation of every financial statement. Revenue, inventory, margins, cash flow, forecasts, ESG metrics, and risk dashboards all depend on trusted data lineage. If data quality fails, the CFO's narrative fails.

At **OrionX Logistics**, a composite supply-chain enterprise, a small manipulation in shipment timestamps affected margin reporting, sales accruals, inventory assumptions, and cash-conversion analysis. The issue was not large in isolation, but it exposed a serious weakness: the company could not prove its numbers quickly enough.

For Kael, cyber security belonged partly to the CFO because a cyber incident can become a liquidity event, reporting event, disclosure event, and trust event.

Strategic Implication

Data integrity strengthens auditability, forecasting quality, Board confidence, and investor communication. Cyber security protects not only systems but financial credibility.

The CFO does not need to become the CIO. But the CFO must ensure that finance-critical data, ERP access, treasury systems, reporting tools, vendor masters, customer masters, and payment workflows are governed with discipline.

CFO Action Plan

1. **Establish a Data Ownership Charter** for finance-critical data elements.
2. **Define the single source of truth** for revenue, margin, cash, working capital, debt, inventory, and ESG metrics.
3. **Map cyber risk to financial exposure** including revenue loss, system downtime, fraud, penalties, and disclosure impact.
4. **Implement continuous data assurance** across ERP, treasury, CRM, SCM, and reporting systems.
5. **Include cyber metrics in finance dashboards** such as access exceptions, incident response time, and critical-system uptime.
6. **Run CFO-led cyber simulations** for ransomware, payment compromise, data corruption, and reporting disruption.
7. **Tie data quality to accountability** through controllership, FP&A, treasury, and system-owner scorecards.

Investor Lens

Auditability | Predictability | Control Maturity | System Resilience

Investors reward companies that can prove the origin, integrity, and reliability of their numbers. Strong data governance reduces uncertainty and improves confidence in management reporting.

CFO KPI Proposition

Data Trust Coefficient
Percentage of finance-critical data elements meeting lineage, accuracy, ownership, and reconciliation standards.

Finance System Resilience Score
Composite measure of uptime, incident response, access control, backup integrity, and recovery readiness.

Cyber Financial Exposure Ratio
Estimated financial exposure from cyber events as a percentage of EBITDA or operating cash flow.

LEVER 7 — Succession Depth | Strengths

Kael Cipher Reflection

A company is not judged only by who leads it today, but by who can lead it tomorrow without panic.

Present Interpretation

Succession depth is a governance strength. Investors, lenders, boards, and rating agencies become uncomfortable when leadership continuity depends too heavily on one individual.

Kael viewed succession as risk management in human form. A company may have strong systems, but if only one person understands key lender relationships, Board narratives, treasury logic, tax exposures, or investor communication, the organisation carries hidden key-person risk.

At **Helix Manufacturing Group**, a composite industrial company, an unexpected CEO transition occurred during a major refinancing cycle. The transition did not damage lender confidence because the CFO office had already developed second-line leaders who could speak to cash flow, capital allocation, operations, and risk. Succession depth protected credibility.

Strategic Implication

Succession depth reduces continuity risk. It protects strategy, Board rhythm, investor communication, lender confidence, and operational execution.

For the CFO, succession planning must extend beyond the CFO role. Treasury, FP&A, controllership, tax, compliance, investor relations, shared services, and digital finance all require backups and leadership pipelines.

CFO Action Plan

1. **Map critical finance roles** by business impact, control ownership, and replacement difficulty.
2. **Build a succession matrix** showing ready-now, ready-soon, and development-stage successors.
3. **Create capability ladders** across FP&A, treasury, tax, controllership, IR, M&A, and digital finance.
4. **Run leadership simulations** where successors present to the Board, lenders, or internal committees.
5. **Integrate succession into risk reporting** as a formal governance indicator.
6. **Link leadership incentives** to bench development and knowledge transfer.
7. **Communicate continuity carefully** to investors through governance language, without exposing confidential succession names.

Investor Lens

Continuity | Bench Strength | Governance Maturity | Leadership Stability

Investors value companies that are not personality-dependent. Deep succession tells the market that strategy, controls, and communication can survive leadership change.

CFO KPI Proposition

Bench Strength Readiness Ratio
Percentage of critical finance roles with identified ready-now or ready-soon successors.

Key-Person Dependency Index
Weighted score of roles where knowledge, relationships, or controls depend heavily on one individual.

Leadership Simulation Coverage
Percentage of identified successors tested through Board, crisis, investor, or operational simulations.

LEVER 8 — Investor Visibility | Strengths

Kael Cipher Reflection

Markets do not fear bad news as much as they fear silence.

Present Interpretation

Investor visibility is the discipline of communicating before uncertainty becomes speculation. It is not public relations. It is financial trust management.

Kael believed investors reward companies that maintain a predictable communication rhythm, explain performance movements clearly, disclose risks honestly, and respond to volatility quickly. When communication is late or shallow, markets often fill the gap with harsher assumptions.

At **Aurum Digital Systems**, a composite technology company, operating margins fell due to raw-material pressure. Instead of waiting for the quarterly call, the CFO issued a clear investor note explaining the margin bridge, mitigation plan, pricing response, and expected recovery path. The company did not avoid market pressure, but it avoided narrative chaos.

Strategic Implication

Investor visibility reduces uncertainty premium. It helps analysts model the business more accurately, gives institutional investors confidence in management, and protects the company during temporary shocks.

The CFO must ensure that investor communication is consistent across filings, earnings calls, presentations, lender updates, press statements, and Board reports.

CFO Action Plan

1. **Build a quarterly investor communication calendar** covering results, guidance, lender reviews, rating-agency updates, and investor meetings.
2. **Create a CFO-controlled guidance framework** with scenario bands, assumptions, and sensitivity drivers.
3. **Standardise earnings communication** around demand, margin, cash conversion, capital allocation, risk, and forward outlook.
4. **Track analyst questions and sentiment** after every major communication cycle.
5. **Respond early during volatility** with short, factual, and controlled updates where appropriate.

6. **Maintain one validated financial dataset** across IR, FP&A, treasury, corporate finance, and leadership.
7. **Train second-line finance leaders** to communicate numbers with clarity and confidence.

Investor Lens

Visibility | Consistency | Clarity | Responsiveness

Investors reward CFOs who reduce uncertainty through timely, precise, and consistent communication. A CFO who shows up before being forced to explain becomes an anchor of trust.

CFO KPI Proposition

Disclosure Predictability Index
Investor communications delivered as per approved calendar divided by total scheduled communications.

Guidance Accuracy Variance
Difference between actual results and guidance midpoint or range, tracked consistently over time.

Investor Query Resolution Time
Average time taken to respond to material investor, analyst, lender, or rating-agency queries.

WEAKNESSES — WHERE VALUE LEAKS

LEVER 9 — Regulatory Exposure | Weaknesses

Kael Cipher Reflection

Regulation does not punish mistakes alone. It punishes organisations that are surprised by what they should have seen coming.

Present Interpretation

Regulatory exposure is one of the quietest weaknesses in an enterprise. It rarely appears dangerous during growth, but when scrutiny begins, it can affect cash flow, shipments, licenses, margins, disclosures, investor confidence, and Board credibility.

Kael viewed regulation as a financial foresight issue, not only a legal matter. A company may have strong revenue, but if its compliance calendar is weak, filings are delayed, sector rules are changing, or regulators are already signalling concern, the CFO is carrying hidden risk.

At **NovaMed Health Systems**, a composite healthcare company, a delayed response to updated pricing rules triggered penalties, shipment restrictions, working-capital stress, and rating-agency concern. The issue did not begin as a liquidity problem, but it quickly became one.

For Kael, regulatory exposure was not paperwork. It was cash-flow risk with legal language.

Strategic Implication

Regulatory exposure weakens valuation because it creates uncertainty. Investors and lenders do not like unclear contingent liabilities, unresolved notices, licensing dependency, tax disputes, ESG compliance gaps, or weak documentation trails.

The CFO must convert regulation from reactive compliance into a forward-looking risk discipline. This means identifying upcoming regulatory shifts, modelling financial impact, assigning owners, and keeping the Board informed before notices become crises.

CFO Action Plan

1. **Build a Regulatory Heat Map** covering tax, labour, environmental, data protection, pricing, licensing, antitrust, and sector-specific exposure.
2. **Create 12-month Regulatory Calendar tracking filings**, renewals, inspections, consultation papers, draft rules, and expected changes.
3. **Run regulatory scenario modelling** for new taxes, pricing restrictions, ESG mandates, licensing delays, data penalties, and compliance capex.
4. **Integrate compliance into monthly close** through pending filings, notices, deviations, remediation status, and potential financial exposure.
5. **Establish CFO–Legal joint ownership** where Legal interprets the rule and Finance quantifies the consequence.
6. **Educate the Board quarterly** on material regulatory changes, exposure, mitigation, and unresolved matters.
7. **Strengthen documentation discipline** so every material position has evidence, approval, ownership, and review history.

Investor Lens

Predictability | Control | Governance Quality | Risk Containment

Investors watch regulatory exposure because it can quickly convert into penalties, business interruption, qualification risk, or valuation discount. A CFO who can show readiness, documentation, and scenario planning reduces uncertainty.

CFO KPI Proposition

Regulatory Compliance Health Index

Weighted score across on-time filings, inspections, notices, regulatory responses, control remediation, and disclosure compliance.

Regulatory Financial Impact Ratio

Total penalties, fines, settlements, and compliance-related losses divided by EBITDA.

Notice-to-Closure Cycle Time

Average number of days between receipt of a regulatory notice and formal closure or resolution.

LEVER 10 — FX & Commodity Vulnerability | Weaknesses

Kael Cipher Reflection

Companies do not lose money on currencies or commodities. They lose money on assumptions left untested.

Present Interpretation

FX and commodity vulnerability can quietly damage margins even when operations appear healthy. The risk is not only exchange-rate movement or input-cost inflation. The deeper weakness is poor exposure mapping, weak pricing pass-through, delayed hedging, procurement–treasury disconnect, and budget assumptions that ignore volatility.

Kael saw FX and commodity exposure as business-model risk. If raw materials, imported inputs, foreign debt, export revenue, leases, capex commitments, or inter-company flows are exposed to market movement, the CFO must know where the risk sits and how quickly it can affect EBITDA, cash flow, and guidance.

At **Titanium Auto Components**, a composite auto-parts company, currency movement and steel-price escalation compressed margins, delayed capex, and weakened investor confidence. The issue was not volatility itself. The issue was the company's inability to pass through, hedge, or explain the impact in time.

Strategic Implication

FX and commodity weakness creates earnings volatility. Investors may accept market movement, but they penalise poor preparedness. If management cannot explain exposures, hedge ratios, pricing clauses, procurement timing, and margin sensitivity, the company appears reactive.

The CFO's role is to convert exposure into a governed system: measured, hedged where appropriate, stress-tested, priced into contracts, and clearly reported to the Board.

CFO Action Plan

1. **Build a Currency and Commodity Exposure Map** covering revenue, purchases, capex, debt, leases, inter-company flows, and supplier contracts.
2. **Create a Hedging Policy Playbook** defining eligible exposures, instruments, coverage ratios, tenors, counterparties, and approval limits.

3. **Establish pass-through governance** through price-reset clauses, surcharge mechanisms, dealer communication, and customer-contract review.
4. **Integrate FX and commodity scenarios into budgets** using base, adverse, and severe cases.
5. **Synchronise Procurement and Treasury** so purchase timing and hedge execution do not move independently.
6. **Run quarterly stress tests** for major currency pairs, interest rates, energy costs, freight, and key raw materials.
7. **Report exposure transparently** to the Board through sensitivity tables, margin bridges, and mitigation actions.

Investor Lens

Hedging Discipline | Margin Stability | Scenario Preparedness | Pricing Power

Investors look for evidence that volatility is understood before it appears in results. A CFO who can show exposure, policy, sensitivity, and mitigation protects confidence even when markets move sharply.

CFO KPI Proposition

FX Exposure Coverage Ratio
Hedged eligible FX exposure divided by total identified FX exposure.

Commodity Cost Variance Ratio
Actual commodity cost variance from budget or approved benchmark divided by budgeted commodity cost.

Pass-Through Efficiency Rate
Value of cost increases recovered from customers divided by total FX or commodity-driven cost increase.

LEVER 11 — Talent Attrition & Capability Gaps | Weaknesses

Kael Cipher Reflection
Companies do not run out of capability suddenly. They lose it one quiet resignation at a time.

Present Interpretation

Talent attrition is not only an HR issue. In finance, it can become a control risk, forecasting risk, reporting risk, audit risk, and Board-confidence risk.

Kael believed that the strength of a finance function depends not on headcount, but on capability depth. A company may have enough people, yet still be fragile if only a few individuals understand treasury models, tax positions, consolidation logic, pricing simulations, investor communication, or critical ERP workflows.

At **Lumina Retail Holdings**, a composite retail group, the exit of several mid-level finance managers delayed monthly close, increased vendor disputes, weakened cash forecasting, and created errors in pricing models. The financial statements were still produced, but the rhythm of trust was damaged.

Strategic Implication

Capability gaps weaken execution reliability. They slow decisions, increase errors, reduce strategic speed, and create dependence on a few individuals. Investors may not see attrition directly, but they eventually see its effects in delayed reporting, missed forecasts, audit observations, and weak operating discipline.

For the CFO, talent stability is part of financial resilience. The finance function must be built as a leadership bench, not a collection of replaceable roles.

CFO Action Plan

1. **Map capability gaps across finance** including FP&A, treasury, tax, controllership, IR, shared services, analytics, and digital finance.
2. **Build a Finance Talent Heat Map** showing attrition risk, capability shortage, succession risk, and critical-role dependency.
3. **Create a CFO-led Talent Council** to review succession, development, hiring priorities, and retention risks.
4. **Rotate high-potential leaders** across plants, audits, treasury, FP&A, M&A, investor relations, and business finance.
5. **Build structured onboarding sprints** so new finance talent becomes effective within 30, 60, and 90 days.
6. **Strengthen mid-management depth** because this layer carries institutional memory and execution discipline.
7. **Link leadership evaluation** to retention, successor development, and knowledge-transfer quality.

Investor Lens

Depth | Continuity | Execution | Discipline

Investors value organisations that are not dependent on a few people. A stable, skilled finance team supports better forecasting, cleaner reporting, faster close, and stronger governance.

CFO KPI Proposition

Critical Role Retention Ratio
Number of high-impact finance roles retained for a defined period divided by total high-impact finance roles.

Capability Gap Severity Score
Weighted score of capability shortages across FP&A, treasury, tax, controllership, IR, shared services, and analytics.

Finance Skill Maturity Index
Assessment of finance-team proficiency across modelling, analytics, digital tools, controls, scenario planning, and business partnering.

LEVER 12 — Legacy Technology Debt | Weaknesses

Kael Cipher Reflection

Legacy systems do not fail overnight. They fail one quiet workaround at a time.

Present Interpretation

Legacy technology debt is financial decay hidden inside systems. It shows up as manual reconciliations, spreadsheet dependency, outdated ERP modules, fragmented workflows, delayed close cycles, duplicate data entry, and inconsistent reporting definitions.

Kael viewed technology debt as a CFO issue because weak systems distort numbers. If revenue, inventory, margin, rebates, vendor balances, customer data, and forecasts are managed across disconnected tools, the company may be producing reports faster than it is producing truth.

At **Arcturus Consumer Goods**, a composite consumer company, outdated systems caused mis posted revenue, provisioning errors, inventory confusion, delayed closing, and unexplained margin leakage. The company did not have one large failure. It had hundreds of small system weaknesses that eventually became a Board-level problem.

Strategic Implication

Technology debt weakens forecasting, controls, working capital, audit quality, and operating speed. It also increases dependency on individuals who know how to "make the system work" through manual patches.

The CFO must treat technology modernisation as a value-protection agenda, not an IT wishlist. The first step is to quantify the cost of manual work, errors, delays, rework, and control exposure.

CFO Action Plan

1. **Conduct a Technology Debt Diagnostic** across ERP, treasury, consolidation, procurement, revenue, inventory, HR, and reporting systems.
2. **Build a 24-month modernisation roadmap** prioritising order-to-cash, procure-to-pay, record-to-report, inventory, FP&A, and revenue assurance.
3. **Create a CFO-owned process architecture** so technology follows process discipline rather than vendor convenience.
4. **Quantify manual work cost** in reconciliations, offline reporting, duplicate entry, journal posting, and exception handling.
5. **Deploy automation in high-volume areas** such as invoice processing, bank reconciliation, credit scoring, and demand planning.
6. **Strengthen master-data governance** across customer, vendor, product, pricing, cost centre, and tax master data.
7. **Report transformation progress to the Board** through benefits realized, risks reduced, adoption, and financial return.

Investor Lens

Process Maturity | System Resilience | Forecast Quality | Execution Discipline

Investors may not inspect ERP screens, but they notice the symptoms of technology debt: delayed reporting, recurring errors, weak forecasts, working-capital instability, and transformation overruns.

CFO KPI Proposition

Legacy System Dependency Ratio

Percentage of core finance processes still dependent on legacy, manual, or spreadsheet-based workflows.

Automation Coverage Index
Number of automated finance processes divided by total finance processes in scope.

Close Cycle Efficiency
Time taken to close books, adjusted for accuracy, post-close corrections, and material rework.

LEVER 13 — Working-Capital Inefficiency | Weaknesses

Kael Cipher Reflection

Liquidity is rarely lost in one crisis. It leaks daily through habits no one challenges.

Present Interpretation

Working capital reveals the company's real operating discipline. It shows whether sales convert into cash, whether inventory reflects demand, whether vendors trust payment behaviour, and whether functions work together or protect their own targets.

Kael saw working capital as one of the most honest indicators of leadership maturity. EBITDA may look healthy, but if receivables stretch, inventory bloats, vendor terms weaken, and cash conversion slows, the company is financing inefficiency.

At **Vesper Consumer Technologies**, a composite business, collections slowed, inventory expanded, vendor credit tightened, debt increased, and planned capex had to be deferred. The problem was not a sudden crisis. It was weak daily discipline across sales, supply chain, procurement, and finance.

Strategic Implication

Working-capital inefficiency reduces strategic freedom. It increases borrowing, raises interest cost, weakens vendor confidence, delays growth investment, and reduces earnings quality.

The CFO must frame working capital as an enterprise issue, not a finance metric. Sales owns collection quality. Supply chain owns inventory quality. Procurement owns vendor discipline. Finance owns visibility, governance, and escalation.

CFO Action Plan

1. **Build a Cash Conversion Cycle Dashboard** tracking DSO, DPO, inventory days, overdue receivables, vendor past dues, and slow-moving stock.
2. **Create a working-capital playbook** covering credit approvals, billing discipline, collections, disputes, inventory rules, and vendor payment governance.
3. **Link sales incentives to cash quality** through DSO, overdue receivables, and collection discipline.
4. **Align procurement KPIs** with payment discipline, vendor sustainability, and negotiated terms.
5. **Run weekly cash war rooms** for top customers, top vendors, disputed invoices, and slow-moving inventory.
6. **Deploy digital tools** for automated reminders, credit scoring, dispute tracking, dynamic discounting, and inventory optimization.
7. **Educate the Board** on cash conversion as a quality-of-earnings indicator.

Investor Lens

Cash Quality | Discipline | Control | Predictability

Investors watch the gap between profit and cash. A company with strong working-capital discipline appears more resilient because it converts performance into liquidity.

CFO KPI Proposition

Cash Conversion Cycle

DSO + Inventory Days – DPO.

Working-Capital Intensity Ratio

Net working capital divided by revenue.

Overdue Receivables Ratio

Receivables overdue beyond the defined threshold divided by total receivables.

LEVER 14 — Ownership Governance Opacity | Weaknesses

Kael Cipher Reflection

Capital flees ambiguity faster than it flees volatility.

Present Interpretation

Markets do not punish founder-led, family-owned, sovereign-backed, or promoter-led companies merely because ownership is concentrated. They punish opacity.

Kael saw ownership governance opacity as a major weakness when related-party transactions are unclear, Board independence appears weak, disclosures are selective, decision rights are concentrated, or minority investors cannot understand how capital is being used.

At **AstraNova Retail**, a composite listed company, routine questions around land transfers between ownership-linked entities and the operating business created investor concern. The issue was not proven misconduct. The issue was insufficient clarity. In capital markets, unclear can become expensive long before illegal is established.

This is why Kael preferred the broader term **Ownership Governance Opacity**. It applies not only to promoters, but to any ownership structure where control, disclosure, and minority-interest protection require extra clarity.

Strategic Implication

Ownership opacity increases the perceived governance risk premium. Investors may discount valuations if they feel that insiders have better information, related-party dealings are not transparent, or the Board cannot independently challenge capital decisions.

The CFO becomes the custodian of "truth symmetry" — ensuring that the Board, investors, auditors, lenders, and regulators receive consistent and complete information.

CFO Action Plan

1. **Reconstruct the related-party map** covering ownership-linked entities, directors, key executives, affiliates, and recurring transactions.
2. **Create transparent transaction protocols** for approval, pricing, disclosure, benchmarking, and independent review.
3. **Launch governance heat maps** covering late disclosures, opaque notes, related-party exposure, and inconsistencies across investor materials and statutory filings.
4. **Strengthen Board packs** so independent directors receive full visibility on capital allocation, vendor concentration, and related-party dealings.
5. **Standardise investor narratives** for unusual cash movements, contingent liabilities, ownership-linked transactions, and material variances.

6. **Strengthen internal audit independence** around ownership-sensitive areas.
7. **Report governance metrics quarterly** on disclosures, audit adjustments, whistle-blower cases, insider-trading controls, and related-party compliance.

Investor Lens

Credibility | Independence | Transparency | Disclosure Rhythm

Investors reward ownership structures that reduce information asymmetry. When the CFO improves clarity around related parties, capital flows, and governance processes, the market can judge the business rather than fear the structure.

CFO KPI Proposition

Governance Transparency Index
Percentage of material governance disclosures meeting defined standards for clarity, completeness, timeliness, and Board approval.

Related-Party Exposure Ratio
Value of related-party transactions divided by total operating costs, revenue, or procurement spend, depending on the exposure type.

Independent Review Coverage
Percentage of material related-party or ownership-sensitive transactions reviewed by independent directors, internal audit, or external advisors.

LEVER 15 — Capex Indiscipline | Weaknesses

Kael Cipher Reflection
Bad capex does not destroy cash first. It destroys credibility first.

Present Interpretation

Capex indiscipline begins when projects are approved on optimism instead of evidence. It appears in inflated demand projections, weak hurdle rates, incomplete execution planning, unclear ownership, missing post-completion audits, and reluctance to stop underperforming projects.

Kael believed capex mistakes are dangerous because they compound slowly. A poor project can consume cash, increase debt, distort working capital, weaken ROIC, distract leadership, and damage investor confidence for years.

At **Meridian Foods**, a composite manufacturing company, a large plant expansion was approved on ambitious demand assumptions. When demand did not materialise, return on capital fell, debt pressure increased, and the Board had to revisit capital allocation discipline. The lesson was clear: the approval document had been more confident than the market reality.

Strategic Implication

Capex indiscipline weakens capital productivity and signals poor governance. Investors tolerate business risk. They are less forgiving when management repeatedly approves projects without post-audit accountability or realistic sensitivity analysis.

The CFO's role is not to block investment. It is to ensure capital is deployed with discipline, monitored with honesty, and stopped when assumptions fail.

CFO Action Plan

1. **Establish a Capital Allocation Committee** with Finance-led review and cross-functional accountability.
2. **Use risk-weighted hurdle rates** based on project type, geography, currency, execution risk, and strategic uncertainty.
3. **Deploy stage-gate controls** so projects move only after demand validation, cost benchmarking, funding clarity, and execution readiness.
4. **Maintain capex dashboards** tracking approved cost, actual cost, timeline, commissioning, throughput, and benefit realisation.
5. **Enforce post-investment audits** comparing actual IRR, payback, ROIC, EBITDA, and cash impact against original projections.
6. **Define exit or redesign triggers** for projects that breach cost, time, demand, or return thresholds.
7. **Link leadership bonuses** partly to capital productivity and post-completion performance.

Investor Lens

Capital Productivity | Execution Discipline | Realism | Narrative Integrity

Investors reward companies that allocate capital with discipline and admit when assumptions change. Capex credibility grows when projects are measured after approval, not celebrated only at announcement.

CFO KPI Proposition

Capital Discipline Ratio
Percentage of completed projects meeting approved hurdle rate, payback, IRR, or ROIC targets.

Capex Variance Index
Actual project cost minus approved project cost, divided by approved project cost.

Post-Completion Audit Coverage
Percentage of material capex projects reviewed after completion against original business case assumptions.

LEVER 16 — Disclosure Depth Gaps | Weaknesses

Kael Cipher Reflection
When disclosures are thin, markets write their own story — and that story is rarely generous.

Present Interpretation

Disclosure depth gaps weaken market trust. A company may comply technically, but if its disclosures do not explain drivers, risks, assumptions, judgements, and future indicators clearly, investors may assume hidden weakness.

Kael believed disclosure is not only compliance. It is capital communication. Investors, lenders, analysts, and directors need enough context to understand what changed, why it changed, whether it is temporary or structural, and how management is responding.

At **Verdant Mobility**, a composite mobility company, revenue declined because of a temporary tooling transition. The annual report gave only a brief explanation, and the market interpreted it as demand weakness. The issue was not only performance. It was narrative absence.

Strategic Implication

Weak disclosure increases uncertainty premium. It can widen analyst variance, slow credit decisions, invite governance concerns, and create avoidable volatility.

The CFO must ensure that disclosures are not merely accurate, but useful. Strong disclosure explains cash flow, margins, debt, segment movement, risks, contingencies, related-party transactions, accounting estimates, and forward indicators with enough clarity for serious investors to interpret the business fairly.

CFO Action Plan

1. **Build a Disclosure Depth Framework** defining minimum explanation standards for risks, cash flow, debt, margins, segments, estimates, and contingencies.
2. **Enhance Management Discussion and Analysis** with driver-level explanations, margin bridges, cash-flow commentary, and sensitivity tables.
3. **Publish forward-looking indicators** such as demand visibility, utilisation, order book, funding headroom, or guidance ranges where appropriate.
4. **Improve related-party transparency** through clear categorisation, commercial rationale, approval process, and exposure quantification.
5. **Upgrade note-level precision** around accounting estimates, provisions, off-balance-sheet items, commitments, and contingent liabilities.
6. **Align disclosures with global expectations** while staying compliant with local reporting frameworks.
7. **Train finance leaders in investor-grade storytelling** for earnings calls, Board packs, lender reviews, and annual reporting.

Investor Lens

Clarity | Continuity | Context | Credibility

Investors reward companies that reduce ambiguity. Strong disclosure does not eliminate bad news, but it prevents misinterpretation and helps the market price the business more fairly.

CFO KPI Proposition

Disclosure Quality Index
Weighted score across narrative depth, risk clarity, note detail, segment explanation, cash-flow commentary, and forward indicators.

Analyst Consensus Variance
Standard deviation of analyst estimates for key metrics such as EPS, EBITDA, revenue, or free cash flow.

Disclosure Query Ratio
Number of recurring investor, auditor, lender, or Board questions caused by unclear disclosures divided by total material disclosures reviewed.

OPPORTUNITIES — THE CFO'S GROWTH LEVERS

LEVER 17 — Digital Transformation & AI Integration | Opportunities

Kael Cipher Reflection

AI will not replace CFOs. But CFOs who ignore intelligence, automation, and data discipline will lose ground to those who use them well.

Present Interpretation

Digital transformation is not a technology project. For the CFO, it is a financial acceleration strategy. When finance processes remain manual, fragmented, or spreadsheet-dependent, the organisation loses speed, accuracy, and predictive power.

Kael viewed AI as a leverage multiplier only when the foundation was strong. Clean data, defined ownership, process discipline, control architecture, and user adoption had to come before ambitious automation. Without that, AI merely accelerates confusion.

At **NovusMax Industries**, a composite multinational, the CFO introduced AI-driven procurement analytics, cash-flow forecasting, anomaly detection, and automated reconciliation. The value did not come from replacing people. It came from freeing finance leaders to spend less time processing data and more time challenging assumptions.

Strategic Implication

Digital finance creates opportunity through speed, accuracy, and foresight. It shortens reporting cycles, improves forecast quality, strengthens controls, and gives management earlier warning signals.

Investors increasingly reward companies that can explain their digital maturity in practical terms: faster close, cleaner data, predictive forecasts, automated controls, lower manual effort, and better decision cadence.

The CFO's job is not to chase technology. The CFO's job is to ensure digital investment improves enterprise judgement.

CFO Action Plan

1. **Create a 36-month Digital Finance Roadmap** covering FP&A automation, smart close, treasury analytics, procurement intelligence, and risk monitoring.
2. **Build an AI-ready data stack** with clean master data, data ownership, governance rules, and model-quality protocols.
3. **Deploy predictive FP&A models** for demand, cash, margin, churn, working capital, and scenario planning.
4. **Automate the close** through auto-reconciliations, journal-entry checks, variance alerts, and exception workflows.
5. **Digitise procurement and payables** using supplier risk scoring, dynamic discounting, invoice automation, and spend analytics.
6. **Embed AI in treasury** for liquidity forecasting, FX exposure tracking, hedge monitoring, and cash-pool optimization.
7. **Train finance teams** in BI tools, analytics literacy, AI interpretation, and control-aware automation.

Investor Lens

Speed | Scalability | Predictability | Control Maturity

Investors do not reward digital transformation because it sounds modern. They reward it when it produces measurable improvements in forecast accuracy, reporting speed, cost efficiency, control reliability, and decision quality.

CFO KPI Proposition

Digital Finance Maturity Score

Weighted score across automation depth, AI adoption, data governance, reporting speed, and control integration.

AI Forecast Accuracy Delta

Improvement in forecast accuracy achieved through AI-supported models compared with prior manual or traditional forecasting.

Digital Close Compression

Reduction in monthly or quarterly close cycle time after automation, adjusted for accuracy and post-close corrections.

LEVER 18 — Green Financing & ESG-Linked Capital | Opportunities

Kael Cipher Reflection

The cheapest capital is not always negotiated in markets. Sometimes it is earned through credibility.

Present Interpretation

Green financing and ESG-linked capital have created a major opportunity for CFOs. As lenders and investors increasingly connect capital terms with sustainability performance, companies that can demonstrate credible ESG progress may gain access to wider pools of capital and better financing conversations.

Kael did not treat green financing as CSR. He treated it as capital structure strategy. If energy efficiency, carbon reduction, safety, governance, and sustainability metrics can be measured, assured, and linked to financing terms, ESG becomes part of the CFO's funding architecture.

At **Solara RenewTech**, a composite clean-energy and infrastructure company, the CFO built a sustainability-linked financing framework tied to measurable decarbonisation, renewable energy use, and safety metrics. The strength was not the label "green." The strength was verified performance and disciplined reporting.

Strategic Implication

ESG-linked capital can improve funding flexibility, deepen investor access, strengthen lender relationships, and reduce reputational risk. But the opportunity works only when claims are credible.

A CFO must avoid superficial sustainability language. Every green bond, transition bond, sustainability-linked loan, or ESG-linked facility should have clear use of proceeds, measurable KPIs, independent verification, and transparent reporting.

Green capital is not free capital. It is trust-priced capital.

CFO Action Plan

1. **Create an ESG-linked financing framework** with measurable KPIs such as carbon intensity, renewable energy mix, safety performance, governance compliance, or supplier ethics.

2. **Engage lenders early** to test sustainability-linked triggers, margin adjustments, and documentation expectations.
3. **Evaluate green, transition, or sustainability-linked instruments** for eligible capex, energy efficiency, renewable adoption, or circular-economy initiatives.
4. **Build verification protocols** using internal audit, external assurance, or independent ESG reviewers.
5. **Prepare a capital savings bridge** showing how ESG-linked financing affects interest cost, tenor, access, or investor demand.
6. **Align treasury policy** with approved ESG investment criteria where commercially sensible.
7. **Report ESG-linked capital performance** to the Board and investors with evidence, not slogans.

Investor Lens

Sustainability | Verification | Funding Access | Long-Term Trust

Investors reward ESG-linked financing when the company shows credible targets, reliable measurement, transparent reporting, and disciplined use of proceeds. Weak verification can damage trust faster than no ESG claim at all.

CFO KPI Proposition

ESG-Linked Capital Ratio
Percentage of total debt or capital raised through green, transition, or sustainability-linked instruments.

ESG Financing Benefit
Measured interest, spread, tenor, access, or demand advantage arising from ESG-linked instruments.

Verification Coverage Ratio
Percentage of ESG-linked financing KPIs covered by internal audit, external assurance, or independent verification.

LEVER 19 — Strategic Alliances & Joint Ventures | Opportunities

Kael Cipher Reflection

Scale is expensive. Shared scale becomes powerful only when trust, control, and economics are designed before signing.

Present Interpretation

Strategic alliances and joint ventures allow companies to grow without carrying the full cost, risk, or time burden of building everything alone. For the CFO, they are not merely partnership arrangements. They are capital-efficiency tools.

Kael viewed alliances through three questions: What capability are we gaining? What risk are we sharing? What capital are we saving or redeploying?

At **AerionTech Mobility**, a composite mobility company, the business entered partnerships with battery, drivetrain, and distribution specialists. The alliance reduced upfront investment, accelerated market entry, and gave the company access to technical capability it could not have built quickly on its own.

But Kael also warned that poorly governed JVs can destroy value. Ambiguous decision rights, weak exit clauses, unclear IP ownership, and uneven reporting can turn partnerships into slow-moving disputes.

Strategic Implication

A well-structured alliance can improve ROIC, reduce capex burden, accelerate innovation, enter new markets, and hedge regulatory or geopolitical risk.

The CFO must ensure that every alliance has a clear financial model, governance structure, tax logic, synergy plan, reporting cadence, dispute mechanism, and exit path.

Partnerships should not be built only on enthusiasm. They must be built on economics and governance.

CFO Action Plan

1. **Define a JV Rationale Matrix** covering capability gap, market access, technology need, regulatory advantage, or speed-to-market benefit.
2. **Build a JV financial model** covering shared capex, revenue scenarios, IP value, currency exposure, profit waterfalls, and exit economics.
3. **Establish governance protocols** for Board composition, reserved matters, audit rights, reporting cadence, and decision thresholds.
4. **Create a synergy realisation plan** covering procurement, technology transfer, customer access, shared infrastructure, and operating savings.
5. **Review tax and transfer-pricing structure** before signing, especially in cross-border arrangements.
6. **Design exit mechanisms** including put-call rights, deadlock resolution, step-in rights, and dissolution provisions.

7. **Communicate alliance outcomes** through MD&A, investor presentations, or Board updates where material.

Investor Lens

Scalability | Capital Efficiency | Governance | Market Access

Investors value alliances when the economic logic is clear and the governance is strong. Poorly structured partnerships create hidden liabilities; well-structured partnerships create capital-efficient growth.

CFO KPI Proposition

Alliance Value Realisation Index
Percentage of committed synergy benefits realized within the approved timeline.

Capital Efficiency Delta
Estimated standalone capex avoided or reduced through partnership compared with the required independent investment.

JV Governance Compliance Score
Adherence to agreed reporting, audit, decision rights, compliance, and escalation protocols.

LEVER 20 — Global Tax Optimisation | Opportunities

Kael Cipher Reflection
Tax is not a shortcut. It is a design discipline that must survive law, substance, and conscience.

Present Interpretation

Global tax optimisation is an opportunity only when it is compliant, transparent, and aligned with real business substance. It should never sound like avoidance. For the CFO, responsible tax architecture is about reducing leakage, avoiding double taxation, improving cash movement, managing disputes, and creating predictability.

Kael believed that many companies do not suffer from high tax cost alone. They suffer from poorly designed entity structures, outdated inter-company agreements, trapped cash, withholding leakage, weak transfer-pricing documentation, and insufficient treaty planning.

At **Solstice Biopharma**, a composite multinational, rapid expansion had created unnecessary entities, inconsistent inter-company charges, trapped cash, and tax uncertainty. The CFO redesigned the tax structure around substance, documentation, treaty eligibility, and compliant cash repatriation. The result was not aggressive tax reduction. It was cleaner governance and better predictability.

Strategic Implication

Responsible global tax optimisation can improve post-tax cash flow, reduce disputes, support capital allocation, improve investor confidence, and reduce earnings volatility.

The CFO must ensure that tax planning is aligned with actual operations, people, assets, risks, IP ownership, decision-making, and value creation. In the current global tax environment, substance matters as much as structure.

A tax strategy that cannot be defended to regulators, auditors, the Board, and investors is not a strategy. It is a liability.

CFO Action Plan

1. **Conduct a global entity heat map** identifying tax leakage, trapped cash, withholding exposure, dormant entities, and BEPS-sensitive structures.
2. **Review treaty eligibility** based on beneficial ownership, substance, documentation, and commercial rationale.
3. **Update inter-company agreements** for services, royalties, loans, procurement, cost sharing, and management charges.
4. **Assess Pillar Two and minimum-tax readiness** where applicable to the group structure.
5. **Use APA and MAP routes** where recurring cross-border transactions carry significant uncertainty.
6. **Align IP location with real activity** such as R&D, decision-making, people capability, and risk ownership.
7. **Create a multi-country tax dashboard** covering ETR, disputes, rulings, exposures, cash repatriation, and documentation status.

Investor Lens

Compliance | Predictability | Tax Transparency | Margin Quality

Investors are increasingly alert to aggressive or opaque tax structures. They reward tax positions that are efficient, documented, transparent, and stable across jurisdictions.

CFO KPI Proposition

Global Effective Tax Rate
Total tax expense divided by global profit before tax, analysed by jurisdiction and key driver.

Tax Efficiency Realisation
Actual compliant tax savings or leakage reduction achieved compared with approved restructuring plan.

Cash Repatriation Efficiency
Percentage of available overseas cash repatriated or redeployed through compliant, low-leakage structures.

LEVER 21 — Investor Analytics & Market Perception Technology | Opportunities

Kael Cipher Reflection

Markets do not reward performance alone. They reward performance they can understand, trust, and model.

Present Interpretation

Investor analytics gives CFOs the ability to understand how the market is interpreting the company. Traditional investor relations often reacts to analyst questions. Modern CFO-led IR uses data to identify perception gaps before they become valuation gaps.

Kael saw market perception as a measurable signal. Analyst model drift, recurring investor questions, call transcript sentiment, fund movement, shareholding changes, short-seller narratives, and media triggers all reveal how the market is reading the company.

At **Luminex Digital Systems**, a composite listed company, investor analytics showed that the market's real concern was not current margins but supply-chain resilience. Once the CFO adjusted investor communication to explain mitigation, supplier diversification, and inventory strategy, the company's narrative became clearer.

Strategic Implication

Investor analytics helps the CFO manage uncertainty. It does not replace honest performance. It helps management explain performance more intelligently.

When the CFO understands analyst assumptions, investor concerns, and narrative blind spots, communication becomes sharper. The company can address real concerns rather than over-explaining the wrong numbers.

CFO Action Plan

1. **Deploy an investor analytics dashboard** tracking analyst sentiment, model assumptions, fund movement, questions, and communication heatmaps.
2. **Track analyst model drift** between external expectations and internal planning assumptions.
3. **Design quarterly narrative bridges** linking performance movement to drivers, actions, risks, and forward visibility.
4. **Monitor misinformation and market rumours** where legally and operationally appropriate.
5. **Build a 360-degree IR dashboard** integrating shareholder movement, liquidity, analyst coverage, sentiment, and volatility indicators.
6. **Conduct an annual perception audit** to test how investors understand strategy, risks, and capital allocation.
7. **Use investor insight to improve disclosure** across annual reports, earnings calls, investor decks, and lender communication.

Investor Lens

Clarity | Consistency | Responsiveness | Transparency

Investors reward companies that communicate intentionally. A CFO who understands market perception can reduce confusion, improve disclosure, and strengthen confidence without overpromising.

CFO KPI Proposition

Investor Sentiment Stability Index
Change or volatility in investor sentiment scores across defined communication periods.

Analyst Consensus Alignment Ratio
Percentage of analyst models falling within the company's reasonable guidance or expectation range.

Narrative Resolution Time
Time taken to address material misunderstanding, misinformation, or recurring investor concern.

LEVER 22 — Talent Branding & Cultural Capital | Opportunities

Kael Cipher Reflection

Balance sheets record value. People create it.

Present Interpretation

Talent branding and cultural capital are often treated as HR language, but Kael saw them as financial levers. A strong talent brand reduces hiring friction, improves retention, accelerates productivity, deepens succession, and strengthens execution reliability.

Companies with weak culture may still hire people, but they struggle to retain judgement. The cost appears through attrition, delays, errors, weak accountability, customer disruption, and leadership fatigue.

At **Meridian Nexus**, a composite high-performing enterprise, talent branding was not built through slogans. It was built through learning systems, internal mobility, ethical leadership, strong manager capability, and visible career paths. Finance measured the economic impact through retention, ramp-up speed, productivity, and succession readiness.

Strategic Implication

Cultural capital becomes an opportunity when it improves execution. If employees trust leadership, understand priorities, and see growth, the organisation moves faster and with less friction.

For the CFO, talent branding must connect with measurable financial outcomes: hiring cost, productivity ramp-up, regrettable attrition, leadership continuity, error reduction, and transformation readiness.

The CFO should not own culture alone, but must help measure its economic consequence.

CFO Action Plan

1. **Define a Talent Capital Framework** covering hiring quality, ramp-up speed, role criticality, retention, succession, and cultural alignment.
2. **Create a regrettable attrition heat map** for high-impact roles and critical capability areas.

3. **Link culture metrics to financial outcomes** such as productivity, quality, customer retention, control failures, and project delivery.
4. **Optimise workforce mix** across permanent, contract, shared services, gig, outsourced, and automation-supported roles.
5. **Establish a Leadership Readiness Index** for critical roles across finance and the wider enterprise.
6. **Co-design employer-brand narrative with HR** to attract high-skill, high-trust talent.
7. **Measure learning ROI** by connecting training investment to productivity, promotion readiness, and execution outcomes.

Investor Lens

Stability | Continuity | Execution Confidence | Leadership Quality

Investors increasingly observe talent signals: leadership depth, attrition, culture, succession, whistle-blower trends, and transformation capability. Strong cultural capital supports predictable execution.

CFO KPI Proposition

Regrettable Attrition Rate
Attrition among high-performing or high-criticality employees divided by total employees in that category.

Leadership Readiness Index
Percentage of critical roles with at least one ready-now or ready-soon successor.

Productivity Ramp-Time Ratio
Time taken for new hires to reach defined productivity compared with internal or industry benchmark.

LEVER 23 — Working-Capital FinTech Partnerships | Opportunities

Kael Cipher Reflection
Cash is not only generated by operations. It is released by design.

Present Interpretation: Working-capital FinTech partnerships can help companies release cash trapped inside receivables, payables, disputes, inventory, and settlement delays. The opportunity is not technology for its own sake. It is liquidity design.

Kael believed many working-capital problems exist because cash flows are poorly designed, not because the business lacks revenue. If billing is delayed, disputes are manual, vendor financing is absent, collections are not digitised, or inventory signals are weak, cash remains trapped.

At **Helion Consumer Brands**, a composite consumer company, the CFO partnered with digital collections, invoice discounting, and dynamic payables platforms. The biggest improvement came not from one tool, but from end-to-end visibility across order, billing, collection, reconciliation, and settlement.

Strategic Implication

FinTech partnerships can improve liquidity, reduce borrowing dependence, support suppliers, shorten cash cycles, and strengthen working-capital governance.

The CFO must ensure these partnerships are integrated with ERP, treasury, credit control, procurement, and risk systems. FinTech should not create another fragmented layer. It should reduce friction and improve control.

CFO Action Plan

1. **Map the full cash-flow chain** from order to delivery, billing, collection, reconciliation, settlement, and reporting.
2. **Partner with payables platforms** for dynamic discounting, supplier financing, and payment-term optimization.
3. **Digitise receivables** through automated reminders, API-based collections, credit scoring, and dispute workflows.
4. **Evaluate invoice marketplaces** where supplier financing can be supported by the company's credit standing.
5. **Build real-time working-capital dashboards** covering DSO, DPO, ageing, disputes, supplier adoption, and cash released.
6. **Use AI / IoT tools for inventory signals** where relevant to reorder points, shrinkage, demand sensing, and stock ageing.
7. **Create a CFO–Treasury FinTech Council** to review platform ROI, risk, adoption, and scalability.

Investor Lens

Liquidity | Efficiency | Predictability | Governance

Investors value FinTech partnerships when they improve cash conversion, reduce manual leakage, strengthen controls, and release liquidity without damaging supplier or customer relationships.

CFO KPI Proposition

FinTech Liquidity Release Ratio
Cash released through FinTech-enabled initiatives divided by baseline working-capital exposure.

Digital DSO Delta
Reduction in DSO attributable to digital collections, credit scoring, and dispute automation.

Supplier Digital Adoption Rate
Percentage of eligible suppliers actively using approved digital payables, discounting, or financing platforms.

LEVER 24 — Intangible Asset Visibility | Opportunities

Kael Cipher Reflection

Modern companies are not valued only by what they own. They are valued by what they know, protect, scale, and repeat.

Present Interpretation

Intangible assets increasingly drive enterprise value, but many remain invisible in statutory financial statements. Data, algorithms, patents, customer relationships, brand equity, proprietary processes, design systems, operating know-how, and culture may influence valuation even when they are not formally recognised as balance-sheet assets.

Kael preferred the term **Intangible Asset Visibility** rather than simple recognition. Not every intangible can or should be recognised under accounting standards. But CFOs can still measure, govern, explain, and use them responsibly in investor narratives, M&A discussions, strategy reviews, and capital allocation.

At **Auralis TechLabs**, a composite digital company, the statutory balance sheet showed only part of the enterprise story. The real value lay in recurring customer behaviour, proprietary algorithms, data assets, platform architecture, and brand trust. The CFO built an intangible operating asset map to help investors understand the company's defensibility.

Strategic Implication

Intangible asset visibility helps the market understand competitive advantage. It can support valuation, M&A premium, partnership negotiations, credit discussion, customer confidence, and internal capital allocation.

The CFO must avoid overstating intangibles. The objective is not to inflate value. The objective is to explain what drives future cash flows, resilience, scalability, and customer loyalty.

CFO Action Plan

1. **Create an Intangible Asset Register** covering data sets, algorithms, patents, platforms, customer cohorts, brand assets, processes, and proprietary tools.
2. **Build customer lifetime value models** by segment, retention, acquisition cost, margin, and repeat behaviour.
3. **Measure R&D and innovation return** through commercial adoption, patent progress, product contribution, and time-to-market.
4. **Develop a Data Capital Score** assessing uniqueness, completeness, monetisation potential, governance quality, and reusability.
5. **Conduct brand equity assessment** through pricing power, customer trust, retention, perception audits, and market position.
6. **Use intangible analysis in M&A** to evaluate IP, platforms, customer ecosystems, cultural fit, and synergy potential.
7. **Integrate intangible visibility into investor decks** using clear, responsible, non-statutory explanations.

Investor Lens

Defensibility | Scalability | Predictability | Innovation

Investors value intangible assets when they can understand how those assets create future revenue, customer stickiness, pricing power, barriers to entry, or operating leverage. The CFO's role is to make intangible value visible without overstating it.

CFO KPI Proposition

Intangible Asset Visibility Index

Weighted score of identified intangible assets based on ownership, protection, measurability, strategic relevance, and governance.

Customer Capital Yield

Revenue from recurring, retained, or high-loyalty customers divided by total revenue.

Innovation Velocity Index

Rate at which new products, features, patents, platforms, or proprietary capabilities move from development to commercial use.

THREATS — WHAT CAN ERASE VALUATION

LEVER 25 — Cyber-Breach Risk | Threats

Kael Cipher Reflection

When a cyber breach occurs, the first system to go down is not the server. It is trust.

Present Interpretation

Cyber-breach risk has become a direct financial threat. A serious breach can damage revenue, customer trust, payment systems, regulatory standing, insurance coverage, lender confidence, and market perception.

Kael viewed cyber risk as more than an IT issue. For a CFO, it is a liquidity, disclosure, control, and valuation risk. If a payment system is compromised, customer data is exposed, treasury workflows are interrupted, or financial reporting systems are corrupted, the damage moves quickly from technology to the balance sheet.

At **OmniSphere Retail**, a composite digital-commerce company, a customer-data breach triggered customer churn, regulatory scrutiny, higher insurance costs, delayed partnerships, and Board-level concern. The breach was technical in origin, but financial in consequence.

Strategic Implication

Cyber-breach risk becomes dangerous because its impact spreads across multiple layers: immediate remediation cost, operational disruption, regulatory exposure, legal claims, customer loss, and investor distrust.

The CFO must ensure cyber preparedness is quantified, stress-tested, insured where appropriate, and reported to the Board in financial language. The key question is not only, "Can IT contain the breach?" The CFO must also ask, "Can the company absorb the financial shock?"

CFO Action Plan

1. **Build a Cyber Financial Exposure Matrix** linking breach scenarios to revenue loss, margin impact, cash disruption, legal cost, penalties, and disclosure obligations.

2. **Run quarterly cyber stress tests** covering ransomware, payment compromise, vendor breach, system outage, data corruption, and customer-data exposure.
3. **Implement zero-trust controls for finance systems** including MFA, privileged-access monitoring, encryption, maker-checker controls, and payment validation.
4. **Assess vendor cyber hygiene** for key technology, payroll, cloud, payment, ERP, and data-processing partners.
5. **Review cyber-insurance adequacy** covering limits, exclusions, response support, jurisdiction, deductibles, and claim documentation.
6. **Integrate cyber metrics into CFO dashboards** through incident attempts, downtime, patch status, access exceptions, and backup integrity.
7. **Strengthen Board oversight** with cyber heat maps, financial exposure curves, remediation plans, and response-readiness updates.

Investor Lens

Resilience | Preparedness | Control Maturity | Disclosure

Investors watch cyber preparedness because one serious breach can alter customer behaviour, increase regulatory cost, weaken management credibility, and change the valuation narrative.

CFO KPI Proposition

Breach Containment Time
Time taken from detection of a material breach or incident to isolation or containment.

Cyber Financial Exposure Ratio
Estimated financial exposure from cyber incidents divided by EBITDA or operating cash flow.

Vendor Cyber Hygiene Score
Weighted assessment of critical vendors based on controls, certifications, breach history, access rights, and incident-response maturity.

LEVER 26 — Climate and Resource Shocks | Threats

Kael Cipher Reflection
When climate shifts, cost structures shift — and cost structures decide survival.

Present Interpretation

Climate and resource shocks are no longer distant ESG concerns. They affect raw material prices, energy cost, water availability, logistics routes, insurance premiums, asset lives, labour productivity, and supply-chain continuity.

Kael treated climate exposure as financial exposure. Floods, heatwaves, droughts, cyclones, water scarcity, carbon pricing, and resource shortages can move quickly into margin pressure, production disruption, asset impairment, and capex reprioritisation.

At **Aquaterra Foods**, a composite agri-FMCG company, climate-related crop failure in key sourcing regions increased input costs, disrupted procurement, compressed margins, and forced emergency buying at unfavourable prices. The company did not suffer because of poor ESG messaging. It suffered because climate volatility had not been financially modelled.

Strategic Implication

Climate and resource shocks threaten valuation when the company cannot explain exposure, resilience, sourcing flexibility, insurance adequacy, and cost pass-through.

The CFO must bring climate into financial planning. This means mapping climate-sensitive inputs, modelling regional exposure, evaluating insurance, funding resilience capex, and reporting climate-linked cost sensitivity to the Board.

Climate risk becomes manageable only when it is translated into cost, margin, cash flow, and continuity.

CFO Action Plan

1. **Build a Climate-Adjusted Cost Model** linking temperature, rainfall, floods, drought, water scarcity, and energy volatility to cost structure.
2. **Conduct climate scenario stress tests** for supply disruption, commodity spikes, water shortage, carbon pricing, logistics rerouting, and plant shutdown.
3. **Diversify supply geography** to reduce dependence on climate-vulnerable regions or single-resource clusters.
4. **Integrate resource-efficiency capex** such as energy efficiency, water recycling, renewable sourcing, and waste reduction.
5. **Evaluate carbon-cost exposure** through internal carbon pricing, renewable contracts, energy procurement, and emissions regulations.

6. **Reassess insurance coverage** for flood, heat, storm, business interruption, climate-linked loss, and parametric products where relevant.
7. **Enhance Board and investor climate disclosures** using regional exposure maps, cost bridges, and resilience actions.

Investor Lens

Exposure | Adaptability | Continuity | Resilience

Investors assess whether climate and resource volatility can damage cash flow, margins, assets, and long-term viability. Strong climate-risk translation gives the market confidence that management understands the financial consequence.

CFO KPI Proposition

Climate Cost Sensitivity Index
Estimated percentage change in cost structure under defined climate or resource stress scenarios.

Resource Dependency Ratio
Percentage of critical raw materials, water, energy, or inputs sourced from climate-sensitive regions or constrained resources.

Climate Shock Recovery Time
Time required to restore normal operations after a climate-linked disruption.

LEVER 27 — Geopolitical and FX Instability | Threats

Kael Cipher Reflection - When borders shake, balance sheets tremble.

Present Interpretation

Geopolitical and FX instability can quickly disrupt revenue, supply chains, cash repatriation, commodity access, sanctions compliance, subsidiary funding, and investor confidence.

This lever is different from normal FX and commodity vulnerability. Here the threat is broader: political instability, sanctions, trade restrictions, export bans, capital controls, currency devaluation, conflict, regulatory retaliation, and trapped cash.

At **Meridian Global Systems**, a composite multinational, sudden sanctions in a key export market created revenue loss, receivable impairment, inventory reversal, FX loss, and cross-border payment difficulty. The issue was not only currency movement. It was a geopolitical shock that travelled through the financial statements.

Strategic Implication

Geopolitical threats are dangerous because they can invalidate assumptions overnight. A budget may be accurate under normal conditions, yet fail when a country becomes inaccessible, a currency collapses, a payment route closes, or a trade policy changes.

The CFO must build a global exposure system that connects geography with revenue, cost, assets, liabilities, cash, vendors, customers, banking partners, and compliance obligations.

CFO Action Plan

1. **Build a Global Exposure Map** covering revenue, cost, assets, debt, suppliers, customers, cash, and banking partners by geography.
2. **Design an FX Shock Absorption Model** showing margin, cash, and covenant impact under major currency movements.
3. **Strengthen hedging discipline** through natural hedges, forwards, options, swaps, layered hedging, and defined exposure corridors.
4. **Reduce country concentration risk** through alternate sourcing, diversified markets, multi-location production, and flexible logistics.
5. **Establish sanctions and regulatory watchtowers** for payments, shipping, data transfer, technology transfer, and restricted-party exposure.
6. **Protect cross-border cash** through repatriation planning, banking diversification, exposure caps, and local liquidity rules.
7. **Create a rapid-response playbook** for export bans, civil unrest, sanctions, trapped cash, currency shocks, and supply interruption.

Investor Lens

Diversification | Stability | Hedging Maturity | Predictability

Investors watch geopolitical concentration because it can create sudden earnings volatility, trapped liquidity, or market-access loss. The CFO who maps exposure and prepares response options protects valuation continuity.

CFO KPI Proposition

Geo-Currency Concentration Ratio

Percentage of revenue, cost, assets, or cash exposed to the top high-risk countries or currencies.

Hedged Margin Coverage
Percentage of material net FX or commodity-linked margin exposure covered by approved hedging or natural offsets.

Cross-Border Cash Resilience Score
Composite measure of repatriation ease, trapped-cash risk, banking diversification, and jurisdictional liquidity access.

LEVER 28 — Succession Vacuum | Threats

Kael Cipher Reflection

When a leader leaves, the company does not lose only a person. It risks losing continuity.

Present Interpretation

Succession vacuum becomes a threat when the organisation depends too heavily on a few individuals. If a CEO, CFO, COO, business head, treasury lead, controller, or technology leader exits suddenly and no credible successor is ready, uncertainty spreads quickly.

Kael believed leadership gaps create valuation gaps. The market may not know the details of internal capability, but it senses hesitation through delayed decisions, suspended guidance, frozen capex, weaker investor communication, and inconsistent execution.

At **Nexarion Infra**, a composite infrastructure company, the sudden exit of a CFO during a refinancing cycle created lender anxiety, rating-agency questions, delayed capital decisions, and weaker analyst confidence. The company's operating assets had not changed, but leadership ambiguity changed the market's reading of risk.

Strategic Implication

Succession vacuum threatens strategy, confidence, culture, and capital access. A company without leadership continuity becomes harder to lend to, harder to value, and harder to trust during stress.

The CFO should treat succession as enterprise-risk management. This includes readiness planning, emergency delegation, leadership simulations, Board visibility, and communication protocols.

CFO Action Plan

1. **Map succession for critical roles** across CXO positions, finance, treasury, controllership, tax, technology, operations, and business units.
2. **Build a 24-month leadership readiness plan** using rotations, stretch roles, Board exposure, crisis simulations, and cross-functional assignments.
3. **Establish emergency succession protocols** defining interim authority for sudden departures.
4. **Ensure Board-level succession review** with documented readiness status, gaps, and development plans.
5. **Monitor critical-talent flight risk** for high-impact roles and succession candidates.
6. **Scenario-test leadership transitions** to assess operational, financial, and communication continuity.
7. **Communicate leadership stability carefully** in governance language without disclosing sensitive internal succession details.

Investor Lens

Continuity | Predictability | Governance | Leadership Quality

Investors fear leadership uncertainty because it can interrupt strategy, capital allocation, lender confidence, and execution rhythm. A strong succession process reduces perceived key-person risk.

CFO KPI Proposition

Succession Readiness Index
Percentage of critical roles with at least one ready-now or ready-soon successor.

Leadership Continuity Coverage
Estimated period for which the organisation can operate without material performance drift after a sudden leadership exit.

Critical-Talent Attrition Risk Score
Weighted risk score for possible exits among high-impact leaders and succession candidates.

LEVER 29 — Reputation Crisis | Threats

Kael Cipher Reflection

When reputation falls, valuation does not merely decline. It loses gravity.

Present Interpretation

Reputation crisis is one of the fastest-moving threats to enterprise value. It may arise from governance allegations, product failure, customer harm, data breach, regulatory action, ESG lapse, executive misconduct, misinformation, or social-media escalation.

Kael saw reputation risk as financial contagion. Whether the allegation is true, exaggerated, or false, the market reacts to perceived uncertainty. Customers pause, distributors hesitate, lenders ask questions, employees worry, and investors reprice trust.

At **Aurelius Consumer Tech**, a composite digital-consumer company, a viral allegation later proved inaccurate. Yet the company still faced customer hesitation, distributor concern, analyst questions, and market-cap pressure because its early response lacked speed and clarity. The issue was perception velocity.

Strategic Implication

Reputation crises damage valuation when management responds slowly, inconsistently, defensively, or without evidence. The CFO must help stabilise facts, quantify exposure, reassure stakeholders, and ensure disclosures are accurate.

Reputation recovery depends on speed, truth, coordination, and proof. The CFO should be part of the crisis room because reputation events often become revenue, liquidity, credit, legal, and valuation events.

CFO Action Plan

1. **Build a Reputation Heat-Signal Dashboard** tracking media sentiment, social chatter, keyword spikes, customer complaints, and investor concerns.
2. **Create a 60-minute crisis response protocol** defining validation steps, spokespersons, approval chain, channels, and first-statement principles.
3. **Coordinate with Legal, Compliance, Communications, and Operations** so public statements are factual, defensible, and aligned.

4. **Run perception stress tests** for governance allegations, whistle-blower claims, ESG lapses, product failures, cyber incidents, and partner misconduct.
5. **Stabilise key stakeholders early** including banks, investors, rating agencies, major customers, suppliers, and employees.
6. **Strengthen root-cause controls** around ethics, product quality, data governance, safety, anti-bribery, and customer protection.
7. **Publish a reputation recovery plan** where appropriate, supported by audits, corrective actions, timelines, and progress updates.

Investor Lens

Transparency | Timeliness | Consistency | Governance

Investors judge reputation crises by the quality of management response. A fast, factual, and well-governed response can contain damage; delay or contradiction can permanently impair trust.

CFO KPI Proposition

Reputation Response Time
Time taken from detection of a material reputation signal to validated internal escalation and first approved response.

Perception Recovery Period
Time taken for investor, customer, employee, or public sentiment indicators to return toward baseline.

Stakeholder Confidence Stability Index
Composite score based on investor feedback, customer sentiment, partner confidence, employee pulse, and lender/rating-agency response.

LEVER 30 — Audit and Ethics Breakdown | Threats

Kael Cipher Reflection
When ethics fail, numbers do not merely lie. They lose the right to be believed.

Present Interpretation

Audit and ethics breakdown is the most severe threat in the CFO universe. It can destroy years of strategy, growth, capital raising, brand building, and investor trust.

Kael believed that audit failure rarely begins with one dramatic fraud. It often begins with smaller compromises: aggressive revenue recognition, ignored control overrides, weak reconciliations, poor documentation, related-party opacity, pressure on auditors, or leadership silence around ethical breaches.

At **Heliotrope Industries**, a composite industrial company, a revenue-recognition issue discovered during review led to restatement, auditor concern, Board intervention, lender questions, and long-term trust damage. The financial amount was painful, but the larger loss was credibility.

Strategic Implication

Audit and ethics breakdown threatens capital access, lender confidence, customer trust, regulatory standing, and leadership legitimacy. Once investors question the integrity of numbers, every past and future disclosure becomes suspect.

The CFO must protect the foundation: integrity, controls, and evidence. The organisation should be able to prove not only what it reported, but how it knew the report was true.

CFO Action Plan

1. **Perform a Control Environment Maturity Audit** across finance, procurement, sales, treasury, inventory, tax, HR, and IT controls.
2. **Implement continuous auditing** through automated reconciliations, anomaly detection, exception testing, and control dashboards.
3. **Strengthen whistle-blower mechanisms** with anonymity, independent investigation, closure tracking, and Board visibility.
4. **Enforce policy discipline** around revenue recognition, inventory valuation, impairment, provisions, related parties, and manual journal entries.
5. **Protect auditor independence** through full data access, transparent communication, and early disclosure of difficult issues.
6. **Create a CFO Ethics Dashboard** tracking control overrides, audit adjustments, conflict-of-interest cases, ethics breaches, and unresolved observations.
7. **Enforce leadership accountability** for repeated control failures, intentional concealment, unethical pressure, or unsupported adjustments.

Investor Lens

Transparency | Governance | Control Strength | Credibility

Investors, lenders, regulators, and rating agencies treat audit and ethics failures as trust failures. One serious breakdown can permanently increase the company's cost of capital.

CFO KPI Proposition

Audit Adjustment Frequency
Number and severity of audit adjustments identified during internal or external audit cycles.

Ethics Compliance Index
Weighted score across ethics training, whistle-blower resolution, conflict-of-interest closure, policy adherence, and disciplinary action.

Control Failure Impact Ratio
Financial impact of control failures divided by EBITDA or operating profit.

---

* For the complete governance and ethics KPI catalogue — auditor-alignment dashboards, internal-control matrices, whistleblower analytics, and continuous-audit KPIs — refer to **THE CFO KPI CODEX**, the author's global system for CFO measurement.

Epilogue 1 — The CFO's Final Reflection

By Kael Cipher

Legacy begins the day you stop seeking credit and start creating continuity.

When I first entered the corner office, the walls felt heavier than the title on my door.
I had inherited a balance sheet, a reputation, and an unspoken expectation — to prove that numbers could lead, not just follow.

In those early weeks, I learned that **control was comfort, but credibility was currency**.
The first 30 days taught me rhythm — cash, compliance, cadence.
The next 60 taught me respect — for systems, for people, for truth.
And by Day 90, I realized a CFO does not *own* performance; he *enables* it.

The following 180 days transformed me from executor to architect.
I no longer managed processes — I designed permanence.
Automation replaced repetition; dashboards replaced dependency.
The company no longer waited for reports; it learned to predict.

By the final quarter of my first year, I discovered what all great CFOs eventually do — that the **true measure of finance is not efficiency, but enlightenment.**
Governance, when practiced with empathy, becomes grace.
Courage, when exercised quietly, shapes culture more deeply than charisma ever could.

Each signature carried a fragment of the future — a decision not for quarters, but for decades.
I had moved from asking, *"What can I fix?"* to *"What will remain when I leave?"*

The Invisible Balance Sheet

Every organisation maintains two balance sheets:
one in numbers, and one in values.
The first records assets that depreciate; the second records **principles that compound**.

My greatest contribution lay on that invisible ledger — the one that doesn't appear in quarterly calls or investor decks.
There, beside goodwill and reserves, lived integrity, discipline, and trust.
Those are the **intangibles that never impair**.

The Recalibration of Purpose

When asked, late into my tenure, what a CFO truly does, I said:

"We don't count money; we count meaning."

The income statement is a reflection of intention — the outcome of thousands of moral choices multiplied by discipline.
The real craft of finance leadership is to make **ethics scalable** — to turn moral instinct into measurable practice.

I began this journey learning to balance books.
I end it learning to balance **power with principle.**

Leadership in Reverse

Most leaders measure success by the change they create while they are present.
I measured mine by **what no longer needed my presence** —
a mature system,
a self-thinking finance team,
a Board that debated openly because trust had replaced theatre.

I had become invisible by design.
And in that invisibility lay influence.

The Universal Lesson

Every first-time CFO, somewhere between their first board meeting and their first ethical test, faces the same turning point:
Will I run the numbers, or will I raise the standard?

My year answered that question quietly.
Finance leadership, when done right, isn't about control — it's about **continuity of conscience**.
And perhaps that's how legacy should end:
not with applause, but with assurance.

Final Reflection

Looking back on those 365 days, I realize I didn't just build a finance function —

I built a **philosophy of stewardship**.

I leave behind **dashboards**, not dependencies.
Playbooks, not personalities.
And **a culture where truth is treated as currency.**

In the margin of my final annual report, I wrote one line — not for auditors or analysts, but for whoever would sit in this chair next:

"The best CFOs don't finish their tenure with a legacy of profits — they finish with a legacy of peace."

Epilogue 2 — The Chair That Remembers You

By Gemma Zessar
The silent ledger of a leader's legacy.

The chair in the corner office has been replaced twice since Kael Cipher's tenure.
The systems he built have evolved, dashboards redesigned, teams promoted, and policies rewritten.
And yet, somehow, that chair still carries his imprint — not the physical one, but the rhythm he left behind.

It wasn't just that Kael stabilised the numbers; **he stabilised thought.**
He taught the organisation to pause before reacting, to measure before deciding, and to listen before concluding.

I remember the morning he presented his one-year blueprint — calm, meticulous, as always.
There were no grand slides, no sweeping declarations — just four sentences that summarised a year of transformation:

"We inherited complexity.
We stabilised the chaos.
We built control.
And we institutionalised clarity."

It was simple — and that's what made it profound.

Kael changed the very language of finance inside **G Z Corporation.**
He replaced *"How much?"* with *"Why now?"*
and *"What if?"* with *"What purpose?"*

The finance team that once worked in silos began thinking like **architects of enterprise value.**
Every decision carried an echo of his principles —
visibility before velocity, truth before timing, and courage before convenience.

In his final quarterly note to the Board, he had written:

"The true measure of a CFO is not the profit earned during his tenure,
but the predictability he leaves behind once he's gone."

When he left, there were no farewells, no long speeches — just a handwritten note on my desk that said:

"Thank you for demanding precision.
It gave meaning to every decision."

That's when I realized — leadership isn't remembered by applause.
It's remembered by **continuity.**

Even today, when someone walks into that office and sits in that chair,
the screens flicker on, the dashboards load, and the numbers start to tell a story Kael once began.

The systems remember him.
The culture remembers him.
And yes — **the chair remembers him too.**

Because somewhere between numbers and narratives,
he had turned **finance into faith.**

Afterword — The Chair Awaits You

You've walked through a year of decisions — numbers, narratives, and nights of quiet calculation.
You've seen how a CFO builds not just reports, but resilience.
Some chapters were about control.
Some were about courage.
All were about conscience.

If you've reached this page, you now carry what every great finance leader must: the ability to balance profit with principle, and power with peace.

This book does not end here.
It simply hands the system — and the story — back to you.

Tomorrow, another balance sheet will open.
Another chair will wait.
And when you take that seat, remember —
you are not inheriting an office.
You are inheriting **trust**.

Carry it forward.
Live it with clarity.
Lead it with courage.
And one day, may your own chair remember you too.

APPENDIX C
BEFORE DAY ONE: THE CFO INTERVIEW

From a Friend's Question to a CFO's Compass

It began with a WhatsApp chat.

My friend Paras, a long-time finance professional, had just been shortlisted for a Deputy CFO role at a large educational institution. He sounded nervous — not about accounting standards or ratios, but about the unknowns: a new industry, different compliance cycles, and an interview that could redefine his career.

He asked, "What should I read — and how do I prepare?"

That simple question revealed a gap few ever address. There are thousands of books on leadership, but very few that show how a CFO actually thinks, speaks, prepares, enters the interview room, and survives the twelve months that follow.

At senior levels, interviews are not about proving what you can do. They are about proving what you can steward.

A CFO is not hired merely to process transactions or close books on time. A CFO is hired to preserve trust — in numbers, governance, liquidity, leadership alignment, and enterprise judgement.

The first shift is therefore mental: move from job seeker to custodian.

Boards want to know whether you can keep the organisation solvent, compliant, balanced, and credible when pressure mounts.

Study the organisation before you study your answers.

Read the financials — not just ratios, but the story behind them. Trace liquidity trends, working-capital movement, debt, deferred income, contingent liabilities, and cash-flow behaviour. If you are entering a new sector, learn how the business model, regulation, audit cycle, and revenue recognition differ.

At the CFO level, you do not prepare for a role. You prepare for their reality.

High-level boards rarely test technical knowledge alone. They test judgement.

Expect questions such as:

- How would you handle a liquidity crunch?
- What if your CEO ignores your warnings?
- When have you chosen principle over pressure?

Frame every answer through Diagnosis → Decision → Discipline: what was the situation, what did you decide, and what did you institutionalise afterward?

A strong candidate also walks in with a first-year narrative. Outline what you would do in the first 30, 90, and 180 days — how you would listen, stabilise, improve, and build trust. That roadmap immediately separates a leader from a survivor.

And when you do not know something, do not pretend.

Honesty builds credibility faster than jargon. A candidate may not know every industry nuance, but he must show the discipline to learn fast, ask correctly, and protect the organisation while learning.

Before entering the room, also learn the organisation's language. Study annual reports, investor briefings, founder letters, press interactions, and repeated strategic themes. The goal is not flattery. The goal is alignment.

Senior interviews often end with another silent test: how you handle your own worth. Negotiate with logic, not hesitation. Base your value on contribution — EBITDA improvement, cost-of-capital reduction, cash-conversion efficiency, governance strength, and risk discipline — not on insecurity or market gossip.

The night before his interview, Paras called again.

We did not discuss ratios. We discussed posture, calmness, and responsibility.

I reminded him: "They are not hiring you to make people happy. They are hiring you to make the right decisions — even when people are not."

That principle sits at the heart of this book.

A CFO is not appointed to please the room. He is appointed to protect the enterprise.

APPENDIX D
BEFORE THE CHAIR: THE PREPARATION PLAYBOOK

Two days before his final interview, Kael Cipher was still travelling.

The flight from Frankfurt to New York was not just long; it was reflective. He had spent the journey reviewing the last ten years of G Z Corporation's annual reports, investor transcripts, and press interviews. The company's complexity fascinated him — an American-headquartered conglomerate with European precision, Asian execution, and a culture known for pushing even senior leaders beyond their comfort zones.

He knew this would not be a conversation about accounting alone.

It would be an interrogation of judgement, clarity, and courage.

Kael's preparation had begun weeks earlier. When the executive search firm first called, he did not celebrate. He researched.

He studied G Z's capital structure, debt-equity ratio, cash-conversion cycle, and the way each business vertical — manufacturing, logistics, and digital platforms — interacted with the group's central treasury.

He mapped liquidity triggers, identified where working capital tightened, and noted which divisions were most exposed to foreign-exchange swings.

He also studied Gemma Zessar's public statements and interviews. Her tone was analytical, direct, and impatient with excuses.

"Every line must connect to purpose," she had once said.

Kael underlined that line in his notes. That was the language she spoke.

G Z Corporation's process was not simple. Before the final board round, candidates had to meet key functional heads.

Kael spent one day each with the Chief Technology Officer, the Head of Supply Chain, and the Chief Human Resources Officer.

The CTO tested his understanding of automation in finance and ERP controls. The Head of Supply Chain wanted to know how he viewed vendor risk and capital locked in inventory. The CHRO probed his philosophy on incentives, ethics, and leadership behaviour.

Kael treated these not as interviews, but as data-gathering sessions.

Each conversation revealed a fragment of the company's DNA — how people thought, how they disagreed, how decisions travelled through layers, and where pressure quietly accumulated.

While waiting at airports, he reviewed investor calls. He listened not only to what management said, but to what analysts repeatedly asked. Those questions revealed hidden stress points: margin pressure, delayed integrations, supply-chain dependency, liquidity buffers, and governance fatigue.

By the time he landed in New York, Kael could almost predict the company's pain points: cash predictability, data uniformity, and decision discipline.

On the hotel desk in Manhattan, he drew a four-column sheet titled First 90 Days.

For the first 30 days, Kael's objective was to listen, diagnose, and secure survival visibility. He would ascertain the actual cash position, immediate and future obligations, critical company commitments, debt maturities, statutory dues, open legal matters, compliance exposures, and any issue that could affect liquidity, reputation, going concern, or organisational survival.

He would also meet key SBU and functional heads — including plant, marketing, sales, supply chain, warehousing, inventory, procurement, taxation, legal, HR, and operations leaders — to understand how the business truly worked beyond reported numbers. Alongside this, he would speak with key bankers, major vendors, important customers, auditors, and internal finance leaders to map pressure points, dependencies, and early warning signals.

The outcome of this phase was not action for the sake of action. It was clarity of current state.

Between Days 31 and 90, his focus would shift to stabilization and communication. He would strengthen the liquidity forecast, create the CFO dashboard, align controllership, and begin earning organisational trust.

From Days 91 to 180, he would optimize and simplify. Debt cost, vendor-payment discipline, policy overlaps, and operating inefficiencies would come under sharper review, with the objective of creating efficiency and measurable savings.

From Day 180 to Day 365, he would partner for growth. The focus would move toward capital strategy, expansion support, investor confidence, and strategic alignment.

He knew no board wanted promises. They wanted phased control.

That night, he went over his notes one last time. He memorized key data points — leverage ratios, free cash flow, market-cap growth — but more than data, he rehearsed silence.

He reminded himself: when you face people who know more, listen longer. When you speak, make it count.

At 6 a.m., he went for a short run around Central Park, his usual ritual before major decisions. The city was still dark, but his mind was clear.

He was not going to G Z Corporation to impress.

He was going there to qualify himself for a standard higher than his own.

As he stood before the mirrored elevator doors later that morning, tie straight, folder in hand, he thought quietly:

"You are not walking in to get the job. You are walking in to prove you deserve it."

That is where every CFO journey truly begins — before the chair, before the title, and before Day One.

APPENDIX E

THE CFO ENTERPRISE DIAGNOSTIC CHECKLIST 30–60–90–180–365 DAY VIEW

The first 30 days are about answering three questions:

1. Can this company survive?
2. How does this company really make money?
3. What does everyone expect me to fix?

DAYS 0–30

Liquidity | Survival | Banking | Compliance | CEO Expectations | Board Expectations | Finance Team | Major Customers | Major Vendors | Top Risks

---

1. Verify actual cash position against reported cash position.
2. Review cash available across all bank accounts and entities.
3. Review immediate cash obligations due within the next 30 days.
4. Review liquidity requirements for the next 3, 6, and 12 months.
5. Review all debt facilities and repayment schedules.
6. Review compliance with banking covenants and loan conditions.
7. Identify working-capital pressure points.
8. Review receivable ageing and collection risks.
9. Review payable ageing and vendor payment obligations.
10. Assess going-concern risks.
11. Review contingent liabilities and commitments.
12. Review tax assessments, notices, appeals, and disputes.
13. Review legal cases and potential exposures.
14. Review regulatory compliance issues.
15. Review pending audit observations and management-letter points.
16. Assess customer concentration risk.
17. Assess supplier concentration risk.
18. Review insurance coverage and major uninsured risks.
19. Review guarantees, letters of comfort, and off-balance-sheet commitments.
20. Identify the top ten events that could materially impact liquidity during the next twelve months.
21. Understand CEO expectations.
22. Understand Board expectations.
23. Understand promoter expectations.
24. Understand investor expectations.
25. Understand expectations of SBU heads.
26. Understand expectations of sales leadership.
27. Understand expectations of operations leadership.

28. Understand expectations of supply-chain leadership.
29. Understand expectations of HR leadership.
30. Understand expectations of the finance team.
31. Assess ERP reliability.
32. Review quality of management information systems.
33. Review reporting timelines and effectiveness.
34. Review month-end close process.
35. Review reconciliation discipline.
36. Review approval hierarchies and bottlenecks.
37. Identify manual workarounds.
38. Review delegation-of-authority matrix.
39. Assess internal-control effectiveness.
40. Review fraud-prevention controls.
41. Review quality of financial reporting.
42. Assess reliability of operational reporting.
43. Identify areas where management decisions are delayed because of poor information.
44. Understand major customer concerns.
45. Understand major supplier concerns.
46. Assess the company's reputation in the market.
47. Understand banker perception of the company.
48. Understand auditor perception of the company.
49. Understand investor perception of the company.
50. Identify reports used by the CEO.
51. Identify reports used by the Board.
52. Identify reports used by business heads.
53. Identify reports that drive decisions.
54. Identify reports that are ignored.
55. Assess reliability of management reports.
56. Assess consistency between finance and business reports.
57. Review month-end closing timelines.
58. Review forecasting accuracy.
59. Review budgeting accuracy.
60. Identify multiple versions of the same information.
61. Identify recurring reporting disputes.
62. Review dashboard quality.
63. Review KPI definitions and consistency.
64. Assess management confidence in reported numbers.
65. What keeps the CEO awake at night?
66. What keeps the Board worried?
67. What worries the promoters most?
68. What worries investors most?
69. What does the business think finance does poorly?
70. What does finance think the business does poorly?

71. Which numbers are trusted?
72. Which numbers are doubted?
73. Which reports drive decisions?
74. Which reports are ignored?
75. Which process frustrates employees the most?
76. Which process frustrates customers the most?
77. Which process frustrates vendors the most?
78. Who are the real influencers?
79. Who are the real blockers?
80. Which decisions are repeatedly delayed?
81. What topic is everyone avoiding?
82. What risk is underestimated?
83. What opportunity is being ignored?
84. If nothing changes, what is most likely to go wrong during the next twelve months?
85. Review the enterprise risk register.
86. Identify the top ten financial risks.
87. Identify the top ten operational risks.
88. Identify the top ten compliance risks.
89. Identify the top ten people risks.
90. Identify the top ten technology risks.
91. Identify the top ten cyber-security risks.
92. Identify the top ten reputation risks.
93. Review customer concentration risks.
94. Review supplier concentration risks.
95. Review dependence on key employees.
96. Review dependence on key customers.
97. Review dependence on key vendors.
98. Assess foreign-exchange exposure risks.
99. Assess commodity-price exposure risks.
100. Assess interest-rate exposure risks.
101. Review litigation and legal risks.
102. Review environmental and ESG risks.
103. Review regulatory risks.
104. Review geopolitical risks affecting the business.
105. Review business-continuity plans.
106. Review disaster-recovery plans.
107. Review insurance coverage against key risks.
108. Assess fraud and misconduct risks.
109. Assess internal-control failure risks.
110. Assess reporting and disclosure risks.
111. Assess acquisition and integration risks.
112. Assess capital-project execution risks.
113. Assess succession and leadership risks.

114. Prepare the Top 10 Enterprise Risk Report.

DAYS 31–60

Business Model | Working Capital | Market Position | Capital Structure | Funding | Promoters | Shareholders | Execution Lags

---

117. Understand how the company generates revenue.
118. Identify the most profitable products.
119. Identify the most profitable customers.
120. Identify the most profitable channels.
121. Identify the most profitable geographies.
122. Identify loss-making products and services.
123. Identify loss-making business units.
124. Review pricing strategy and pricing power.
125. Understand gross-margin and contribution-margin drivers.
126. Review plant utilisation levels.
127. Review manufacturing economics and capacity constraints.
128. Review supply-chain vulnerabilities.
129. Review inventory ageing and slow-moving inventory.
130. Review inventory write-off history.
131. Review approved capital projects.
132. Review ongoing expansion projects.
133. Review major contracts and long-term commitments.
134. Identify major value-leakage areas across the business.
135. Understand the company's position within the industry.
136. Identify the company's top competitors.
137. Understand key industry trends affecting the business.
138. Review recent market-share movement.
139. Assess customer demand trends.
140. Assess supplier market conditions.
141. Review commodity-price risks impacting profitability.
142. Review foreign-exchange risks impacting the business.
143. Understand industry-specific regulatory requirements.
144. Identify upcoming regulatory changes.
145. Review industry growth forecasts.
146. Review industry profitability benchmarks.
147. Identify major external threats to business continuity.
148. Identify major external opportunities available to the company.
149. Review current capital structure.
150. Review debt-to-equity position.
151. Review all borrowing facilities.
152. Review unutilized credit facilities.
153. Review upcoming refinancing requirements.
154. Review cost of debt across facilities.

155. Review cost of capital assumptions.
156. Review treasury investment positions.
157. Review foreign-currency borrowings.
158. Review hedging policies and effectiveness.
159. Review lender concentration risks.
160. Review banking relationships.
161. Review financing restrictions and covenants.
162. Review shareholder funding arrangements.
163. Review intercompany funding structures.
164. Review capital-allocation practices.
165. Review dividend history and expectations.
166. Review share-buyback commitments, if any.
167. Review capital expenditure funding plans.
168. Assess adequacy of funding for future growth.
169. Understand promoter priorities.
170. Understand Board priorities.
171. Identify areas where promoter and Board expectations differ.
172. Review shareholder expectations.
173. Review investor concerns raised during the last twelve months.
174. Understand historical governance issues.
175. Review related-party transaction history.
176. Review shareholder communication practices.
177. Review major investor presentations.
178. Understand expectations regarding growth.
179. Understand expectations regarding profitability.
180. Understand expectations regarding cash generation.
181. Understand expectations regarding capital allocation.
182. Understand expectations regarding governance.
183. Identify sensitive topics involving ownership or governance.
184. Identify projects currently delayed.
185. Identify projects significantly over budget.
186. Identify projects consistently missing timelines.
187. Review execution bottlenecks across functions.
188. Identify recurring operational issues.
189. Review major customer complaints.
190. Review major vendor complaints.
191. Identify recurring quality issues.
192. Identify recurring service failures.
193. Review inventory-related execution issues.
194. Review procurement-related execution issues.
195. Review supply-chain execution gaps.
196. Review manufacturing execution challenges.
197. Review commercial execution challenges.
198. Identify decisions that repeatedly get delayed.

199. Identify areas where accountability is unclear.
200. Review cross-functional coordination effectiveness.
201. Identify departments operating in silos.
202. Review performance-review mechanisms.
203. Identify the top ten execution risks facing the business.

DAYS 61–90

Strategy | Culture | Team Capability | Digital Readiness | Risk Register | Initial CFO Outputs | 90-Day Action Plan

---

204. Identify key-person dependencies.
205. Assess succession readiness.
206. Identify high-performing leaders.
207. Identify weak leadership positions.
208. Understand informal reporting relationships.
209. Understand informal power structures.
210. Identify critical talent-retention risks.
211. Review the company's stated vision and mission.
212. Review the current business strategy.
213. Assess whether leadership is aligned on strategy.
214. Identify the top five strategic priorities.
215. Review progress against strategic objectives.
216. Assess whether budgets support strategy.
217. Assess whether capital allocation supports strategy.
218. Identify initiatives consuming significant resources.
219. Identify initiatives creating measurable value.
220. Identify initiatives that should be stopped.
221. Review market-expansion plans.
222. Review new-product development plans.
223. Review acquisition and partnership plans.
224. Assess competitive positioning.
225. Assess growth assumptions used by management.
226. Assess profitability assumptions used by management.
227. Identify major strategic risks.
228. Identify major strategic opportunities.
229. Assess execution capability against strategy.
230. Prepare an initial strategic assessment summary.
231. Understand how decisions are really made.
232. Identify formal decision makers.
233. Identify informal decision makers.
234. Identify key influencers within the organisation.
235. Identify individuals who can block decisions.
236. Understand relationships between key leaders.
237. Assess trust levels between functions.

238. Assess trust levels between business and finance.
239. Identify recurring internal conflicts.
240. Identify politically sensitive topics.
241. Review history of major organisational disputes.
242. Review history of leadership changes.
243. Understand employee perception of finance.
244. Understand management perception of finance.
245. Identify areas where finance is viewed as a business partner.
246. Identify areas where finance is viewed as a policing function.
247. Identify cultural strengths.
248. Identify cultural weaknesses.
249. Assess openness to change.
250. Document major cultural and political observations.
251. Review finance organisation structure.
252. Review finance headcount by function.
253. Assess capability of direct reports.
254. Assess capability of finance leadership team.
255. Identify top performers.
256. Identify high-potential employees.
257. Identify critical resource gaps.
258. Identify weak performers.
259. Assess succession readiness for key roles.
260. Identify single-person dependencies.
261. Review treasury team capability.
262. Review controllership team capability.
263. Review FP&A team capability.
264. Review taxation team capability.
265. Review internal-control capability.
266. Review business-finance capability.
267. Review training and development practices.
268. Review employee retention trends.
269. Review recent resignations in critical roles.
270. Prepare an initial talent and capability assessment.
271. Review ERP platform and stability.
272. Review ERP utilization levels.
273. Assess data quality across major systems.
274. Assess master-data governance.
275. Review cybersecurity controls impacting finance.
276. Identify automation opportunities.
277. Review reporting automation levels.
278. Review dashboard quality and usability.
279. Review forecasting tools and methodologies.
280. Assess quality of business intelligence systems.
281. Review AI initiatives currently underway.

282. Review automation initiatives currently underway.
283. Identify manual finance processes suitable for automation.
284. Assess month-end close automation opportunities.
285. Assess treasury automation opportunities.
286. Assess reporting automation opportunities.
287. Review cybersecurity controls impacting finance systems.
288. Review data-access controls.
289. Review system-integration challenges.
290. Assess digital maturity of finance function.
291. Assess digital maturity of business functions.
292. Prepare an initial digital-finance roadmap.
293. Prepare CFO Arrival Report.
294. Prepare liquidity and survival assessment.
295. Prepare working-capital assessment.
296. Prepare governance and compliance assessment.
297. Prepare business-model assessment.
298. Prepare stakeholder expectation map.
299. Prepare organisational capability assessment.
300. Prepare digital-finance assessment.
301. Prepare enterprise-risk summary.
302. Identify top ten enterprise risks.
303. Identify top ten value-creation opportunities.
304. Identify top ten quick wins.
305. Identify top ten long-term transformation opportunities.
306. Prepare CFO priorities for the next 90 days.
307. Prepare CFO priorities for the next 180 days.
308. Prepare CFO priorities for the next 365 days.
309. Review findings with CEO.
310. Review findings with Board Chairperson.
311. Align expectations with key stakeholders.
312. Finalize and launch the 90-Day Action Plan.

DAYS 91–180

Revenue Leakage | Operational Economics | Plant Efficiency | Yield Analysis | Job Work | Third-Party Processing | Margin Improvement

---

311. Review product-wise gross margins.
312. Review customer-wise profitability.
313. Review channel-wise profitability.
314. Review geography-wise profitability.
315. Review sales returns and credit notes.
316. Review customer claims and deductions.
317. Review pricing deviations and unauthorized discounts.
318. Review scheme settlements and rebate structures.

319. Review unbilled revenue and billing delays.
320. Review collection delays and overdue accounts.
321. Review inventory write-offs and obsolescence.
322. Review slow-moving and non-moving inventory.
323. Review inventory shrinkage and stock losses.
324. Review procurement-price variances.
325. Review material consumption variances.
326. Review yield losses in manufacturing operations.
327. Review process losses against standards.
328. Review scrap generation levels.
329. Review scrap disposal and scrap realization.
330. Review rework costs and quality-failure costs.
331. Review rejection percentages.
332. Review machine-utilization levels.
333. Review capacity-utilization levels.
334. Review production-efficiency measures.
335. Review conversion-cost trends.
336. Review labour-productivity measures.
337. Review warehouse and storage inefficiencies.
338. Review freight and logistics costs.
339. Review dispatch and distribution inefficiencies.
340. Review job-work arrangements and controls.
341. Review third-party manufacturing arrangements.
342. Review toll-processing economics.
343. Review subcontracting profitability.
344. Review transfer-pricing impact on profitability.
345. Review product-mix optimisation opportunities.
346. Identify the top ten revenue leakages.
347. Identify the top ten cost leakages.
348. Identify the top ten operational inefficiencies.
349. Identify the top ten margin-improvement opportunities.
350. Prepare the Revenue Leakage & Value-Creation Report.

DAYS 181–365

Transformation Roadmap | Value Creation | Systems Upgrade | Governance | Leadership Agenda | Board-Level Execution

351. Prepare the CFO Arrival Report.
352. Prepare the Enterprise Diagnostic Summary.
353. Prepare the Stakeholder Expectation Map.
354. Prepare the Enterprise Risk Report.
355. Prepare the Revenue Leakage & Value-Creation Report.
356. Prepare the Liquidity & Survival Assessment.
357. Prepare the Organisational Capability Assessment.

358. Prepare the Digital Finance Assessment.
359. Prepare the 90-Day Action Plan.
360. Prepare the 180-Day Transformation Roadmap.
361. Prepare the 365-Day Leadership Agenda.
362. Present findings to the CEO.
363. Present findings to the Board or Audit Committee.
364. Align priorities with key stakeholders.
365. Launch the execution plan.

Note: The time buckets in this checklist are indicative. Some items may naturally move earlier or later depending on the organisation's size, industry, ownership structure, complexity, urgency, reporting cycle, sub-functions, available data, date of joining, and immediate business priorities. The checklist should be adapted to the CFO's actual context rather than followed mechanically.

Glossary of CFO Terms

A Practical Language Map for Financial Leaders

A CFO's language is not limited to accounting. It moves through treasury, risk, taxation, governance, capital markets, technology, strategy, operations, and leadership judgement.

This glossary is designed as a quick reference for aspiring and first-time CFOs. It does not replace detailed technical study, professional advice, or jurisdiction-specific guidance. Instead, it helps the reader become familiar with terms commonly used in boardrooms, finance reviews, investor discussions, audit meetings, and strategic decision-making.

Use this glossary as a language map — not merely to memorize definitions, but to think more clearly as a financial leader.

GLOSSARY INDEX –

A Practical Language Map for Financial Leaders

1. **Treasury, Liquidity and Cash Management**
   13-Week Cash-Flow Forecast · Liquidity Buffer · Cash Pooling · Working Capital Limit · Bridge Loan · DSCR · Interest Coverage Ratio · Covenant · Cash Forecast Accuracy · Factoring · Cash Trap
2. **Working Capital**
   Working Capital · Cash Conversion Cycle · DSO · DIO · DPO · Receivable Aging · Inventory Aging · Bad Debt Provision · Dynamic Discounting · Supply-Chain Finance · Credit Approval Matrix

3. **Capital Allocation and Investment Decisions**
   Capital Allocation · Capex · Opex · WACC · NPV · IRR · Payback Period · Hurdle Rate · ROIC · Post-Completion Audit · Stage-Gate Approval
4. **Board, Governance and Controls**
   Board Pack · Audit Committee · Executive Summary · Internal Control · Management Letter · Delegation of Authority · Related-Party Transaction · Whistle-Blower Mechanism · Tone at the Top · Management Override · Segregation of Duties
5. **Risk Management and Compliance**
   Risk Appetite · Risk Register · Risk Heat Map · Black Swan Event · Grey Rhino Event · Business Continuity Plan · Disaster Recovery Plan · Fraud Triangle · AML · Anti-Bribery and Corruption · Cyber Risk · Continuous Controls Monitoring
6. **Forex, Hedging and Financial Exposure**
   Foreign Exchange Exposure · Natural Hedge · Forward Contract · Option Contract · Hedge Ratio · Mark-to-Market · Speculative Position
7. **Tax and Transfer Pricing**
   Direct Tax · Indirect Tax · Withholding Tax · Deferred Tax Asset / Liability · Transfer Pricing · Arm's-Length Principle · CUP · TNMM · APA · MAP · BEPS · Country-by-Country Reporting
8. **Mergers, Acquisitions and Investor Readiness**
   Due Diligence · Data Room · Term Sheet · Enterprise Value · Equity Value · Goodwill · Earn-Out · Synergy · Integration PMO · IPO Readiness · Investor Information Memorandum · Equity Story
9. **Digital Finance, Data and Systems**
   ERP · MIS · RPA · Master Data · Data Governance · Dashboard · Predictive Analytics · AI Governance · Audit Trail · System Integration
10. **Leadership, Strategy and CFO Judgement**
   Strategic CFO · Operational CFO · Business Partnering · Finance Transformation · Stakeholder Management · Decision Velocity · Enterprise Value · Stewardship · Leadership Optics · CFO Legacy

Treasury, Liquidity and Cash Management

13-Week Cash-Flow Forecast

A short-term cash visibility tool showing expected inflows, outflows, opening balances, closing balances, and liquidity gaps over the next thirteen weeks. It helps the CFO anticipate pressure before it becomes a crisis.

Liquidity Buffer

The minimum cash or immediately available funding the company keeps to meet operating, debt, payroll, statutory, and emergency obligations.

Cash Pooling

A treasury arrangement where cash from multiple entities or accounts is consolidated to improve visibility, reduce idle balances, and optimize borrowing.

Working Capital Limit

A short-term borrowing facility provided by banks to support day-to-day business needs such as inventory, receivables, and operating expenses.

Bridge Loan
A temporary loan used to meet immediate funding needs until a longer-term financing arrangement is completed.

Debt Service Coverage Ratio — DSCR
A ratio that measures whether the company generates enough cash to meet principal and interest obligations. It is commonly monitored by lenders.

Interest Coverage Ratio
A measure of how comfortably a company can pay interest on its borrowings from operating earnings.

Covenant
A financial or non-financial condition imposed by lenders or investors. Breach of a covenant can trigger penalties, higher monitoring, repayment demands, or renegotiation.

Cash Forecast Accuracy
The comparison between projected cash movement and actual cash movement. A disciplined CFO monitors forecast accuracy to improve treasury reliability.

Factoring
A financing method where a company sells its receivables to a third party to receive cash earlier, usually at a discount.

Cash Trap
A situation where accounting profits exist but cash is blocked in receivables, inventory, restricted accounts, or delayed collections.

Working Capital

Working Capital
The capital required to run daily operations. It generally represents current assets minus current liabilities.

Cash Conversion Cycle — CCC
The number of days it takes for a company to convert investment in inventory and receivables back into cash, after considering supplier credit.

Days Sales Outstanding — DSO
The average number of days customers take to pay the company after sales are made.

Days Inventory Outstanding — DIO
The average number of days inventory remains in the business before being sold or consumed.

Days Payable Outstanding — DPO
The average number of days the company takes to pay its suppliers.

Receivable Aging
A report that classifies unpaid customer invoices by age, such as 0–30 days, 31–60 days, 61–90 days, and above 90 days.

Inventory Aging
A report showing how long inventory has remained unsold or unused. It helps detect slow-moving, obsolete, or overstocked items.

Bad Debt Provision
An accounting estimate created for receivables that may not be collected.
Dynamic Discounting
A payment arrangement where suppliers offer discounts in exchange for early payment.
Supply-Chain Finance
A financing solution where suppliers receive early payment through banks or platforms, while the buyer may continue to enjoy extended payment terms.
Credit Approval Matrix
A structured authority framework defining who can approve customer credit limits, payment terms, and exceptions.

Capital Allocation and Investment Decisions

Capital Allocation
The process of deciding where the company's financial resources should be invested, retained, reduced, or withdrawn.
Capital Expenditure — Capex
Spending on long-term assets such as plants, equipment, technology platforms, infrastructure, or major expansion projects.
Operating Expenditure — Opex
Recurring expenditure required to run the business, such as salaries, rent, utilities, maintenance, subscriptions, and administrative costs.
Weighted Average Cost of Capital — WACC
The blended cost of debt and equity used to evaluate whether investments are creating value above the company's cost of capital.
Net Present Value — NPV
The present value of future cash flows from a project after deducting the initial investment. A positive NPV generally indicates value creation.
Internal Rate of Return — IRR
The rate of return at which a project's NPV becomes zero. It is used to compare investment attractiveness.
Payback Period
The time required to recover the initial investment from project cash flows.
Hurdle Rate
The minimum acceptable return a project must generate before capital is approved.
Return on Invested Capital — ROIC
A measure of how efficiently the company generates returns from the capital invested in the business.
Post-Completion Audit
A review conducted after a project is completed to compare actual cost, timing, returns, and benefits against the approved business case.

Stage-Gate Approval
A capital control process where funding is released in phases only after predefined milestones are achieved.

Board, Governance and Controls

Board Pack
A structured set of documents presented to the board, usually including financial performance, risk updates, strategic matters, decisions required, and management commentary.

Audit Committee
A board-level committee responsible for oversight of financial reporting, internal controls, audits, compliance, risk, and governance matters.

Executive Summary
A concise summary highlighting the key issues, risks, decisions required, and management recommendations.

Internal Control
A process, policy, or system designed to prevent errors, fraud, misstatements, unauthorized transactions, or operational failures.

Management Letter
A letter issued by auditors highlighting control weaknesses, process gaps, observations, and recommendations.

Delegation of Authority — DOA
A formal framework defining approval powers for spending, contracts, hiring, investments, payments, and commitments.

Related-Party Transaction
A transaction between the company and persons or entities connected to promoters, directors, management, group companies, or other related parties.

Whistle-Blower Mechanism
A formal channel that allows employees or stakeholders to report fraud, misconduct, ethical violations, or governance concerns.

Tone at the Top
The ethical and governance culture set by the board, CEO, CFO, and senior leadership.

Management Override
A situation where senior management bypasses or manipulates controls, policies, or accounting judgement.

Segregation of Duties
A control principle ensuring that no single person controls all stages of a transaction, such as initiation, approval, recording, and payment.

Risk Management and Compliance

Risk Appetite
The level and type of risk the company is willing to accept while pursuing its objectives.

Risk Register
A structured record of key risks, owners, impact, likelihood, mitigation plans, and escalation triggers.

Risk Heat Map
A visual tool that plots risks based on likelihood and impact.

Black Swan Event
A rare, unexpected event with severe consequences.

Grey Rhino Event
A highly probable and visible risk that is often ignored until it becomes damaging.

Business Continuity Plan — BCP
A plan that helps the company continue critical operations during disruption.

Disaster Recovery Plan — DRP
A technology-focused recovery plan for restoring systems, data, and IT operations after failure, breach, or disaster.

Fraud Triangle
A framework explaining fraud risk through three factors: pressure, opportunity, and rationalization.

Anti-Money Laundering — AML
Policies and controls designed to prevent the movement, concealment, or use of illegally obtained funds.

Anti-Bribery and Corruption — ABC
Controls and policies designed to prevent bribery, improper payments, kickbacks, and corrupt practices.

Cyber Risk
The risk of financial, operational, legal, or reputational loss caused by data breaches, system attacks, unauthorized access, or technology failure.

Continuous Controls Monitoring — CCM
Technology-enabled monitoring of transactions and controls on an ongoing basis.

Forex, Hedging and Financial Exposure

Foreign Exchange Exposure
The risk that currency movements may affect revenue, costs, assets, liabilities, margins, or cash flows.

Natural Hedge
A situation where foreign currency inflows and outflows offset each other without using financial instruments.

Forward Contract
A contract to buy or sell foreign currency at a predetermined rate on a future date.

Option Contract
A financial instrument giving the right, but not the obligation, to buy or sell currency at a specified rate.

Hedge Ratio
The percentage of foreign currency exposure covered through hedging instruments.

Mark-to-Market — MTM
The process of valuing financial instruments based on current market prices.

Speculative Position
A currency or derivative position taken without underlying business exposure, usually to profit from market movement. A prudent CFO avoids speculative treasury behaviour.

Tax and Transfer Pricing

Direct Tax
Tax charged directly on income or profits, such as corporate income tax.

Indirect Tax
Tax charged on goods and services, such as GST or VAT.

Withholding Tax
Tax deducted at source when making certain payments, especially cross-border payments such as royalties, interest, fees, or services.

Deferred Tax Asset / Liability
Accounting recognition of future tax benefits or future tax obligations arising from timing differences between accounting and tax treatment.

Transfer Pricing
Pricing of transactions between related entities within the same group, such as goods, services, royalties, loans, guarantees, and cost allocations.

Arm's-Length Principle
The principle that related-party transactions should be priced as if they were conducted between independent parties.

Comparable Uncontrolled Price — CUP
A transfer pricing method comparing the price charged in a related-party transaction with the price charged in a comparable independent transaction.

Transactional Net Margin Method — TNMM
A transfer pricing method that compares net profit margins from related-party transactions with margins earned by comparable independent companies.

Advance Pricing Agreement — APA
An agreement with tax authorities that determines the transfer pricing method for future related-party transactions.

Mutual Agreement Procedure — MAP
A mechanism under tax treaties to resolve double taxation or transfer pricing disputes between jurisdictions.

Base Erosion and Profit Shifting — BEPS
Tax planning strategies that shift profits to low-tax jurisdictions without sufficient

economic substance. CFOs must ensure tax efficiency does not become governance risk.

Country-by-Country Reporting — CbCR

A reporting requirement for large multinational groups showing revenue, profit, tax paid, employees, and economic activity across jurisdictions.

Mergers, Acquisitions and Investor Readiness

Due Diligence

A structured investigation of a target company's financial, legal, tax, operational, commercial, technology, and human capital position before a transaction.

Data Room

A secure repository of documents shared during due diligence, such as contracts, financials, tax filings, litigation records, employee data, and corporate documents.

Term Sheet

A document outlining the key commercial and legal terms of a proposed transaction.

Enterprise Value — EV

The total value of a business, generally including equity value plus debt, minus cash.

Equity Value

The value attributable to shareholders after considering debt and cash adjustments.

Goodwill

An intangible asset arising when a company pays more than the fair value of identifiable net assets acquired.

Earn-Out

A transaction structure where part of the purchase price is paid later if the acquired business achieves agreed performance targets.

Synergy

The additional value expected from combining two businesses, such as cost savings, revenue growth, market access, or operational efficiency.

Integration PMO

A Project Management Office established to manage post-merger integration, timelines, accountability, synergy tracking, and Day 1 readiness.

IPO Readiness

The process of preparing a company for listing, including governance, financial reporting, internal controls, investor communication, compliance, and management discipline.

Investor Information Memorandum — IIM

A document prepared for potential investors or lenders containing business overview, financials, strategy, risks, management profile, and investment rationale.

Equity Story

The narrative explaining why investors should believe in the company's future value creation.

Digital Finance, Data and Systems

Enterprise Resource Planning — ERP
An integrated software system used to manage finance, procurement, inventory, sales, manufacturing, HR, and other business processes.

Management Information System — MIS
A structured reporting system used by management to review performance, trends, variances, and key business indicators.

Robotic Process Automation — RPA
Technology that automates repetitive rule-based tasks such as reconciliations, invoice processing, data entry, and report generation.

Master Data
Core business data such as customer codes, vendor codes, product codes, tax codes, chart of accounts, and employee records.

Data Governance
The framework for managing data accuracy, ownership, access, security, consistency, and usage.

Dashboard
A visual reporting tool that summarizes key performance indicators and helps management track business health.

Predictive Analytics
Use of data, models, and technology to forecast future outcomes such as cash flows, demand, defaults, or risk patterns.

AI Governance
Policies and controls governing the use of artificial intelligence to ensure accuracy, transparency, accountability, data protection, and ethical use.

Audit Trail
A record showing who performed a transaction, when it was performed, what changed, and who approved it.

System Integration
The connection of different technology systems so data flows accurately across functions.

Leadership, Strategy and CFO Judgement

Strategic CFO
A CFO who goes beyond reporting and control to influence capital allocation, business strategy, risk, growth, investor confidence, and enterprise value.

Operational CFO
A CFO focused strongly on systems, controls, processes, cash discipline, reporting, and execution reliability.

Business Partnering
The CFO's role in working with operations, sales, HR, supply chain, and technology teams to improve decisions through financial insight.

Finance Transformation
The redesign of finance processes, systems, roles, reporting, automation, and capabilities to make finance more strategic and efficient.

Stakeholder Management
The ability to manage expectations and communication with the board, CEO, investors, lenders, auditors, regulators, employees, and business heads.

Decision Velocity
The speed at which an organisation makes and executes decisions without damaging quality, governance, or accountability.

Enterprise Value
The broader value of the company as seen through financial performance, strategy, risk discipline, governance, people, systems, and market confidence.

Stewardship
The responsibility to protect the organisation's resources, reputation, governance, and long-term sustainability.

Leadership Optics
How the CFO's behaviour, tone, decisions, and communication are perceived by the board, leadership team, employees, investors, and external stakeholders.

CFO Legacy
The systems, culture, controls, people, judgement standards, and decision discipline a CFO leaves behind after moving on from the role.

Closing Note

The modern CFO is expected to understand more than numbers. He must understand the language of risk, capital, governance, technology, people, and trust.

Technical knowledge can be deepened through study and specialists. But judgement is built through repeated exposure to the right questions.

This glossary is meant to support that journey — from knowing the terms to understanding the responsibility behind them.

BECOMING THE CFO

The First 90 Days and Beyond

Decoding the DNA of Financial Leadership for First-Time CFOs

FCA Shriharsh Sonar

www.ingramcontent.com/pod-product-compliance
Lightning Source LLC
LaVergne TN
LVHW052222200926
848481LV00001B/182